SOCIAL CHANGE AND THE INDIVIDUAL

To My Wife, Ann

Grading of tobacco leaves ready for baling

SOCIAL CHANGE
AND THE
INDIVIDUAL

A study of the social and religious
responses to innovation in a
Zambian rural community

by

NORMAN LONG

PUBLISHED FOR
THE INSTITUTE FOR SOCIAL RESEARCH
UNIVERSITY OF ZAMBIA
BY
MANCHESTER UNIVERSITY PRESS
1968

© 1968 NORMAN LONG
Published by the University of Manchester at
THE UNIVERSITY PRESS
316–324 Oxford Road, Manchester 13

Distributed in the U.S.A. by
HUMANITIES PRESS, INC.
303 Park Avenue South, New York, N.Y. 10010

G.B. SBN 7190 1025 X

Printed in Great Britain by Butler & Tanner Ltd., Frome and London

FOREWORD

Sociologists and Social Anthropologists are fortunate in that, if they are shrewd, they can at once contribute to the development of their subject and to the development of the welfare of mankind. This book is an example of such a dual contribution.

This, however, is only one of the reasons why I am delighted to write a foreword to it. Since 1949, when Max Gluckman, a former director of the Rhodes-Livingstone Institute, started the department of Social Anthropology and Sociology at the University of Manchester, there has been a fruitful interaction between the scholars of that university and sociological studies in Central Africa. General fruits of this include A. L. Epstein's recent *The Craft of Social Anthropology* (Tavistock Press, 1967), Turner's collected papers published under the title of *The Forest of Symbols* (Cornell University Press, 1967) and Mitchell's forthcoming study of social networks. Dr. Long's book here introduced is the latest of a series of highly *specific* studies of the greatest *general* importance. I regard the fifteen books of this type published by the Rhodes-Livingstone Institute since 1951 as both a remarkable achievement and a magnificent legacy to the new University of Zambia and what has now become the Institute for Social Research within it. The influence of the most recent, Van Velsen's *The Politics of Kinship* (Manchester University Press, 1964) is beneficially clear in the present work. If future research continues to hold to the principle that the understanding of general problems requires specific studies, future contributions both to science and welfare will match those of the past.

A third reason for pleasure at the publication of this book is the very explicit way in which it relates sociological theory to empirical research. This is especially noticeable in the chapters on prestige and on Religion and Social Action, and to some extent may be seen as redressing a balance not always perfectly achieved in publications of the R.L.I. in particular and of social anthropologists in general (cf. Worsley, *The End of Anthropology*: paper presented at the 6th World Congress of Sociology, Evian, 1966).

Fourthly, although the research here described was done both before independence and before the establishment of the University of Zambia, Dr. Long revised and rewrote his thesis as a book while on secondment from Manchester to the Sociology section of the School of Humanities and Social Sciences in the new university. It is therefore, in one sense, the culmination of a line of work associated with the R.L.I., and, in another, the first fruits of Zambian sociology. That such continuity is both desirable, fruitful and possible is a tribute to many, of all ethnic groups, both politicians and scholars, on both sides of independence and symbolizes perhaps the determination of Zambia to combine the best of the past with its vision of a truly autonomous future.

Finally, to intrude a personal note, happy circumstances decreed that when I returned to Manchester in 1960, Dr. Long was one of the first two postgraduate students whom I taught, although I soon realized that my knowledge of African sociology was inadequate to his needs and passed him on to those who had something to teach him. Another happy circumstance found me in Lusaka for the final stages of the book's preparation. I may therefore claim to have been present at both conception and birth, even if I played no part in providing nourishment during the necessarily long gestation.

Dr. Long here sets out to document in detail, in one district, the kinds of socio-economic changes that were taking place as Zambia approached, achieved and consolidated independence. He shows the factors responsible for the emergence of various new social forms. He is truly sociological in examining the differential response to change of different social categories within the population, whether objectively defined in terms of classical variables of age, sex and marital status, occupational status, religious affiliation, ethnic origin, stage in life cycle and cultural background or more subjectively by the local classification of the people themselves. I find myself particularly fascinated by the way he uses (in Chapter VI) the formal methodology of prestige ranking (following Mitchell), side by side with the more uniquely specific technique of situational analysis (in Chapter VII) to illuminate the meaning and significance of local terms: *Mucinshi* —the kind of respect between specific categories of kin; *bukankala*, that due to headmen and chiefs; and *bucindami*, less specifically tied to special relationships. This leads him on to the consideration of such categories as *bawina*, the wealthy man; *basambashi*, the man with a high standard of living who is said to govern himself (*kuiteka mwine*); *basambilia*, the educated man who possesses wisdom and looks like a *bwana* (a term once used for Europeans and now for anyone of high status, or within the United National Independence Party); *nshimishi*, ordinary villagers, alternatively *cicommoni* and disrespectfully referred to as *kamushi*, country bumpkins, and finally, the vital category within the Zambian scene, *bena tauni*, townspeople.

This last concept and its significance to policy and development cannot be overstressed. As Dr. Long says (p. 166), such 'a man does not necessarily have to have spent much time actually residing in town, so long as he exhibits the right attributes of the "townsman" as perceived by the people of the parish. Thus, for example, a teacher may have only visited town to see friends and relatives and may not have lived or worked there for any lengthy period, but is still regarded as a "townsman"; and the same may be true of an agricultural demonstrator or peasant farmer.'

Now it is true that President Kaunda and the philosophy of Zambian Humanism speak out firmly against class and prestige divisions, but development must not only be based on knowledge of where it is to lead but also where it starts from. The class, status and prestige divisions of Zambia have, until now, been little charted, but they nevertheless exist. Nor are they the products of individual disordered minds. They emerge out of and are generated and reinforced by social relations of the kind and at the level described by Dr. Long in such passages as his account of the visit of Pati, NaBombwe and Eliza to the village.

They emerge also out of the work relations described elsewhere in this book and in forthcoming publications by Kapferer and others. To change these concepts and attitudes it is necessary to change the social and work relations which gave rise to them. This is the central problem of development.

The kind of detailed, objective, and, in a sense, outsider's account which sociologists can give us is indispensable to those who wish even to reverse a trend, let alone fundamentally to change society.

The efforts of independent government to halt the drift (or the rush) to the towns and to regroup rural villages will be as fruitless as previous similar attempts by the B.S.A. Company, Colonial and Federal governments, unless there is a sophisticated appreciation not merely of social attitudes but also of how they are concretely formed in real-life situations.

The same considerations apply, of course, to the discussions of the role of matrilineal kinship and its obligations which pervade every part of Dr. Long's book. It is too facile to say that in Zambia, or at least on the direct evidence of this book, in Serenje district, at the village level, all men are 'brothers'. 'They help each other as kin, let us extend this way of behaving to society as a whole; let the urban learn from the rural.' For Dr. Long shows clearly that men are not automata, as less observant anthropologists have implied. They exercise a choice of which norms they follow, and a choice of which kin relations they emphasize or reject. It is of the essence of rural kin relationships in sharp contrast to the totally proletarianized town-dweller that to include one man or woman in the benefits of co-operation may well be to exclude another.

This exclusive, rejecting aspect of kin behaviour is accentuated, as Dr. Long shows, by the urban-rural seeming confusion of norms and property. The villagers of Serenje are not wedded to pre-industrial values. They live in industrial society. There is much coming and going from Kabwe, and even the Congo and Rhodesia. But each detailed case study shows that these values and customs are among the armoury of arguments to be deployed when fighting over the distribution of such meagre spoils of industry as come to Kapepa.

The language of rural kinship humanism is not 'all men are brothers', or even 'all kin are brothers' but 'those men are my brothers who are genealogically suitable and also mutually agree to enter into brotherly property relations'. In peasant society, at least, kinship is a device for restricting the distribution of scarce loving-kindness, not for scattering it at large.

These observations add particular interest to Dr. Long's Chapter VIII, concerning Religion and Social Action, for here he shows, carrying the analysis of Weber empirically further, that it is not merely the ideology of Jehovah's Witnesses that gives them entrepreneurial advantage. Membership of the sect, like membership of the Quakers in eighteenth-century England or Jews in mediaeval Europe, provides a quasi-kinship relationship independent of genealogy which reduces the constraints of kinship-limited co-operation. Put bluntly, while non-Witnesses can trust only their kin (and not always them), Witnesses can trust both kin and fellow Witnesses. When this is tied to the Protestant Ethic of getting on, it gives Witnesses a formidable edge over their competitors for both wealth and corporate identity. This has already led, in Malawi, and to some extent in Zambia, to their prophecy that they would be persecuted becoming only too true. Once again, like the Jews in mediaeval Europe or the Quakers at the outset of British capitalism, punishment for worldly success is interpreted by persecutors and persecuted alike in terms of a difference in religious or quasi-religious ideology (Witnesses do not allow their children to salute the flag or to sing the national anthem). Mwape's statement (p. 29) that the land was God's, not the Chief's, echoes down the centuries from the struggles of the mediaeval burgesses.

Thus far, I have been concerned with the ways in which Dr. Long relates socio-economic and social change. In the early chapters of the book he is concerned with the other side of the equation, namely the relationship between economic and socio-economic change. The recognition that changes in the economy change socio-economic categories and only then social relations seems to me an important advance on the view which sees social changes too directly caused by the economic. (See Frankenberg, 'Economic Anthropology: One Anthropologist's View', ed. Firth, *Themes in Economic Anthropology*, Tavistock Press, 1967; T. S. Epstein, *Economic Development and Social Change in South India*, Manchester University Press, 1961.) In the long run, it is possible to eliminate the middle sociological term and perhaps the usefulness of sociologists as many economist-planners seem anxious to do. But reactions to economic development are not long run but immediate and may be sufficiently devastating to bring development to a halt.

In this part of the book, Dr. Long shows how subsistence-based axe agriculture (small circle *citeme*) is being gradually replaced by cash-cropping and the use of the plough. He suggests that changes in the organization of agricultural labour are leading to changes in the attitudes to land holding and the emergence of smaller, differently composed residential groupings. He further examines whether this was not in fact inevitable for ecological reasons and is here able to draw on another side of the Rhodes-Livingstone Institute's activities, the ecological studies set in train by W. Allan and continued in Serenje by the late D. U. Peters.

These findings again are of very general significance. They provide a necessary, if not sufficient, causative background to the rise of new forms of status evaluation and the possibly increasing frequency of conflict relations within small groups of close matrilineal kinsmen. Both these features I have already made some comment upon.

Secondly, they touch the interests of government at two points. If the scatter of settlements is, as Dr. Long suggests, ecologically determined, this presents yet another difficulty, in this district at least, to the policy of rural resettlement and regrouping. A difficulty stated and analysed is that much more easily overcome. Finally, Dr. Long shows that the role of the village headman has radically changed since Gluckman, Barnes and Mitchell's classical study (in *Africa*, xix, 1949), a finding which obviously bears on the future of rural administration.

In this foreword, I have touched on a few only of the many themes which Dr. Long has skilfully woven into this book. I have said nothing of, for example, his stimulating discussion of the relationships of structuralism and situational analysis, or the difficulty of capital accumulation by agriculture alone, or the implications of labour migration, or the contrast made by Lala between those on block farms—slaves of the government—and those who are described as 'headmen of their farms'. These and other topics with which he deals are also of interest both to administrators and professional sociologists and anthropologists.

The University of Zambia emphasizes its commitment both to the real needs of Zambia and to the world of scholarship. In publishing this book I feel that we are contributing to both.

Furthermore, I hope that just as T. S. Epstein on India (1961), Barth on *The Role of the Entrepreneur in Social Change in Northern Norway* (Norwegian University Press, 1963) and Worsley on Saskatchewan ('Bureaucracy and Decolonization: democracy from the top', ed. Horowitz, *The New Sociology*, 1965), all teach useful lessons for the understanding of Zambia, so the relevance of Long on Zambia will be recognized far outside our own boundaries.

RONALD FRANKENBERG
Professor of Sociology
University of Zambia

Lusaka, 1968

CONTENTS

ILLUSTRATIONS

Plates

Maps

Figures

Tables

Appendix

Genealogies

ACKNOWLEDGEMENTS

This book is based on a period of field research carried out in Serenje District, Zambia, between January 1963 and May 1964, and aims to analyse only those factors affecting social and economic change in the immediate pre-Independence period. Since then major changes have taken place in the structure of local government and new agricultural policies have been formulated. However, it lies outside the scope of the present study to discuss these more recent developments and when using the present tense I refer to the situation existing in 1963–4.

My research was financed by a Commonwealth Scholarship, though I also received assistance from the Rhodes-Livingstone Institute (now the Institute for Social Research, the University of Zambia) which made available to me one of their research assistants, and from the University College of Rhodesia which provided transport. I would like to express my debt to these various bodies and thank Professor Alastair Heron, former Director of the Institute for Social Research, and Professor Clyde Mitchell, formerly of the University College of Rhodesia, for solving some of the difficulties of operating on a very slim budget.

Prior to my field study I spent about 16 months of postgraduate studies in the Department of Social Anthropology, the University of Manchester, where I received training, guidance and intellectual stimulation from many staff and fellow students. I am most grateful to Professor Max Gluckman, Professor V. W. Turner (now of Chicago University) and Dr. E. L. Peters for their generous help during this time and also for the many useful discussions I have had with them on my field material.

Throughout my stay in central Africa I was supervised by Professor Mitchell and I owe a special debt to him for his unfailing assistance and encouragement both during fieldwork and later while writing up. He has made many constructive criticisms and has shown keen interest in the sociological problems explored. I also wish to acknowledge the help I received from Professor A. L. Epstein (now of the Australian National University) who guided me through the difficult early months of analysing my data.

Several other colleagues have indirectly contributed to this book. Dr. van Velsen made a number of pertinent suggestions during the field research and my fellow research workers at the Institute for Social Research provided an excellent milieu for the discussion of specific problems at intervals during my stay in Zambia. I am especially grateful to Mr. Bruce Kapferer for the many long and stimulating discussions I have had with him throughout the research. Whilst in Manchester I also had the benefit of discussion with Mr. D. Boswell, Mr. J. Lee, Mr. B. Sansom and Mr. R. Werbner.

During our stay in Serenje District my wife and I were given hospitality by many persons, both in the villages and at the Administrative Centre. To mention only a few, Mr. and Mrs. L. Pretorius and Mr. and Mrs. T. Robb at the Teachers' Training College, Mr. D. Alexander who was a District Officer, and Dr. and Mrs. C. Musk of Chitambo Mission regularly provided open house to two weary field workers whenever they needed a break. We also made many friends in Chibale Chiefdom and it was largely through the good offices of the Chief and his councillors that our stay was made so enjoyable. Lupalo, the village headman, together with the members of his village, were perfect hosts and gave us entrée into village life at a rather tense time in the history of Zambia. My wife and I express our deepest gratitude for the companionship of Lupalo and his kin and our thanks to the innumerable villagers, farmers, storekeepers and others in the parish who made us so welcome. We also received wise counsel from the Rt. Hon. Mr. Pirie Kapika and from the late Mr. Mateyo Kakumbi.

Very special thanks extend to Mr. Titus Musonda who was my field assistant for most of the time, and to Mr. Alexander Machamanda who first introduced us to Serenje and to the people of his home area. Mr. Musonda, with his considerable research experience, proved an ideal co-worker and an immensely shrewd judge of social situations. It would have been impossible to have collected much of the data without his help. Mr. Machamanda likewise gave me the benefit of his knowledge of the area and the people and made a number of very useful suggestions as to the significance of particular observations.

The final draft for the book was prepared during a year's teaching at the University of Zambia. This made revision somewhat easier as I was able to revisit the area to check some of my data. I hope later to publish an account of the developments in Serenje following Independence. During my year in Lusaka I had valuable assistance from Professor R. Frankenberg who commented extensively on the manuscript.

Finally, and most importantly, I wish to express my inestimable debt to my wife, Ann, who shared both the hardships and rewards of fieldwork and also the many excitements and tribulations associated with writing up. Throughout she has given me every encouragement and has made many incisive comments on the structure of the argument.

NORMAN LONG

Lusaka, January 1968

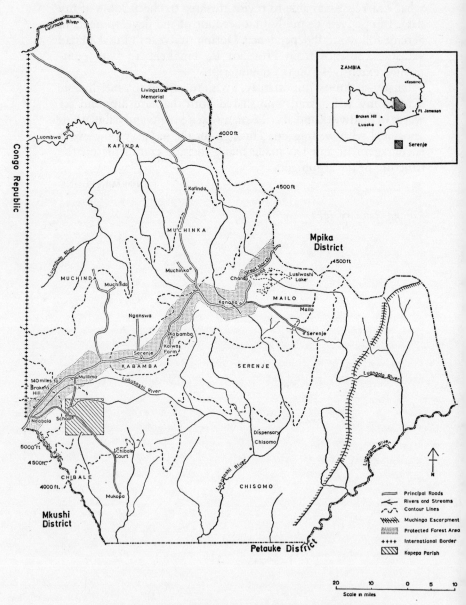

Map legend:

Principal Roads
Rivers and Streams
Contour Lines
Muchinga Escarpment
Protected Forest Area
International Border
Kapepa Parish

Scale in miles

MAP I. Serenje District showing the location of Kapepa Parish

CHAPTER I

INTRODUCTION

The problem and setting

It has long been a feature of anthropological monographs on rural peoples in Africa to include some account of the changes incurred by their involvement in wider social, economic and political structures, but frequently the anthropologist has attempted to 'deal with social change at the end of an analysis mainly devoted to the structure and equilibrium of the traditional tribal system' (Gluckman, 1965a, p. 286). Gluckman suggests that the reason for this is that 'most tribal systems have in fact absorbed *many* changes into their traditional equilibrium'. While I do not wish to dispute the validity of this statement, it seems that nowadays in many fieldwork situations this predilection for so-called 'traditional tribal systems', with only minimal treatment of the emergence of new modes of behaviour and values, results in an unwarranted weighting in favour of the 'fascinating complexities of tribal systems' and fails to take sufficient account of the development of new parameters for social action. The present study, then, attempts to shift the emphasis away from problems arising out of the exposition of so-called 'traditional' institutions to problems posed by the presence of new factors making for social change.

It is impossible, even within a carefully circumscribed unit for analysis, to present a rounded account of all aspects of social change. A more realistic objective is that of showing the inter-connections between certain types of change and continuity. Here I shall concentrate on the social responses to economic change in a small rural community in Zambia and discuss only those components in the situation which seem relevant to this theme.

The material for this book was collected in Serenje District, in the Central Province of Zambia, in 1963–4. The area delimited for intensive research roughly coincided with the administrative Parish of Kapepa.[1] Kapepa Parish lies in the north-western sector of Chibale Chiefdom, some twenty-odd miles east of the boundary

[1] This is a pseudonym, as are also the names of the settlements and their inhabitants that appear elsewhere in the book.

between Serenje and Mkushi Districts, and within easy reach of the Great North Road (see Map I).

Chibale Chiefdom is one of eight Lala chiefdoms recognized by the administration in Serenje District and is situated on the plateau which forms the Congo–Zambesi watershed. The Lala of Serenje are part of a wider complex of peoples found on both sides of the Congo–Zambia border marking the eastern extremity of the Congo pedicle. Lambo (1948, p. 233) estimated that about 10,000 Lala were living in the Congo in 1946, and more recent censuses for Zambia indicate that a further 60,000 are divided between the administrative districts of Serenje and Mkushi (*Census for Northern Rhodesia*, 1963). The total *de facto* population for Chibale Chiefdom in 1963 was 9,238 persons, of whom just over 1,000 were resident in Kapepa Parish. The population is fairly evenly spread throughout the chiefdom as there are few natural barriers to settlement.

Like the Bisa and Bemba to the north, the Lala claim to have come originally from Luba country, in the Congo, somewhere around the turn of the eighteenth century, and their migration seems to have been linked in some way to the collapse of the Luban Empire (Munday, 1961, p. 8). They reached their present habitat towards the end of the eighteenth century, after first moving south-eastwards through what is now Mwinilunga District and the Copperbelt, and then north-eastwards across the Luapula River to the fringes of the Bangweulu swamps before trekking south on to the plateau region. The evidence suggests that the original migrants moved in fairly small kinship groups and that the gradual drift of population from the Bangweulu swamp region has continued until relatively recent times (Munday, 1940, p. 438).

Like the rest of the plateau, Chibale Chiefdom has a general elevation of about 4,000 ft. above sea-level, rising to about 5,000 ft. along the Luangwa Valley escarpment in the extreme south. The area is well watered, with numerous perennial streams, and has an average annual rainfall of between 35 and 40 inches. The rains are mostly confined to a single wet season which commences in November and lasts until April. The mean maximum temperature is 78°F, rising to about 85°F for the months of October and November, just before the rains break. The soils are mainly of a light sandy nature with occasional pockets of better light-reddish and brown loams. The vegetation is of the *Brachystegia* woodland variety, with stony outcrops in the more hilly places and grassy plains around the rivers (Trapnell, 1943).

Important agricultural changes have occurred in Kapepa Parish in recent years. From about 1950 onwards, plough methods of cultivation have been steadily replacing the traditional form of ash cultivation known as the *citeme*, or 'small-circle' *citemene*, system; and this has led to the development of a category of farmers producing a surplus of food crops for sale. More recently Turkish tobacco was introduced as a cash crop and has been successfully grown by both commercial farmers and ordinary village cultivators.

Agricultural development has brought about an overall increase in the prosperity of the area and has led to increased capital investment by labour migrants hoping to benefit from the expanding economy. At the time of fieldwork, a notable feature of Kapepa Parish (as compared to adjacent areas) was the large number of brick settlements and stores which had sprung up. There were also two diesel engine grinding mills serving the neighbourhood and several locally owned cars and lorries making regular trips to Broken Hill (Kabwe) and the Copperbelt towns.

Connected with these changes has been a change in settlement patterns. Prior to about 1950, the basic residential unit was the village composed of a group of matrilineally related men and women, together with others attached by varying ties of kinship and affinity. But since then villages have tended to fragment into smaller settlements based on a nuclear or three-generation extended family, or on a small group of uterine siblings and their descendants. From a census I took in 1963, just under half the total *de facto* population was residing in settlements other than recognized villages; and a high proportion of commercially oriented farmers and storekeepers had set up by themselves away from their close matrilineal kinsmen. This suggested that large matrilineal descent groups were somewhat incompatible with cash-crop farming and the accumulation of wealth above subsistence needs, and that they were giving way to smaller types of residential units, though the situation was further complicated by the introduction of the parish system[1] of local government which legalized the setting up of small settlements away from the village.

[1] For a description of this see pp. 84–6, 140–2.

Another aspect of change, and one closely related to the various socio-economic changes mentioned above, was the emergence of new patterns of social status. New criteria for evaluating status—wealth, education and leadership in certain non-indigenous associations (e.g. a church or political party)—were tending to replace the more traditional forms. Village headmanship, it was said, was a title only and no longer carried any special privileges. Few people, it seems, considered it a position worth striving for.

These observations indicate that at the time of fieldwork Kapepa Parish was experiencing marked social and economic change. Hence it no longer seemed legitimate to try and circum-scribe one's main field of study in terms of 'the problems posed by the structure of traditional villages', as Turner does in a study of Ndembu social structure (Turner, 1957, p. 10). A broad aim of the present study was to document the kinds of socio-economic changes taking place and to indicate the factors responsible for the emergence of various new social forms. It was also intended to examine the question of the responses to change shown by differ-ent social categories within the population.

Throughout the analysis that follows emphasis will be given to the problem of how far economic innovation has brought about concomitant changes in the social organization and values of the people. It will be argued, for instance, that the move from a subsistence-based axe agriculture to one where cash-cropping and the use of the plough are becoming increasingly important, has led to certain changes in the organization of agricultural labour and in attitudes towards land holding, and has also stimulated the emergence of smaller, differently composed, residential groupings. Similarly, the decline in the position of the village headman, the rise of new forms of status evaluation and the hostilities that now arise within a small group of close matrilineal kinsmen will be attributed in part to the development of new, achievable, econ-omic objectives.

On the other hand, however, some attention will also be given to the problem of whether any significant shifts were already taking place in the economic environment, social organization and values of the people at the time of the introduction of these new forms of production and wealth, and to whether these might have facilitated the acceptance of new modes of socio-economic organization. Hence, when discussing agricultural change, I shall briefly assess the ecological changes occurring in Serenje District and argue that the acceptance of a more settled form of agriculture was partly a response to the rapidly deteriorating ecological situation which could no longer support the *citeme* system of cultivation. Likewise, it will be necessary, when analysing the proliferation of small settlements, to examine the effects that the parish system has had on the position of the village headman and the break-up of villages.

Apart from documenting the major dimensions of social and economic change in the parish, I have tried also to examine the implications of this for individuals involved in concrete social situations and to analyse the strategies adopted by particular social innovators. This is especially evident in the chapter on the dynamics of farm management but it is implicit throughout other parts of the study, for example, in the discussion of the struggles which arise over power and prestige within a small group of kinsmen and affines analysed in Chapter VII. By 'social innovator' I mean someone who manipulates other persons and resources, discovers new channels for exploitation or utilizes 'traditional' relationships and values, in an attempt to achieve some new type of goal, or who devises novel means to attain some already recognized end.

Leaving aside the terminological difficulties of just what kinds of activity should properly be described as 'innovatory', what emerges from this type of orientation is that one can meaningfully study the processes of social change taking place within a community by focusing on those types of social situations which exhibit most clearly the operation of new parameters for action.[1] Close attention can then be given to the kinds of decision made by individuals in relation to specific issues, to the question of how their choices are restricted by a host of different, though possibly interrelated factors, and to the unintended consequences that may arise from their actions. Such an approach, I suggest, facilitates both an understanding of how particular innovators have built upon, or utilized already existing ties, allegiances and sentiments, whilst at the same time showing how new forms of social coalition

[1] A somewhat similar view is expressed by Barth (1963, p. 1), who suggests that the study of entrepreneurship is of key importance for the anthropologist interested in questions of social stability and change.

are formed and new attitudes formulated. Hence in the long run, we arrive at not only an account of newly emerging forms of organization and leadership but also at an appreciation of the extent to which there is continuity with forms of organization which the people themselves categorize as being 'customary'.

The last part of the study discusses the relationship between religion and social action. In the earlier chapters it emerges that Jehovah's Witnesses occupy a prominent place in the economic organization of the parish. They in fact constitute an important group of socio-economic innovators. Most of them live outside the village in small settlements based on a nuclear or small extended family, and a high proportion of them at commercial farms or stores. Proportionately more of them are exploiting the new economic opportunities made available through the introduction of new farming methods and cash-crop production, and more practise additional non-farming trades, such as bricklaying or carpentry.

Is there then some kind of relationship between being a member of this sect and participating in certain forms of social and economic action? Chapter VIII explores this problem and tests the general Weberian thesis about the ways in which a religious ideology can influence social and economic behaviour. To do this it is necessary to enquire into the religious organization, ethic and social recruitment of Jehovah's Witnesses in Kapepa and discuss the relationship between religious conversion and socio-economic mobility.

Analytical approach

Most anthropological studies of social change have worked with some notion of what Gluckman (1958) calls 'successive equilibria' and consist of a series of synchronic structural analyses of the major social groupings, social positions and institutional frameworks of a given social system at successive time-periods (e.g. Barnes, 1954; Fallers, c. 1956). From this it is possible to indicate the nature and degree of structural change that has taken place between the various time-periods, though ideally this kind of study can only satisfactorily be accomplished if reliable and detailed historical data exist or if the anthropologist is making a replication study. A major difficulty in much research is that often the account given of previous structural arrangements is far too sketchy and too idealized to provide much of a baseline for assessing the magnitude of changes that have occurred.

Yet, even granting an adequate baseline, there remain a number of analytical limitations in this approach. Firstly, to present cross-sections of the social structure at different points in time may enable one to deduce the magnitude of structural changes that have occurred between various equilibria, but this in itself provides no convincing assessment of the factors responsible for change, nor does it provide a basis from which to offer prognoses about probable lines of development. A conventional structural analysis, because of its concern for the consistency and continuity of social relationships, tends to give analytical priority to describing the ways in which exogenous factors have been incorporated into, or have impinged on, a pre-existing structure of relationships and values (generally referred to as the traditional system). It does not trace out in detail the ways in which the presence of these new elements are themselves giving rise to new types of social situations, relationships and values. Nor can it give adequate coverage of the variability and flexibility of particular social systems, or handle the question of social innovation.[1]

The intrusion of new factors, such as new forms of technology, obviously set in operation a number of social processes which may, perhaps slowly through time, have widespread repercussions on existing institutional forms. It should be theoretically possible, therefore, by focusing on the ways in which, say, technological innovation is affecting the range of choices open to individuals placed in particular situations, to hypothesize about what long-term structural effects are likely to result if such new components find a more permanent place in the system, or at least to analyse the new sets of relationships occasioned by such a change. Similarly it might also be possible to predict what kinds of innovation will be acceptable to the general populace, or to certain sections of it, if other things remain constant. However, to construct theoretical models of this type one needs to develop modes of analysis outside the strictly structural frame of reference.

In an introductory note to his book *The Politics of Kinship* (1964) van Velsen presents a statement of the general characteristics of structuralism as shown in the works of Evans-Pritchard, Fortes and their students, and discusses some of its inherent analytical

[1] For further discussion of these problems see Moore, 1963, Chapter I.

limitations. Van Velsen deduces that there are, broadly speaking, three salient aspects of structuralism: its concern for relations between social positions or statuses rather than with actual social relations and hence its tendency to over-emphasize consistency and formal rules, its assumption of homogeneity, and thirdly, its concern for the stability of the society or community studied.

Van Velsen considers that the first of these characteristics has a serious limitation in that it aims at presenting an outline of the social morphology in terms of a schema of social positions organized in persons and corporate groups and does not show how 'actual observed behaviour fits into the structural frame' (van Velsen, 1964, p. xxv). In order to handle this problem the anthropologist needs also to take into account behaviour which structuralists would normally designate as 'exceptional' and not relevant to their analyses. One way of doing this in van Velsen's opinion is to use 'situational analysis' or the 'extended-case method' as an integral part of one's study. This type of case-study approach aims, through the exposition and analysis of a series of concrete social situations, to highlight the variability and flexibility inherent in any social system by showing how exceptions and variations are in fact accommodated within the overall structure. This means of course that situational analysis is complementary to structural analysis and is not an alternative model.

His comments on the other aspects of structuralism are brief but to the point. He suggests that Fortes' delimitation of the field in terms of 'homogeneous and relatively stable societies' is probably related to the method's emphasis on consistency (Fortes, 1953, p. 29). If the analytical construct stresses the regularities and interdependencies between parts of a system and largely excludes consideration of problems relating to the variability and flexibility of the system studied, then it tends also to make assumptions about homogeneity and stability. Hence in situations where these types of assumptions cannot so easily be made the model is redundant, unless modified in some way. Van Velsen's solution is to make greater use of the extended-case method as developed by Mitchell (1956) and Turner (1957).

These comments by van Velsen seem directly pertinent to the limitations the structural approach has, I suggested, for the study of social change. Structural analysis enables one to identify and describe the interconnections between different social institutions;

and it may allow one to make *post hoc* statements about the kinds of structural changes which have occurred between two or more time-periods. But it cannot adequately deal with the problem of how change is generated, neither can it satisfactorily handle situations where 'we are not dealing with an integrated cultural system but with one in which quite disparate systems of belief may co-exist' (Mitchell, 1960, p. 19). To analyse problems of this nature it seems better to work with the more flexible notion of a social field or fields, and to employ a type of situational or extended-case method to help determine the more important structural and situational components.

By 'social field' I mean an area of social life defined in relation to certain types of social action. Thus, 'economic field' refers to all those activities, relationships and values which affect the production, distribution and consumption of goods and services; and 'political field' to all those concerned with the distribution of power in a society. The idea of a *field* of activity is wider than what we normally mean by an economic or political *structure* for it refers not only to those institutional arrangements specifically designed to attain certain economic or political ends, but also takes into account other kinds of relationships and values that may be utilized for the same purpose.[1] The heuristic advantage of such a concept is that it covers both the important structural features (which to some extent limit the range of choices open to individuals) while at the same time giving attention to what Firth (1964, p. 17) has called the 'organizational elements'—the processes by which individuals choose between alternative courses of action and manipulate various norms and values in order to justify them.

To talk of a social field then is to specify one's problem and social area for analysis.[2] It remains the task of the analyst to identify those clusters of highly interconnected relationships that exist within a social field and to examine how far behaviour in one field affects relationships in others. To do this he will need to explore in detail the ramifications of particular actions, making

[1] For discussion of this difference see Bailey, 1960, pp. 10–12.

[2] Barnes, for example, in his study of a Norwegian fishing community, isolates three main fields—the territorial, the industrial and the field of interpersonal relations—and discusses their interconnections (Barnes, 1954, pp. 39–58). See also Epstein (1958, p. 232) and Mitchell (1960, p. 32; 1966, p. 57).

some assessment of the determinants of behaviour in different types of social situations. This means that sufficient weight can be given to the variability of social systems for one is not solely interested in formulating statements about overall structural regularities. One also attempts to explain how deviations from the norm (ideal or statistical) arise, or to show how new types of social situations, relationships and values are emerging, perhaps with a view to deducing the direction of change.

In the present study I have attempted to operationalize this notion of the social field by isolating for analysis three main fields of action which exhibit marked degrees of variability and change: the economic (Chapters II and III), the residential (Chapters IV and V), and that involving the evaluation of social status (Chapters VI and VII). Within these analytically separable fields one can then isolate sets of interdependent variables. For example, it is possible to identify the necessary requisites (both material and social) associated with commercial plough agriculture in Serenje and to demonstrate how change in one factor affects changes in the levels of other resources. Or similarly, one may examine the principles governing residential affiliation for different types of residential grouping and discuss the nature of their interconnections. This procedure enables one to describe the structural regularities of different dimensions of social life without positing the existence of a single, interdependent socio-cultural system or a total social structure. In addition it allows one to explore, through situational analysis, the ways in which new social and economic factors are affecting the type and range of choices open to individuals, and clears the way to a more thorough appreciation of the sources and conditions of change.

My use of situational or extended-case analysis differs somewhat from that of Turner and van Velsen. These latter both show how 'individuals actually handle their structural relationships and exploit the element of choice between alternative norms according to the requirements of any particular situation' (van Velsen, 1967, p. 148). Here, however, I have attempted to go beyond this, and where possible, have used case material to generate hypotheses about the relations between various factors and how these influence the patterns of behaviour and decisions made by actors in situations of similar type. Some of these hypotheses are then tested out over a wider body of data and given some quantitative form. This enables me to generalize my conclusions so as to arrive at statements about the kinds of components, or sets of relationships, involved in certain types of social situations and how these are interrelated. Moreover, since the analysis concentrates primarily on situations which depict most clearly the operation and influence of new factors, this procedure allows one to make generalizations about the sociological implications of socioeconomic change.

CHAPTER II

CHANGING PATTERNS OF AGRICULTURE

Traditionally the Lala have practised a form of ash cultivation known as the *citeme* (pl. *fiteme*), or 'small circle' *citemene* (pl. *fitemene*), system growing finger millet as the staple crop and supported by a variety of crops grown in secondary hoed gardens (*mabala*). The *citeme* system has been described as a variant of the *citemene* system used by the Bemba; but whereas the Bemba pollard the trees and stack the branches in large circles for burning, the Lala fell them at breast height and make small circles (*iminda* or *myunda*), or, if there is a plentiful supply of large branches, they stack them in long narrow strips (*bakulakula*). Cutting begins in April or early May and lasts until the end of August, and during this time people live in temporary grass encampments (*nkutu*) built close to the cutting areas, as the *citeme* gardens are usually several miles from the permanent settlements. After the trees have been felled the branches are left to dry and later stacked to form *iminda* and *bakulakula*. This task should normally be completed by the end of September in good time for the first rains. Then, shortly before the rains are due (that is, in late October or early November), the piles of branches are fired to ensure that only a minimum of ash is lost. This also reduces the risk of weed seeds accumulating in the ash patches. The millet seed is sown in early December. An unsown border is usually left along the margin of each ash circle where pumpkins or gourds are planted. The garden areas are then fenced off to protect the maturing crop from predatory game, though this has been discontinued in some areas as game became scarcer. From now on periodic inspections are all that are necessary until May or June when the millet is harvested. After harvesting, the grain is stored in grain bins (*amatala*), built close to the *citeme* gardens for convenience. Small quantities are collected from time to time and carried to the permanent settlements for pounding. A few *fiteme* may be used for a second season for groundnuts, or groundbeans, but generally only those which are closest to the permanent settlements. In this case each household is allocated a certain number of ash patches for planting.

PLATE I

(a) *above:* landscape showing effects of *citeme* system

(b) *below:* newly-cut *citeme*. The branches are left to dry before they are piled to form *iminda* or *bakulakula*

PLATE II

(a) *left:* harvesting of finger millet from *citeme* garden

(b) *below:* pounding of finger millet

A wide variety of hoed gardens (*mabala*, pl. *ibala*, sing.) are cultivated where sorghum, maize, beans, groundnuts, cassava, sweet potatoes and other vegetables are grown. These gardens are found both on upland soils and along the dambo[1] margins. In the case of upland sites, the area is first cleared of trees and bush and the branches laid in circles as for *citeme*. The branches are usually burnt at about the same time as the *citeme* gardens. The ash circles are then planted with sorghum, or with finger millet if for some reason the household is short of millet. The intervening ground is made into mounds which can be planted with a number of different crops. The usual arrangement, however, is for beans or groundnuts to be planted in the first year, with cassava roots around the base of each mound. The beans or groundnuts are harvested in April. Then at the beginning of the next rainy season sorghum is sown and this is reaped in the following May or June. Thereafter the garden is left to cassava, individual roots being dug up as required. Cassava, having a lengthy maturation period of about 18 months, is normally ready for use immediately after the sorghum has been harvested.

Other types of hoe-cultivated gardens also require brief mention. Occasionally, separate mounds are prepared in the wetter dambo margins and planted with cassava in March or November. This kind of garden is called *citaba*.

Again maize and beans may be grown on seepage sites within the dambos. These gardens are usually dug in June or July. The grass and turf is hoed into small circles and burnt when dry in August. Maize and pumpkins are then planted. The maize is harvested very early (in December or early January) because the wetness of the soil removes the need for dependence on the main rains for the growing season, and after it has been gathered beans are usually planted. This particular garden, *cisebe*, is very popular throughout Serenje District, and in some parts it provides the only reliable supply of maize, the upland soils often being too sandy for the crop. One other dambo garden of some importance is the *fibunde* beds. These are dug on the upper flanks of the dambos and used for Livingstone potatoes.[2]

In 1946 a survey of the agricultural system in Serenje District

---

[1] A dambo is a treeless, grassy and often swampy plain.
[2] For a fuller account of the indigenous form of agriculture practised among the Serenje Lala, see Peters, 1950.

c

was undertaken by the late David Peters, who concluded that the *citeme* system of cultivation was on the point of breakdown in that there was a serious shortage of sufficiently well regenerated trees available for cutting (Peters, 1950). This he attributed to the fact that the density of population had exceeded the critical population or land-carrying capacity of the system. Under *citeme* cultivation the critical population was calculated to be about six persons per square mile, but the actual overall population density for the district was 7·3, rising to 8·2 in Chibale Chiefdom and to 11 in Mailo Chiefdom in the eastern part of the district. Hence the woodlands were being consumed at a phenomenal rate. 75 per cent of all trees felled were not fully regenerated, the average age of growth being about 17 years. Peters estimated that a tree would require something like 35 years to regenerate after having been cut at breast height. Moreover, from the measurement of 44 *fiteme* areas, it was calculated that the mean size of woodland area cut per *citeme* was 17·3 acres and Peters suggested that the acreage would increase as fewer large trees were available. Though greater reliance might be placed on the various subsidiary gardens for the provision of staple requirements, all the evidence pointed to the inevitable extinction of the *citeme* system on the Serenje plateau.

In 1958 a follow-up study was made by the agricultural staff at Serenje to test the general validity of Peters' work (Smyth, 1958). The original study was found to be reasonably predictive of subsequent trends. In the intervening 12 years the average woodland area cut had increased to about 25 acres, though there was found to be considerable variation throughout the district. The maximum regeneration period possible at the rate of consumption at that time was calculated to be 17·8 years for the whole district, slightly higher than Peters' figure. Comparison of the size of *citeme* and subsidiary gardens revealed that in areas where the average area of *citeme* cut was smallest, the average subsidiary garden was the largest. Peters had estimated that the average area per household devoted to subsidiary gardens was about 1½ acres. The 1958 study, however, draws attention to a wide range in size and concludes that the area devoted to subsidiary gardens is related to the size of *citeme* cut. For example, in Muchinka Chiefdom the average *citeme* was 34·28 acres and the average for hoed gardens only 1 acre, but in Kabamba Chiefdom the *citeme* covered only 16·49 acres and the hoed gardens 5·4 acres. The figures for the southern part of Chibale (the only area sampled) were 24·66 acres of *citeme* as against 1·2 acres of hoed gardens.[1]

Towards the end of his report Peters discusses the question of long-term agricultural development. One of the recommendations he makes is for a more permanent system of agriculture based on livestock production together with dry season wheat, vegetables, beans and groundnuts. He writes,

It is difficult to combine finger millet grown as the staple crop under a *chitemene* system with a permanent system of agriculture (perhaps on irrigable sites) in most areas. Nevertheless, as the importance of the former declines, the number of areas where a more permanent agriculture can be practised will increase and the village site become also more permanent. . . . Since one of the main features of the plateau is the plentiful supplies of permanent water, long term developments may be looked for in livestock production and dry season wheat and vegetable growing . . . the Broken Hill [Kabwe] market, and even that of the Copperbelt, should prove within economic distance for much vegetable produce. Beans, groundbeans and groundnuts should be of much greater importance as rain-grown crops for sale (p. 86).

He also suggests that even if the average hoed acreages at present cultivated are near the possible limits for the population in its present physical condition, it would be possible to increase the acreage with the use of ploughs.

Following Peters' study attempts were made to improve the *citeme* system by introducing interplanting of sorghum and cassava and by encouraging the adoption of large circle methods. Experiments had shown that the Bemba large circle system provided much higher yields of finger millet, chiefly because the border wastage on large circles is far less. Yet despite the efforts of the Agricultural Department to bring about such changes the Lala were generally unresponsive and the attempt was abandoned in 1953.

Efforts were also made to get people to cultivate more extensive hoed gardens. Native Authority orders had been issued in the

[1] 34·28 acres for Muchinka Chiefdom seems an incredibly large area and one suspects that the author may not always have ascertained accurately the boundaries between individual *citeme* gardens. Yet despite this the general pattern remains clear enough.

1940's requiring all adult males to cultivate special gardens each year for cassava and maize. This met with little resistance, for in many areas people had in effect already started cultivating larger subsidiary gardens to meet their basic requirements, no longer satisfied by their *citeme* gardens. Cassava had originally been introduced into Serenje District through contact with the peoples of the Bangweulu swamp fringe and had been cultivated as a standby crop for many years. This suggests that the Lala had for some time been reacting and adjusting to growing land degeneration by reducing their *fiteme* areas and at the same time increasing the acreage under hoe cultivation.[1]

A more radical move was made when the Agricultural Department set up a number of 'peasant farming' blocks in various parts of Serenje. The original aim of the scheme was 'to anchor the African to the land, to concentrate population, to improve agricultural practice and soil conservation and so to open the way to further development' (*Review of Ten Year Development Plan*, 1948). It was hoped that despite the poor soil conditions the scheme might nevertheless help to pave the way to wider agricultural change and alleviate the pressure of population on land occasioned by the *citeme* system. This plan was part of a wider attempt to foster the transition from subsistence to commercial production in African rural areas throughout Northern Rhodesia. At the same time as farming blocks were being demarcated in Serenje so they were at Katete in the Eastern Province, and at other places in the Eastern, Central and Northern Provinces (Coster, 1958, pp. 4–6).

Under the peasant farming scheme selected cultivators were invited to move out of their villages and settle on specially sited 10-acre plots. In Serenje, five localities were chosen, one being in Kapepa Parish, Chibale. It was intended that each block would initially have ten farmers who would be issued with oxen, plough and farming implements. Every three years another 10 acres would be added to each plot until the ninth year when each farmer would then have a total of 40 acres of land. Each year,

---

[1] See Allan, 1965, p. 113. He also argues that migration westwards into the uninhabited or sparsely inhabited woodlands between the Lala and Swaka peoples helped to alleviate this problem. The same argument might hold for the early period of labour migration from the district though, as Peters shows, by the mid-1940's even this did not improve the situation much.

however, a total of 10 acres only would be under cultivation: thus every 10-acre plot would be worked for three years and rested for nine. By the end of 1949, 49 farms had been opened on the five Serenje blocks and a total of 330 acres was already under cultivation.

In the first year of joining the block the farmer is under close supervision and is taught modern methods of agriculture and soil conservation, and thereafter he continues to receive regular technical assistance and advice from trained agricultural demonstrators. In addition he is offered credit facilities so that he can acquire various items of capital equipment and cover the costs of stumping and clearing the land. On arrival he is issued with one plough with yoke and chains, one shovel and fork, one harrow and one scotch cart, plus two oxen and two cows, which he is required to pay for on a system of ten annual repayments. The total loan would be in the region of £120 in value. Later he may be encouraged to purchase a planter, a ridger, a wheelbarrow and a small hand grinding machine.

In 1958, agricultural policy shifted its emphasis from 'block' to 'individual' farming. This made it possible for individuals not living on the blocks to be registered as peasant farmers. Originally it had been hoped that farming blocks would become permanent centres for community development. It was envisaged that a kind of village would evolve around the nucleus of a group of about 50 farmers wherein would live various non-farming specialists, such as carpenters, blacksmiths and storekeepers. But the scheme did not develop in this way. To most farmers the block farms simply provided an opportunity to learn the techniques of plough cultivation and the means to acquire the necessary equipment. They moved to the farming block to serve a form of apprenticeship, after which they sought to set up their own individual farms outside the direct control of the Agricultural Department. In Chibale in 1964 it was still a popular notion that those who remained on the block farms were 'the slaves of the Government' (*abasha babuteko*), whilst those working their own farms were their own masters (*basulutani bafwamu*), literally, 'headmen of their farms'. The Agricultural Department also found that returning labour migrants often brought with them sufficient savings of their own to purchase all or some of the basic equipment and it was felt that these men should likewise be given the benefits of technical help if they wanted it. Thus, since about 1958, there has been a steady increase in the number of 'individual farmers' as against 'block farmers' and by March 1963 only six of the 25 registered peasant farmers in Kapepa Parish were living at the block, and only one other farming block in Serenje was still in existence.

Like the block farmers, individual farmers may apply for loans for farming equipment and for stumping. However, most have already practised plough cultivation for a year or two prior to their registration as peasant farmers and have had to meet some of the establishment costs themselves. Indeed this appears to be one criterion by which the Agricultural Department judges the suitability of applicants. Once registered, then individual farmers receive the same technical assistance from agricultural field staff as do the block farmers. They are regularly visited by agricultural emonstrators who advise on crop rotation and on the use of kraal and green manure, and who give short courses on the handling of oxen and plough.

Where axe has given way to plough, the land is normally cleared and stumped between January and April, ready for ploughing which commences at the beginning of the next rainy season. It is recommended that kraal manure be spread over the plots some time before ploughing, though only a few farmers were observed to do this. A cereal crop like maize, sorghum or millet is sown in late November or early December and this is harvested in the following May or June. Weeding is a major task and is done throughout January, February and March. In the second year, the field may be used for planting another grain crop and in the third, a legume such as groundnuts or groundbeans. It is then left fallow for three or more years. Where green manure crops are grown these should be ploughed under in March. Few farmers have under plough at any one time more than 12 acres, the average being in the region of eight, but their wives also grow a variety of produce like sweet potatoes and cassava in hoed gardens.

In 1963 all but one of the registered peasant farmers in Kapepa produced a surplus of food crops (maize, beans, groundnuts and vegetables) which were transported to Broken Hill (Kabwe) and the Copperbelt towns for sale. For instance, I found that their average annual income from the sale of maize and beans in 1963 amounted to £20 9s. The amounts ranged from £7 10s. to about

£57. There appeared to be no significant difference in the levels of productivity of block and individual farmers.

In 1958 Turkish tobacco was introduced as an experimental cash crop and the soils were found to be particularly favourable. Tobacco was first grown by peasant farmers but was later extended to include all kinds of cultivators. In 1963 there were 44 growers in Kapepa, most of them growing about half an acre. Of these, 20 were registered peasant farmers, three were storekeepers and the remaining 21 ordinary subsistence cultivators.[1] Their average income from tobacco in 1963 was about £35, though the more successful growers received between £70 and £100.

Work on tobacco begins in November with the preparation of nursery beds sited on the dambo edges and the ploughing or hoeing of a main garden on more upland soil. Seedlings are planted in mid-November and treated with insecticides and fungicides and kept well watered. From mid-January until the end of February transplanting to the main garden takes place. The top soil is first treated with fertilizer. Reaping begins in mid-March and lasts until the end of July. The leaves are picked daily by hand as they ripen and are graded according to size and threaded on strings ready for curing. This task takes up most of the day and is sometimes continued by firelight in the evenings. The leaves are then strung on racks and sun-dried. Later the cured tobacco is stored in a vacant house or a grass shed to await baling, which begins in time to catch the first tobacco sales in early June. Each tobacco grower transports his tobacco to special baling centres where there are agricultural demonstrators to assist with the job. Baling continues throughout July and August, as it is desirable that the tobacco should be baled only a few days before each sale. In the following year the old garden is normally planted with a grain crop and a new tobacco garden prepared.

Broadly speaking, most farmers earn about £25 per annum from the sale of food crops, about £35 from tobacco, and perhaps a further £10 from other sales (e.g. beer, vegetables, chickens). This gives a rough figure of about £70 gross. Out of this they

[1] I have defined subsistence cultivator as someone whose surplus of food crops (if any) is insufficient for external marketing. In a majority of cases he also practises non-plough cultivation. In contrast, a peasant farmer is a small-scale commercial farmer who sows his crops with the specific aim of producing a surplus for sale.

will probably have to pay about £10 in loan repayments and reserve another £10 for hiring labour during the next year. A good slice of the remaining £50 will be earmarked for paying off debts incurred at local stores and for rewarding persons (usually kinsmen) who have contributed free labour or services during the preceding year. This shows that the rate of capital accumulation is likely to be rather slow unless the farmer has other sources of income. Many farmers do practise some non-farming trade in their spare time and many also receive regular financial assistance from wage-earning relatives in town.

The introduction of plough methods and of Turkish tobacco as a cash crop have wrought significant changes in Kapepa Parish. Though plough agriculture was initially practised only by peasant farmers, it has spread to other sections of the community and has become increasingly popular with the development of the tobacco crop. A census I made in March–April 1963 showed that out of 214 male cultivators in the parish 136 (64%) continued to employ *citeme* methods, 52 (24%) were engaged in plough cultivation, and the remaining 26 (12%) used a combination of both. Thus, though a majority still rely on traditional methods, there has over the last 15 years been a marked trend away from traditional forms of agriculture.

Organization of labour

All forms of agricultural production are closely associated with the household unit. The household among the Lala is generally referred to as 'our house' (*kwesu*) and can be defined simply as a group of persons receiving their food from a common domestic hearth and usually cultivating a common set of gardens. From the analysis of households in Kapepa it was found that two main kinds of grouping predominated: that consisting of a single nuclear family (i.e. a man, his wife and unmarried children) and that made up of an uxorilocal or sometimes bilateral extended family (i.e. a man, his wife, his unmarried children and one or more of his married daughters, possibly also sons, and their spouses and children) but seldom having more than three or more adult women or more than two adult men in one household. In theory, marriage is uxorilocal for the first few years, during which the husband works for his parents-in-law. He cuts a *citeme* garden for them or assists with ploughing, and cultivates secondary gardens;

but being part of their household he has no exclusive right to any portion of the produce resulting directly from his labours and receives his food from his mother-in-law's fireplace. Only later when the young couple have children are they allowed to establish their own separate household. This nuclear family will subsequently develop into an uxorilocal extended family when the man's daughters marry and bring their husbands to work for him.

Under the *citeme* system of cultivation there is a fairly clear-cut division of agricultural tasks between the sexes within the household. The felling of trees, the clearing of the undergrowth and the construction of the fence around the *citeme* garden are male tasks, while women are responsible for the gathering and piling of the branches, and for the harvesting of the millet crop. Sowing is a joint effort, the man scattering the seeds and his wife following behind covering them with earth. The firing of the piles of branches is generally undertaken by the man assisted by his wife or others in the household. Each *citeme* garden is cut individually by each adult male member of the household, though occasionally collective work parties are organized. The 'owner' of the *citeme* announces that on such-and-such a day beer will be available for all those who help him cut his *citeme*. The work party will assemble early in the morning and will fell trees until a fair day's work has been completed. They will then return to the settlement to drink beer. Nowadays workers are often paid instead with money or salt. There is no regular pattern for recruiting workers for *citeme* work of this sort, most work parties being composed of a rather heterogeneous collection of kinsmen and neighbours.

A woman is normally helped by some of her close female matrikin when she harvests the millet crop, and in return she will assist them when their crops ripen. She may also be assisted with the piling of branches by these same kin. The group of female matrikin involved are usually other members of the same household (i.e. they will be her daughters, sisters, or mother), but it may include members of different households. Sometimes too, affines or unrelated persons will help each other, or a woman who has no man to cut for her will provide labour in return for millet grain. Such work arrangements between various women, however, are mostly on a fairly *ad hoc* basis.

The initial clearing of the bush for the hoed gardens is again a male task, while the sowing, weeding and harvesting are undertaken by the wife assisted from time to time by other women, usually matrikin. The making of mounds is a joint task. Dambo gardens are cultivated entirely by women.

Under plough agriculture the household remains the basic labour unit, but often the fairly strict division of labour between sexes is less marked. This is related to the greater need for co-operation among members of the household which ploughing demands and also to the increased labour input associated with commercial production.

Although ploughing is mostly considered a male task, frequently a wife and an elder daughter are asked to lend a hand if no other males are available. A minimum of two but preferably three persons are needed to accomplish the task successfully: one to hold the plough, one to lead the oxen and one to goad them on. Thus women will sometimes assist with leading and goading on the oxen and may also take turns at holding the plough. Holding the plough is a relatively skilled and heavy job and requires a fair amount of experience to handle it properly, but no social stigma attaches to a woman performing the task as there would be if she undertook to cut her own *citeme*. Occasionally too, co-wives will assist one another with ploughing.

Similarly the planting, weeding and harvesting of crops under plough cultivation are often undertaken jointly by the husband and wife, though links with various female matrikin may still be utilized as with *citeme* methods. The cultivation of tobacco is a joint household task, all members of working age participating throughout its production and children from about the age of nine upwards providing essential labour during the picking and stringing stages.

The change from a subsistence-based agriculture to one of cash-cropping, however, has brought with it certain innovations in the organization of labour.

Many cash-crop farmers use casual contract labour for such tasks as stumping and harvesting. In 1963–4 labourers were mostly paid a standard rate of about 2s. a day or the equivalent in kind (e.g. salt or flour). Sometimes matrikin of the farmer or his wife were asked to lend a hand on the understanding that they would receive the same basic pay as non-kinsmen and would be expected to complete the same work tasks. In other cases, matrikin were recruited at a slightly lower rate of pay and promised some share of the produce when harvested. In addition, most farmers had regular herdsboys working for them, often their own or their sister's sons. In return the farmer provided food and clothing for the boy and had an arrangement with him whereby after so many years he would be given a cow for his services. Similarly a farmer may decide to reward his wife for the many years of labour she has contributed to the farm by transferring to her ownership a few head of cattle and some farming implements. Most farmers said this was in recognition of her having performed many arduous tasks which some might consider unbecoming to her sex. Having handed over the property, the farmer sometimes finds that this acts to his disadvantage, for frequently the wife will pass it on to a uterine brother or to some other male matrilineal kinsman to hold in trust for her should she later be divorced. In fact I recorded two cases where divorce had ensued and where the women had left their husbands to start their own peasant farms. Yet despite this difficulty, most of the larger, more established farmers in the parish had rewarded their wives in this way.

Tobacco cultivation requires a large labour input throughout its production and especially during the processing stages. Turkish tobacco has a high value to weight ratio and is therefore a suitable cash crop for more distant rural areas where heavy transport costs make it uneconomic to market bulky crops. A recent agricultural report (Maclean, 1962) estimates that with skilled production the gross annual income per acre of tobacco would be in the region of £80. Moreover its production needs little in the way of capital equipment or land. But, on the other hand, Turkish tobacco does require a great deal of constant attention and manpower to produce a high-quality leaf. It has been calculated that about 694 man-days per acre of the crop are required to handle all stages of production which span a period of about eight months from mid-November until mid-July. In comparison, Burley tobacco requires only 298 man-days, groundnuts 122 and maize 86. Furthermore, like most leaf crops there are peak requirements at various times during the year.

It is usual for tobacco growers to employ some extra labour at the picking, stringing and baling stages. Some are employed on a casual piece-work basis, the standard rate for stringing leaves being a penny a string, others receive the daily rate of 2s. a day, and a few may be taken on for the whole season. This latter category normally receives some proportion of the income from the crop. Moreover, since tobacco is seen purely in terms of cash return, many households operate a system whereby each one of the adults, and in some cases adolescent boys and girls too, receive some share of the price fetched by the tobacco. Also an unmarried son, or perhaps a second wife, is at liberty to cultivate his or her own separate garden of tobacco and will generally be allowed to keep the profits.

Contract labour is not exclusively confined to the peasant farming group. Those subsistence cultivators who can afford it may occasionally employ others on a daily basis to assist with the cutting of their *citeme* gardens or they may hire a local farmer to plough for them, paying £2 10s. or £3 per acre. Thus, one farmer finds it more remunerative to plough for others than to concentrate on growing a surplus of crops for sale. Storekeepers also rely on hired labour for the cultivation of small gardens (*fiteme* or ploughed) to meet some of their food requirements.

The labour requirements of *citeme* and plough methods of cultivation differ somewhat. Peters writes in his report that under the *citeme* system,

The labour requirement is very low, and is discontinuous. The maximum labour requirement is at and not long after harvest and is at a minimum after planting (i.e. in the 'hunger season'). The man's labour can be, and usually is, restricted to three months' tree cutting in the year. . . . Together with tree felling and the lopping off of branches the biggest labour requirement is in the carrying of the branches to the burning sites. In comparison with the Northern *Chitemene* system, where all branches are carried to one large site, the small circle method shortens the distance of carriage almost to a minimum, with corresponding lightening of the labour required (Peters, 1950, p. 72).

At no stage in the agricultural cycle does the system demand the co-operation of large numbers of men or women. Thus a household unit consisting of say one man, his wife and two adult daughters (and perhaps one resident son-in-law) should normally be sufficient to meet all labour demands. Indeed it would be unlikely for a household of this size to call in additional workers at harvesting time or to assist with the piling of branches. The same would be true for hoed gardens since they also require a relatively low labour input.

The adoption of plough methods does not automatically result in an increased labour input, except during the initial years of establishing plough cultivation when stumping is a major task. But by using the plough larger acreages can be brought under cultivation for an equivalent amount of labour and these larger acreages imply a heavier labour demand at weeding and harvesting time. A household unit consisting of two men and two women, with up to four small children, will normally be sufficient to complete the necessary tasks to meet the subsistence requirements for the family, though to do so they will have to operate a system of joint roles with little sexual division of labour, and they must of course possess the necessary farming expertise. If, however, the farmer (as is the case with almost all plough cultivators) genuinely aims at producing some surplus of crops for sale, then he will probably need to recruit additional labour for weeding and harvesting and perhaps also at other times. Many farmers do this by taking on hired hands. In the next chapter I shall examine in detail how it is that farmers recruit the necessary labour and shall analyse more closely the question of the composition and deployment of the regular labour force at farms. One point I shall develop is that the composition of labour units is related to the level of labour input from the farmer's own household, which varies according to the stage of family development. It also relates to the opportunities which exist for recruiting other forms of labour.

Earlier I drew attention to the large labour input required for tobacco production. A study by the Agricultural Department showed, for example, that one acre of tobacco requires the work of three adults working full time on it throughout its production to produce a reasonable crop. Thus a major difficulty with Turkish tobacco is that it demands a persistent effort on the part of the growers over a period of about eight months. Also several of its operations clash with the labour requirements of various food crops. The seed-bed activities coincide with the ploughing and planting of grains like maize, millet and sorghum, and the picking and stringing process cuts across the harvesting period for these crops. For those who practise *citeme* cultivation, the whole of the harvesting, curing and baling period occurs at the same time as the cutting of *fiteme*, when many people are away living at temporary encampments at some distance from the village. Thus its production seems more compatible with plough or hoe agriculture and for this reason has tended to make *citeme* methods less attractive to those who become growers. This is supported by the fact that almost all of the 21 growers, who were not peasant farmers, had either recently purchased a plough and oxen or managed to borrow these items from some kinsman or friend, or they had found sufficient cash to hire a farmer to plough a tobacco plot for them. In the latter case, their tobacco garden was planted with a grain crop in the second year and this reduced the amount of *citeme* which had to be cut.

Another factor making for the acceptability of plough agriculture is the general ecological situation. Like the rest of Serenje plateau, the area of good woodland in Kapepa suitable for *citeme* has diminished drastically over the past 30 years due to increased pressure of population. In 1963–4 I estimated that the density of population in the parish was about ten persons per square mile, which was well above the carrying capacity for the *citeme* system. It was also found that most *citeme* cultivators were travelling about five miles from their permanent settlements in search of good cutting areas, as compared with the figure of $2\frac{1}{2}$ miles given by Peters. Most of the trees felled were of less than about 20 years re-growth, which was below the number of years needed for complete regeneration. Thus, we can see that as the process of land degeneration proceeds so a larger input of labour and time is required to obtain the same food requirements: much more time is expended commuting between the cutting areas and settlements and far larger acreages have to be cut. In some parts of the district these changes have been met by adjustments taking place within the framework of the traditional system of agriculture. For example, in Muchinka Chiefdom, where I worked for a short time, people now spend a longer period cutting their *fiteme* than they did in the past and grow more cassava in their secondary gardens. Cassava has a lower labour requirement than other crops like sorghum and maize, and this compensates for the greater amount of time spent on *citeme* gardens. An alternative solution to the problem is exemplified in Kapepa Parish, where in some sections of the community there has been a technological change-over from axe to plough. Providing some fertilization is used finger millet yields from ploughed fields are as good as obtained from ash circles. The slightly better reddish soils of the parish, when compared with other parts of the plateau, respond well to plough agriculture and the heavy fertilization of tobacco fields offers an excellent base for the cultivation of a grain crop in the second season.

System of land holding

Under the system of *citeme* cultivation traditionally practised by the Lala no groups or persons had an interest in a particular piece of land for an indefinite period of time. Land rights were vested in the individual as a member or citizen of a particular chiefdom, but each individual could cultivate any tract of uncultivated land within the chiefdom providing no one had already established prior rights over it. The chief was described as 'the owner of the land' (*mwine mpanga*) but only in the sense that he acted as custodian of the land for the people of his chiefdom. He had no right to dispossess people of their land nor did he allocate specific plots or delegate such powers to the village headmen under him. Essentially his title referred to the political control he exercised over the people in his chiefdom—he was entitled to demand allegiance from anyone settling within his area—and to the ritual role he performed on their behalf to ensure the fertility of soils and to bring rain.

It was customary on joining a village to ask the headman to advise on a suitable area for cultivation but theoretically an individual could choose any unoccupied tract and delineate his own boundaries. In the case of *citeme* this was done by pollarding trees at widely spaced intervals along the boundaries of the area one wished to cut, and by doing so one established a prior claim to it. *Citeme* gardens might be several miles from the settlement depending on the availability of good woodland. Unlike the *fiteme*, secondary gardens were generally close to the village and close to each other. Boundaries were marked by footpaths between them, but where two villages were close together the gardens of one village might be interspersed with those of the other. Once an individual had started cultivating a certain area he had full rights to its use until he abandoned it. He also had prior rights to vacant and unused land adjacent to his own gardens, and any dispute that might arise over the use of this land was normally settled on the grounds that the first to cut trees or cultivate in the area had land rights there. Women were not excluded from having rights in land and older children might also cultivate their own gardens. Everyone had an equal claim on other natural resources such as water, firewood and game, though the bushland immediately surrounding a village was generally held to be for the use of the inhabitants of that village and would be the grazing ground for their domestic livestock.

The same basic principles of land tenure hold for today. The chief remains the custodian of the land but nowadays has few ritual functions to perform. Any newcomer to his chiefdom has to seek permission to cultivate and this applies equally to subsistence cultivators and to registered peasant farmers living outside the farming block. Block land is administered by the Agricultural Department on behalf of the Local Authority. The tenant is given the right to use the land for so long as he remains on the block.

The development of a more settled form of agriculture with the use of the plough has as yet brought no major changes to this system of land tenure. But there are signs that peasant farmers are beginning to attach a new value to land. When farms are established neither the chief nor the Agricultural Department (except for the block farms) is responsible for demarcating farm boundaries. Thus boundaries remain vague and are often a source of friction between adjacent farmers and between farmers and other cultivators. This is illustrated in the following two disputes, the first concerning the making of a farm boundary and the second over the use of a tract of land close to a dambo area.

Farm boundary dispute

Mwape had been authorized by the chief to establish a new farm in the newly opened Protected Forest Area near the Great North Road. After selecting a site for his house and commencing building the dwellings and cattle kraal, he set about cutting a wide pathway through the woodland, encircling his settlement. This, he claimed, marked the extent of his farm land to be used for gardens and grazing.

Shortly after Mwape had settled in, Chisenga arrived. He also had permission from the chief to start a farm within the Protected Forest Area. The site he chose was on the opposite side of the stream from Mwape.

Friction between them arose over the grazing of Chisenga's crops by

PLATE III

(a) *above:* stringing of newly-picked tobacco leaves by children
(b) *below:* tobacco drying racks. The tobacco is threaded on string and hung up for sun drying. At night and during showers the racks are covered with plastic sheeting to protect the tobacco from rain and dew

PLATE IV

(a) *above:* Saini Moloka farm
(b) *below:* herdsboy controlling oxen during a break in ploughing. The plough is in the left foreground

Mwape's cattle Chisenga had cultivated a small garden of maize and beans on Mwape's side of the stream, though it was nearly a mile from Mwape's settlement and gardens. On two separate occasions the garden was extensively damaged by Mwape's cattle. On the first, Chisenga had politely asked Mwape to ensure that the herdsboys kept closer watch over the beasts to prevent it happening again. Mwape had replied tersely: 'This is my land. This is not the time of the year for me to keep my cattle shut up in the kraal. I can chase you from this land.' Not wishing to become involved in a bitter argument Chisenga let Mwape have his say and then returned to his own farm. But when the cattle grazed the crop for a second time he decided to take the case to the chief's court.

At the court, the main question for discussion was not the damage incurred to Chisenga's crops but the fact that Mwape had 'tried to be big, like a chief' and had claimed too large an area of woodland for his own use when Chisenga also needed land. Moreover the point was made that boundary disputes could not be solved simply by arguing that one had already marked out the boundaries of one's farm and that was that. Only the chief could grant rights in land and only he could resolve boundary disputes. Why had Mwape cut a boundary round the farm without first seeking the permission of the chief and why had he not tried to come to some agreement with Chisenga over boundaries? Mwape's reply to these charges was that in the final analysis he believed the land was really God's, not the chief's. (Mwape was in fact an ardent Jehovah's Witness.)

The hearing ended at this point with Mwape being threatened with eviction from his farm unless he took a different attitude.

Dispute concerning land rights

One day Santi, a rather successful farmer, was dismayed to find that a neighbouring cultivator, Kamfwa, was felling trees on the dambo margins on the other side of the stream to his own farm. He tried in vain to stop Kamfwa who was apparently cutting a *citeme* garden. Santi argued that although he had no gardens yet on that side of the stream, he had planned to open up some in the coming year because there was not enough good soil on this side to allow for expansion. When he had spoken to Kamfwa about this, Kamfwa replied that Santi had shown no signs that he intended using it and therefore had established no prior rights over the area. If Santi wished to dispute this then they should go to the chief's court as Mwape and Chisenga had done previously. Santi, however, was very unwilling to do so as he realized that the case would almost certainly go against him. Instead he approached the Agricultural Officer who was on a visit to his farm, but the Agricultural Officer was unhelpful and said the matter lay outside his jurisdiction. Then in a final effort Santi went over to Kamfwa and read aloud to him the Local Authority agricultural rule forbidding the felling of trees within 30 yards of a stream. Not surprisingly, however, this failed to produce the desired effect and so Santi gave up worrying about it.

Most farmers cultivate plots within close proximity to their farm settlements and regard any unused land in a certain radius as being within the bounds of their farm for future use as gardens and to serve as grazing grounds for their cattle. They also cultivate the same set of gardens over a long period and invest considerable labour and capital in them. Because of this many feel they should have the right to dispose of their land either through sale or by making a will. I found no instance of farmers attempting to sell their land but I did record a case where the original farmer left the farm and received payment from the next occupier for the standing crops, for the farm buildings and for the labour expended on stumping. Legally the farmer could not sell his land so instead claimed a cash payment for the various improvements he had made.[1] This emphasizes the point that farmers attach great value to land as an economic asset.

Similarly, although a registered peasant farmer has the right to nominate a successor to his farm in the event of his death or his abandoning it, the successor may not enter the farm or take over the fields without the prior approval of the chief. This means that there may be competing claims on the farm from the farmer's close matrilineal kinsmen (brothers and sisters' sons) and from his own sons. The former would argue that under the traditional Lala matrilineal system it is they who are the rightful heirs, not the farmer's sons. In most cases where this arises the deciding factor taken into account at the chief's court is who has contributed most to the development of the farm. If the farmer's sons, then they inherit the property, but if not then it usually goes to matrikin. One case was solved by allowing the farmer's sons to claim the

[1] For similar practices among people in other parts of Zambia see Allan, 1965, p. 369.

farm property and gardens while the rest of the deceased's personal property (his furniture, clothing and motor-car) was divided among his matrikin.

Non-farming occupations

So far I have sketched in the main features of the changing agricultural system in Kapepa Parish and have examined the impact that new techniques of cultivation and cash-cropping have had on the organization of labour and on the system of land holding. I now describe briefly the emergence of small-scale business enterprises and other opportunities which exist for earning cash locally.

With agricultural development came the opening of a number of stores along the road leading through the parish to Chibale's Court. In 1963 there were eight stores and two diesel engine grinding mills. All but one had been established within the last decade.

Four of the eight stores and both of the grinding mills were established by returning labour migrants with savings of their own derived from long periods of urban wage employment; and of the remaining four stores, one is owned by a man who continues to work in town and who relies on the assistance of various matrikin to manage his enterprise. The others were financed largely by profits from cash-crop farming.

Like the rest of Serenje and most parts of Zambia, Kapepa Parish has over the past 50 years been a regular supplier of male labour for the towns of south and central Africa. Peters (1950, p. 5) recorded that 41·5 per cent of adult males of the district were absent from it in 1946. Most of these would be in urban employment. By 1960, according to official government figures, the rate had risen to 64 per cent, due partly to increased employment opportunities on the mines and in industry and partly to the poor economic situation existing at home. District Officers' tour reports for the mid-1950's, suggest that in this respect Kapepa Parish was probably no exception.

Yet by 1963 there appeared to be a distinct drop in the proportion of men absent. My own estimate, based on detailed genealogical enquiries, indicated that just over 50 per cent of adult males were away from Kapepa. Moreover the age structure for the resident male population showed a rather surprising bulge for the 25-34 year age categories, which suggested that although most young men spent an initial period in urban employment they were now less inclined to return to town for additional trips. One reason for this could have been the increased opportunities existing at home for earning cash.

The eight stores in the parish vary in the quality and range of goods stocked. Four of them are rather small and stock mainly non-perishable foodstuffs, such as tea, sugar, coffee, jam, tinned meat and tinned milk, and other household items like soap, razor blades and a small selection of children's clothes and trousers, blouses and shirts. The owners of these four stores do not own vehicles and have to rely on other storekeepers or vehicle owners living in the vicinity to transport their orders from town. This generally involves them in fairly high transport costs, as the vehicle owner is in a strong bargaining position and may ask anything up to about £5 per order for bringing goods from Broken Hill (Kabwe), some 150-odd miles, or from one of the Copperbelt towns, 180 miles or more. In addition, the vehicle owner might also make a small profit on the goods themselves as he may be entrusted with the job of buying them from one of the Indian wholesale dealers. In view of this, it is perhaps significant that three of these storekeepers have recently started growing Turkish tobacco which they hope will enable them to buy vehicles.

The remaining four stores stock a very wide range of goods, foodstuffs, clothing, household items, etc. All of the storekeepers have their own motor vehicles (one owns two lorries) and make regular weekly trips to the towns and back, carrying goods and persons and the weekly supply of paraffin, soft drinks, bottled beer and town-brewed millet or maize beer and bread, etc. Two of them employ regular drivers at a rate of between £2 and £3 per trip.

Although it was difficult to obtain systematic information on the profits from storekeeping, I was able roughly to compare the levels of income and expenditure for the small as against the large stores. From this I calculated that the annual profit (after deducting the amounts spent on re-stocking and transportation) for the small stores was somewhere between £50 and £60, whereas for the larger stores it was in the region of about £150.

The clientele for each of the stores varies somewhat according to its geographical location and size. The larger stores attract persons from a wide area and persons of high status, like teachers and various other government employees, who obtain goods on a monthly credit system. The smaller stores tend to attract customers with whom the storekeeper is personally well acquainted. This is especially the case with some of the smaller stores owned by Jehovah's Witnesses. Here the storekeeper will often use his church connections to attract customers, though he may not offer them any preferential treatment.

The two grinding mill owners combine farming with the grinding of maize and millet for local consumption. Those in the community who have sufficient cash prefer to take their grain for grinding rather than pound and grind it themselves, a lengthy and arduous task. The charge for grinding is normally about 4s. per *debbi* (i.e. a four-gallon tin). One of the grinding mill owners has recently opened a small store and hopes to expand this side of his business when he has more capital.

Other non-farming specialist occupations in the parish are bricklaying, carpentry, tailoring, sawing and metalwork, but these are practised only on a part-time basis. As yet a small amount of remuneration derives from such trades but they are important as an extra source of income. The building of a two-roomed brick house, for example, will usually cost about £6 and a bricklayer may build two or three a year. Tailoring is mainly associated with the stores. It is a common sight on a warm day to see the storekeeper, or someone employed by him, seated on the verandah of his store building operating a treadle or hand sewing machine and making shirts or dresses.

Economic differentiation

Agricultural development in Kapepa Parish has brought about a diversification of the rural economy. Prior to 1950 the economy was almost entirely subsistence-based and people relied on cash remittances from migrant kinsmen in town to pay their taxes, to purchase clothing and to pay for school fees, etc. There were few opportunities for earning cash locally. In a good year a man might sell a very small surplus of maize or millet or some other produce to persons less fortunately situated, or he might brew millet beer for sale. But it would be exceptional if a man earned as much as £5 from these miscellaneous sales. Since 1950, however, the growth of commercial agriculture with Turkish tobacco has led to increased circulation of locally earned cash and to greater investment by returning labour migrants, as manifested in the growing number of stores, grinding mills and commercial farms. All this has meant a general increase in the prosperity of the area, though the effects of economic change have been somewhat uneven. Thus, while recognizing that economic expansion is taking place, it is equally important to note that a majority of individuals continue to be oriented primarily towards subsistence production, though far greater opportunities exist for earning cash (e.g. by practising some non-farming skill, by brewing beer for sale or by working at one of the peasant farms) than did in the past.

Table I: Primary occupations of adult males in Kapepa Parish in 1963

Whether or not tobacco grown	Occupations				Totals
	Subsistence Cultivator	Peasant Farmer	Store-keeper	Govern-ment Employee	
Tobacco	21 (9·8)	20 (9·3)	3 (1·4)	—	44 (20·5)
No tobacco	158 (73·8)	5 (2·4)	5 (2·4)	*2 (0·9)	170 (79·5)
TOTALS	179 (83·6)	25 (11·7)	8 (3·8)	2 (0·9)	214 (100·0)

Percentages in brackets

* Chief's Messenger

Table I gives a breakdown of the adult male population of the parish in terms of a number of occupational categories. From this it can be seen that 73·8 per cent of all males are still firmly rooted in subsistence production, though the recent recruitment of tobacco growers from among the village population suggests further expansion of the cash sector of the economy in the future if the market for Turkish tobacco remains stable.[1]

Tables II and III attempt to provide a fuller picture of the degree of economic differentiation in Kapepa. I was not able to collect detailed household budgets of income and expenditure but during my census I made inventories of the major items of property owned by all individuals in the parish. From this data I have

---

[1] Since this was written Turkish tobacco production in Serenje has suffered a major setback. In 1966–7 there was a considerable reduction in the number of growers. I cannot examine the reasons for this recession as the relevant data are not yet available. My analysis refers only to the situation in Kapepa Parish up to May 1964 when I left the area.

constructed two indices of economic status, using a modified Guttman scale analysis. Guttman's method rates persons (or units) on a continuum according to whether or not they are associated with a pattern of attributes and makes the assumption that the selected attributes can be ranked in order of significance, such that if a person is associated with the first item then the probability is that he will be associated with the rest. If he is associated with the second and not the first then it is probable that he will be associated with the third, fourth, fifth, etc., and so on. Here, then, I have analysed the combinations of property items associated with particular individuals and on the basis of this have placed them into one of three broad economic status categories, which I have labelled 'high', 'medium' and 'low'.[1]

Preliminary analysis suggested that there were two rather separate kinds of property items which did not necessarily intercorrelate: those associated with farming, such as ploughs, farming

Table II: *Economic status categories: first cluster of property items*

Occupation	Economic status			Totals
	High	Medium	Low	
Subsistence cultivator	2	59	97	158
Sub. cult. growing tobacco	3	12	6	21
Peasant farmer	5	—	—	5
Peasant farmer growing tobacco	20	—	—	20
Storekeeper	—	3	2	5
Storekeeper growing tobacco	—	3	—	3
Government employee	—	2	—	2
TOTALS	30	79	105	214

High: (1) Those possessing all five items.
                (2) Those possessing all but grinding machine.
                (3) Those possessing cattle, plough and bike only.
Medium: (1) Those possessing plough and bike only.
                (2) Those possessing bike only.
Low: Those possessing none of the five items

[1] A fuller account of the methodology used is contained in Appendix under Tables V and VI.

implements, and cattle; and those of a more general type. In the processing of the data therefore I have worked in terms of two separate clusters of property items, a farming cluster and a con-sumer-durables cluster, comprising five items each.

Table II gives the results for the first cluster which included, in order of significance, (1) hand grinding machine, (2) farm imple-ments other than plough, (3) four or more cattle, (4) plough, (5) bicycle. The table shows that just over 14 per cent of the male population fall into the high status category and that occupational status is a fairly reliable indicator of high economic status for this cluster. Of the 30 individuals falling into the high category, 25 are peasant farmers, three are subsistence cultivators who have recently taken to growing tobacco, and the remaining two, subsistence cultivators who possess the requisite farming equipment but have not yet produced any surplus of crops for sale. The storekeepers and subsistence cultivators growing tobacco fall mostly into the medium status category, and the majority of subsistence culti-vators proper into the low category.

Table III: Economic status categories: second cluster of property items

| Occupation | Economic status | | | Totals |
	High	Medium	Low	
Subsistence cultivator	I	59	98	158
Sub. cult. growing tobacco	4	13	4	21
Peasant farmer	—	2	3	5
Peasant farmer growing tobacco	4	14	2	20
Storekeeper	5	—	—	5
Storekeeper growing tobacco	2	1	—	3
Government employee	—	1	1	2
TOTALS	16	90	108	214

High: (1) Those possessing all five items.
(2) Those possessing all but motor vehicle.
(3) Those possessing furniture, sewing machine and brick house only.

Medium: (1) Those possessing sewing machine and brick house only.
(2) Those possessing brick house only.

Low: Those possessing none of the five items.

Table III shows the results for the second cluster which consisted of (1) motor vehicle, (2) radio, (3) Western-type furniture, (4) sewing machine, and (5) brick house. Here the proportion of persons falling into the high economic status category is considerably less, only 16 (or 7·5 per cent) out of 214. Of these 16, seven are storekeepers, five are subsistence cultivators and only four peasant farmers. This suggests that storekeepers tend to invest in consumer-durables and that only a few farmers are able to invest equally in farming equipment and in major consumer items. The proportions of subsistence cultivators falling into the high, medium and low categories remain roughly the same for both clusters.

Comparing the results for the two clusters of property items we find that some individuals have invested in farming items and some in consumer goods, and only a very small group of persons (only six) can be regarded as of high economic status by both sets of criteria. As would be expected, there is a large group who consistently fall into the lower status categories. Yet despite this generally low level of material wealth, agricultural change has produced a number of important shifts in the economy of the parish.

In concluding this chapter I want to draw attention to a major aspect of the situation, and one which I shall have occasion to re-examine at different points in the analysis which follows. This is the differential response patterns of Jehovah's Witnesses as against the rest of the population. If, for instance, we compare Jehovah's Witnesses (who number some 91 individuals out of 497 adults in the parish) with the rest of the population who are mostly non-Christians, we find that they differ significantly in terms of residence, occupation, skills, type of agriculture practised and economic status.

Comparing the residence patterns for Witnesses and non-Witnesses one finds that of the 91 Witnesses, 74·7 per cent live outside the village in small settlements, as against only 40·1 per cent of non-Witnesses. Moreover, of these Witnesses just under half live at peasant farms and stores (see Table I, Appendix) compared with only 19·9 per cent of non-Witnesses. Consistent with this is the fact that proportionately more male Witnesses follow occupations from which they derive some regular local cash income. Of the 47 male Witnesses, 12 are peasant farmers, four are storekeepers and a further eight combine subsistence cultivation with tobacco production. Of the 167 male non-Witnesses, only 19·2 per cent fall into these cash-income categories (see Table II, Appendix).

Again there is a marked difference between the two groups with regard to additional trades practised. Considering bricklaying, carpentry, sawing, tailoring, metalwork, driving and shoe-repairing as skills, then 57·5 per cent of male Witnesses are skilled and only 21·6 per cent of non-Witnesses (see Table III, Appendix). Proportionately more Witnesses practise some form of plough cultivation and more grow tobacco. 46·8 per cent of Witnesses use plough methods exclusively and 21·3 per cent cultivate by a combination of plough and *citeme*. In contrast, only 17·8 per cent of non-Witnesses use the plough and 9·7 per cent a combination of plough and *citeme* (see Table IV, Appendix). As for tobacco growing, 18 out of the 44 growers are Jehovah's Witnesses.

Some measure of their economic prominence is gauged by considering the ownership of various items of property. Individual Jehovah's Witnesses own the only two diesel engine grinding mills and four out of the six motor vehicles in the parish. Also proportionately more of them possess cattle and farming implements and various consumer items, such as radios, Western-type furniture, sewing machines and brick houses (see Tables V and VI, Appendix).

The pattern which emerges is that a substantial number of Jehovah's Witnesses are utilizing the new economic opportunities made available in Kapepa through the introduction of new farming techniques and cash-crop production, and have moved out of their villages to start farms or stores. Furthermore, several of them have achieved high economic status in the community.[1]

[1] For an explanation of this see Chapter VIII.

CHAPTER III

THE DYNAMICS OF FARM MANAGEMENT

To set up as a peasant farmer one needs to have ready command over, or access to, certain basic resources, such as land, labour, capital and expertise, but for any one individual there will always exist a number of alternative ways of acquiring these. Thus to understand the dynamics of farm management one has to focus on the specific socio-economic situation in which a man finds himself and examine how far his choices have been restricted by the presence or absence of certain critical factors. Since any particular organizational form is in part the result of a multitude of previous decisions it is also necessary to analyse the enterprise as a sequence in time, so that the relationships between various factors can be examined at several stages of its development. It is very important, therefore, to adopt a diachronic case-study approach,[1] though as one hopes to draw some general conclusions from the material it is also important to set these case studies within some analytical framework.

The first part of this chapter gives an account of the establishment and growth of three farming enterprises, documenting the various material and social assets which each of the farmers possesses and examining the kinds of strategies they use to achieve their objectives. This is designed to show how changes in the levels of resources available to particular farmers and/or changes in their farming objectives lead to changes in the pattern of farm organization; and also highlights other sociological components of the farm situation. It is argued, for instance, that the range of choices open to a particular farmer at any one moment in time is not only determined by what he already has in the way of capital and expertise, or by the previous decisions he has made, but also by

[1] Recent work by agricultural economists has also emphasized the importance of the case-study approach. Clayton (1964, Chapter 5) argues that the intensive study of 'typical or commonly-found farm situations' enables one to construct plans of optimal resource combinations for individual farmers or for farmers of the same type. Here I explore the sociological components of the 'farm situation' and do not discuss economic farm planning as such.

the network of multifarious social ties which link him with other actors in the situation, who, like him, have their own particular assets and their own expectations.

In the second part of the chapter I widen the study to include all 24 peasant farms in Kapepa and focus on observable differences in the pattern of farm organization.[1] Here I present a synchronic analysis of the farms in the parish in terms of the composition and deployment of their labour force, and show that differences in labour organization are closely related to differences in resource availability and to differences in the social characteristics of the farmers themselves.

The first case study describes the setting up of a farm by a recently returned miner with considerable capital resources of his own. The farm is analysed first as a developing enterprise, showing how the farmer's strategies of management changed over time as he faced the problems of recruiting a permanent labour force and as he acquired the necessary farming expertise. I then discuss the fission of the farm which took place in 1963–4 and argue that the hiving off of various groups was closely related to the question of labour deployment and economic assistance at the farm.

SAINI MOLOKA FARM

Phase I: establishment of the farm: 1958–60

The owner of the farm, Saini Moloka (see Genealogy I, C6), returned from Broken Hill (Kabwe) in 1958 at the age of 53, after completing about 25 years' work at the mine. He brought with him £397 personal savings and gratuity with which to start a farm. Prior to this in 1949, his younger brother, Petro (I, C8), had been granted a block farm under the peasant farming scheme and had received oxen and farming implements on a loan basis. Petro, however, remained there for only two years, for in 1951 he left to manage a store for an Indian businessman in Broken Hill (Kabwe) for whom he had previously worked. The farm and small store (which he had opened near to the block farms) were entrusted to his sister's son, Sakishi (I, D3). But although Petro sent money regularly to Sakishi to help pay off the loan and to keep the store running, Sakishi proved such a bad manager of both enterprises

[1] At one of the farms there are two registered peasant farmers who run a joint farm, hence 24 peasant farms but 25 registered peasant farmers.

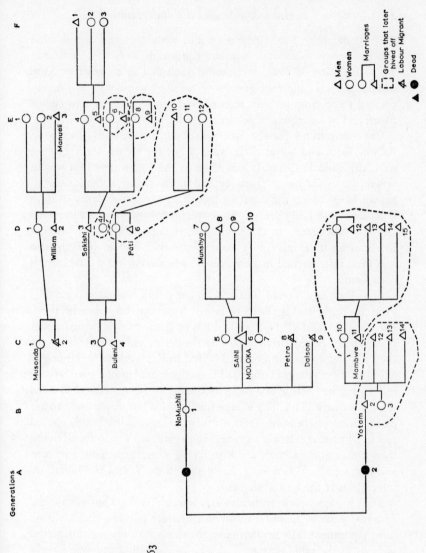

Genealogy I, April 1963
Saini Moloka Farm

that by the time Saini arrived on the scene the store was defunct and the payments for the oxen and equipment were well in arrears. There had, at one time, been some discussion as to whether Saini should take over the management of Sakishi Farm but he had finally decided to open up his own tract of land and acquire his own equipment, and to be quite independent of Sakishi.

The site selected for the farm was about a mile and a half from Sakishi Farm and about three miles from the motor track leading to Chief Chibale Court. It was close to the headwaters of a stream where the soils range from typical light sandy upland soils to brown loams along the dambo edges. There was also plenty of light woodland with fairly decent grass coverage for pasturage for livestock and few other farms in the immediate vicinity. The site was chosen for Saini by his classificatory mother's brother, Yotam (I, B2), who had been instrumental in persuading Saini to retire and establish his own farm.

Over the years, Yotam, a man in his late sixties, had made occasional visits to Broken Hill (Kabwe) to see Saini and his other brothers, Petro and Daison (I, C9), and had kept them well informed about home affairs, particularly concerning the health and general welfare of their old and widowed mother, NaMushili (I, B1), who was living at Sakishi Farm. Yotam's father had been the headman of a very famous old village in Chibale and Saini and many of his matrikin had lived there for many years. The village finally broke up in the early 1950's on the death of the headman and Yotam and his nuclear family moved to a nearby village. Being a stranger in the village, Yotam found living there rather unsatisfactory and kept trying to persuade Saini to return and start a farm. When Saini finally did return, Yotam and his family joined him at the new settlement.

Saini brought back with him considerable savings but within the first two years he spent far more on consumer durables than on basic farm equipment. His major items of expenditure during this period were as in the table on page 44. The balance of £117 was largely spent on food, beer, gifts, clothing, etc., so that by late 1960 he was obliged to take on a government loan of £133 in order to obtain additional farming implements and livestock. These included one scotch cart, one harrow and eight head of cattle. The loan was repayable over ten years.

Several local farmers were hired to plough for him, at the standard rate of £3 per acre. Four of the ten acres cleared and ploughed were

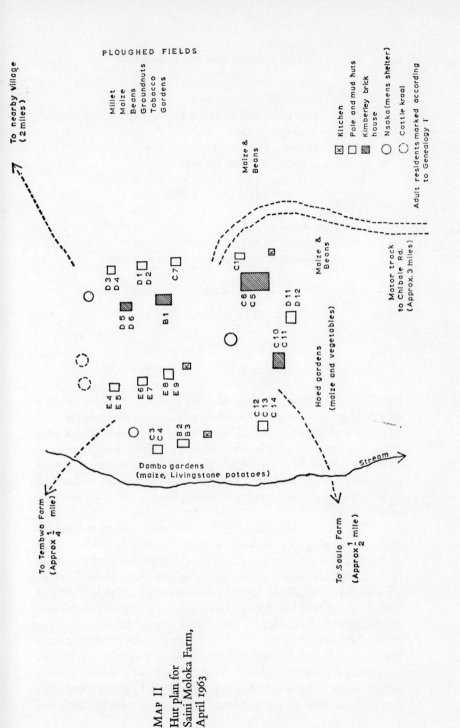

PLOUGHED FIELDS

Millet
Maize
Beans
Groundnuts
Tobacco
Gardens

Maize & Beans

Maize & Beans

To nearby village
(2 miles)

Kitchen
Pole and mud huts
Kimberley brick house
Nsaka (mens shelter)
Cattle kraal

Adult residents marked according to Genealogy I

Motor track to Chibale Rd.
(Approx. 3 miles)

D 3
D 4

D 1
D 2

C 7

C 1

C 6
C 5

D 11
D 12

D 5
D 6

B 1

C 10
C 11

Hoed gardens
(maize and vegetables)

E 4
E 5

E 6
E 7

E 8
E 9

C 12
C 13
C 14

C 3
C 4

B 2
B 3

Dambo gardens
(maize, Livingstone potatoes)

Stream

To Tembwa Farm
(Approx ¼ mile)

To Saulo Farm
(Approx ½ mile)

MAP II
Hut plan for
Saini Moloka Farm,
April 1963

	£
Second-hand motor-van (crashed and written off)	83
Sewing machine	45
House construction:	
corrugated iron roofing	30
timber	5
window frames	12
transport costs	6
labour	11
2 oxen	36
1 plough	6
Stumping	16
Ploughing of 10 acres	30

Total Expenditure	£280
Original Savings	£397
Balance	£117

for Yotam. Stumping was undertaken by groups of villagers working on a daily basis, and a track for motor vehicles was cut from the farm to the nearest point on the Chibale Road by local schoolboys who received payment in salt. He also employed a skilled bricklayer to build his three-roomed Kimberley-brick house and a carpenter to prepare the timber sections. Each task was carried out on a strictly contractual basis and none of those employed were related to him by kinship or affinity.

During these initial years Saini devoted some time to training his oxen and learning to plough. Apart from the help he received from agricultural demonstrators in the area and from farmers who worked for him, his chief instructor was a sister's daughter's son, Manueli (I, E3), who was living at Sakishi Farm. Manueli spent a good deal of time at Saini Farm teaching him how to handle oxen, how to hold the plough and telling him about what the other block farmers did on their farms, the kind of rotation of crops used, and how they deployed their farm labour. Yotam and his sons and Mambwe (I, C11), his son-in-law, were all inexperienced in plough cultivation and not of much use when it came to the techniques of farming, but they did provide some additional labour. One of Yotam's sons became the regular herdsboy and another tried his hand at ploughing. Harvesting was not a major task because Saini had only three acres under cultivation each year and his wife and teenage daughter were able to do the job satisfactorily themselves. Yotam cultivated about two acres per year and had his daughter and son-in-law and their children to help him. The son-in-law also cut a *citeme* millet garden. At this stage Saini's and Yotam's gardens were devoted mainly to maize and beans and their wives hoed stream-side gardens for growing various vegetables. Looking back on these years, Saini describes them as the time when he had to buy bags and bags of maize flour from the local stores in order to supplement what they produced themselves.

Phase II: expansion: 1961–3

Towards the end of 1960, Saini's mother, NaMushili (I, B1), his uterine sisters (I, C1 and C3) and the small descent groups associated with them, Sakishi (I, D3) and his married daughters and their spouses, arrived at Saini Farm to settle. Prior to this, they had all lived at Sakishi Farm. The immediate cause of this move was that, after several attempts to get Sakishi to pay back some of the debts incurred by Petro and himself, the Agricultural Department decided that he should be asked to leave the farming block and return most of the equipment and cattle that he had obtained from them. NaMushili tells the story of how one day, quite without warning, Sakishi sent Manueli to Saini Farm to collect the scotch cart which Saini had recently acquired from the Agricultural Department, so that they might transport all their belongings from their farm to Saini's. Some of the details of the eviction remain obscure, but Sakishi and his kin moved to join Saini Farm in the latter part of 1960.

Saini did not try to prevent their settling at his farm and seems to have welcomed them. Even though Sakishi Farm had never been a financial success, Sakishi and the others did have a good deal of agricultural experience between them which they could pass on to Saini, and they also constituted a reasonably skilled labour force. In addition to Sakishi and Manueli, there were three young men (I, D6, E7, E9) married into the farm whose fathers were peasant farmers. Sakishi's eviction was quickly seized upon by Saini as offering a solution to some of his problems of labour and lack of expertise. As for Sakishi, he needed the co-operation of Saini in order to survive as a plough cultivator. After handing back some of the equipment and livestock, Sakishi was left with one plough, one ox, and two cows. This meant

E

that he was short of one ox for ploughing and would have to borrow from someone if he were to continue. Saini was the obvious choice.

Genealogy I shows the composition of Saini Farm during the 1961–3 phase. Saini married a second wife towards the end of 1962. Table IV gives the crop acreages under plough and the types of other gardens cultivated for the households living at Saini Farm in April 1963. From this it can be seen that Saini had by far the largest number of acres devoted to the plough though all households had some ploughed gardens.

Table IV: Types of gardens for households at Saini Moloka farm: April 1963

Households	Crop acreages under plough					Produce grown in hoed gardens	*Citeme* gardens
	maize	beans	ground-nuts	millet	tobacco		
Saini:							
senior wife	4	$\frac{1}{2}$	$\frac{1}{2}$	2$\Big\}$	$\frac{1}{2}$	Vegetables only	None
second wife	3	$\frac{1}{2}$	$\frac{1}{2}$	1			
Sakishi	2	1	—	1	$\frac{1}{2}$	Groundnuts and vegetables	None
Musonda	1	1	—	—	$\frac{1}{2}$	Maize, ground-nuts and vegetables	None
Buleni	1	—	—	—	—	Maize, beans, groundnuts and vegetables	Cut by D6
Yotam	1	—	—	—	—	Maize, beans, groundnuts and vegetables	Cut by C11, D12
William	1	—	—	—	—	Maize, beans, groundnuts and vegetables	Cut by D2

The following arrangements were made for ploughing. Saini, Manueli and Sakishi worked together in one group. They would firstly plough Saini's gardens and then move to Sakishi's, and Musonda's (I, C1). Manueli worked on behalf of his maternal grandmother, Musonda, a divorcee. Sometimes also, Saini would work with Manueli and Saini's first wife (I, C5). They would plough the first wife's gardens and then move on to Musonda's. Later when Saini married a second wife (I, C7) she also took turns at leading the oxen when her gardens were being ploughed. Sakishi would occasionally plough with his two sons-in-law (I, E7 and E9). Others at the farm were given the chance to use the equipment and oxen when Saini and Sakishi had finished with it. Yotam would sometimes work with one of his sons and his son-in-law, Mambwe (I, C11); and another group consisted of Buleni (I, C4) and his wife, assisted by Pati (I, D6), their son-in-law.

The sowing and weeding of the gardens was carried out mainly by those women whose menfolk regularly teamed together for ploughing, but the harvesting of crops required some extra input of labour. Each of the household heads (Saini, Sakishi, Musonda, Yotam, Buleni and William (I, D2)) made their own arrangements for this. All but Saini and Musonda called in female matrikin on a reciprocal work basis. Saini and Musonda took on hired female labour from neighbouring villages and paid them in kind (i.e. salt and millet flour).

In 1961 Saini began growing Turkish tobacco, and two years later Sakishi and Musonda followed suit. The main tobacco gardens were located together in one large plot of about 1½ acres in order to facilitate ploughing. The team for ploughing consisted of Saini, Sakishi and Manueli. The preparation of the plots, the planting and the processing of the tobacco, however, were the responsibility of the individual growers. Saini was regularly assisted by his two wives and teenage daughter, Munshya (I, D7), and employed outside labour during the picking and stringing stages. Musonda was helped by her daughter (I, D1) and her husband, and by Manueli and Yotam's eldest son (I, C12) during the peak period. The latter two received a few shillings 'pocket' money for their efforts. Sakishi had his wife and daughter (I, E4) working with him regularly, with additional hired hands from nearby villages during the picking and stringing stages.

Phase III: fission: November 1963–June 1964

The work arrangements apparently continued quite satisfactorily until November 1963 when Musonda complained of not getting a fair deal over ploughing. She argued that because Saini and Sakishi had priority over the use of the equipment, her gardens were not ploughed until later in the season and were much smaller. She therefore suggested paying Saini £2 per acre for ploughing her gardens. This had important consequences, for Saini then made the rule that no one could use his oxen or equipment or expect him to plough for them unless they also paid. Following this, Musonda and Yotam both paid Saini for plough-ing their gardens at the rate suggested, though Sakishi was not re-quired to do so as he had some equipment of his own. The result of this was that ploughing for others was no longer seen primarily as an obligation arising within the context of matrilineal kinship sentiments but more in the form of a commercial contract. This change in the nature of work relationships was symptomatic of a more general discontent on the farm at the time.

1963 was the critical year for the fission of the farm, for by the end of it several groups had either moved away or had made plans to move. Yotam's son-in-law, Mambwe (I, C11), obtained the chief's permission to move out and establish his own settlement in the newly opened Protected Forest Area some five miles from Saini Farm. Mambwe had repeatedly negotiated with the Agricultural Department for a loan for oxen and equipment but had been turned down, it was said, because equipment was easily available at Saini Farm. Mambwe had three cows and had re-applied for a loan which he hoped this time would be successful. He set up his new settlement in November 1963. Earlier in the year, Buleni's son-in-law, Pati (I, D6), left the farm together with his wife and children and moved back to his father's settlement. Pati's father is a peasant farmer who had joined the farming block in 1949. He had recently opened up a new site, also in the Protected Forest Area, where his son joined him. Sakishi's son-in-law (I, E9) also left Saini Farm in 1963 and moved to join his mother, a divorcee, who is the owner of a peasant farm. Another son-in-law (I, E7) left shortly after Mambwe and built a settlement a short distance from him. By December 1963, Yotam's family were making plans to leave the farm. Yotam's sister's daughter who was returning from the Congo where she had been married for many years was going to join them. A few years ago her brother had been killed in a mine accident and she had received some of the compensation money, with which she purchased ten head of cattle. Her mother, who was living in a village near to Saini, planned to join them at the new settlement. So by April 1964, many of the houses at Saini Farm were empty and Sakishi's wife had recently gone to live at Mambwe's settlement, though her husband refused to leave the farm.

Although Mambwe undoubtedly wished to have his own farm, the occasion for his move arose over a dispute concerning the grazing of crops by his three cattle. NaMushili, Saini and Sakishi asked that compensation be paid for the damage done to their maize crops. Mambwe refused to pay and was backed up by Sakishi's wife who is his classificatory sister's daughter. This sparked off a series of quarrels between Sakishi's wife and other women at the farm, particularly with the two wives of Saini, and eventually Sakishi's wife told Mambwe to go to the chief and register his own settlement. Mambwe agreed to do this and hoped that Sakishi would later settle with his wife at the new settlement. During the quarrels Sakishi's wife did not confine her remarks to the question of the grazing of the crops but aired her general grievances about the low standard of living she suffered at the farm and about the lack of respect shown to her by others. On a later occasion, during a fierce argument she was having with her husband over whether she should go and visit her mother and leave Sakishi stringing tobacco, she cursed the old woman, NaMushili, for interfering in her marriage and struck her across the face with a stick when the old woman tried to calm her down. She also cursed Sakishi for not providing for her in the way that Saini cared for his wives and compared the standard of living of the women in Saini household with that of her own. She left the farm that night, against the wishes of her husband, saying that she was going to her mother's to fetch food, but she actually spent the night at Mambwe's settlement and has remained there since. Sakishi appears to have accepted the situation and occasionally visits his wife though he stubbornly refuses to leave Saini Farm permanently himself.

The moving out of the farm by Pati (I, D6), and Sakishi's sons-in-law (I, E9 and E7) was not directly caused by the quarrels developing between Sakishi's wife and others at the farm, though the fact that their wives are all close matrikin of Sakishi made their relationship to his wife, who is mother-in-law to E9 and E7, a somewhat tense and delicate one. However, each of them had completed two or more years' service to their in-laws and were probably already intending to return to their fathers' farms, where the opportunity for economic advancement would be greater.

By April 1964, Yotam's family were in the process of building houses for the settlement they would move to when Yotam's sister's daughter arrived from the Congo. During the past two years there had been a lot of tension between the Yotam group and Saini, Sakishi and NaMushili. Yotam and his sons and Mambwe all felt that Saini had seriously neglected his obligations to them, and pointed to Saini's decision that they should pay him for ploughing as a clear indication of this. Yotam himself was particularly upset that Saini should ask for money when it was he who persuaded Saini to take up farming in the first place. He also claimed that they had put a good deal of labour into the farm: his sons had been herdsboys and had occasionally helped with the ploughing and preparing of Saini's gardens. Yet despite this Saini had never rewarded them in any way substantially. They had been offered the use of the plough and oxen but only after the rest had completed their gardens; and their living at the farm had, they claimed, positively handicapped Mambwe in his attempt to secure an agricultural loan. On the other hand, Saini maintained that Yotam and his family had been somewhat of a drain on the resources of the farm. Yotam was old and not very able-bodied and had not been able to assist him greatly and nor had the others. When recounting the establishment of the farm, Saini seldom mentioned the help he had received from Yotam, and instead told how he, Sakishi and Manueli developed it. He also argued that since he started growing tobacco about three years ago he had never had any assistance from Yotam's family in the processing of it which required no special skills. He had had to employ outside help.

One incident illustrating the lack of co-operation between Yotam and Saini concerned the breaking out of the cattle from Saini's kraal at night. One morning the herdsboy, Yotam's son, went to let the cattle out, only to find them missing, and so Saini and the boy immediately set out to locate them. They returned later with no success. That day Saini was due at Serenje Boma for a farmers' meeting and so he asked Yotam to take charge of the search. Yotam was very reluctant but eventually went off to try and find them. Some hours later, after a long and arduous search, the herd was driven back into the kraal. On his arrival back at the farm, Yotam was very disagreeable and complained bitterly about the whole affair, saying that Saini should never have gone to the meeting. They were not Yotam's cattle and why should he be given the responsibility of finding them. A quarrel ensued between Yotam and NaMushili who supported Saini, during which Yotam cursed both her and her son for not caring for their matrikin. Yotam is also said to have hinted that his own father's death and the subsequent break-up of the village were the work of NaMushili, who was herself a renowned sorceress (*mfwiti*). Tempers had cooled by the time Saini arrived back from Serenje and so he avoided antagonizing the parties involved. Later, however, he made an oblique reference to the general state of affairs at the farm when he described at a beer drink how he had been the first man to arrive in Chibale 'as a European, with plenty of money, bicycles and corrugated steel', and how people flocked to his farm because of his wealth. He went on to comment that he welcomed the prospect of being on his own now that many of the people were moving away, and said that his brother, Petro, had been making plans to retire from Broken Hill (Kabwe) and establish another farm close to Saini's. When Petro arrived Saini would help him set up his enterprise and instruct him in plough methods. They would then assist one another in the organization of their farms and might later open a joint store. This he thought would be a far better arrangement than any he had previously made with other kin.

Commentary and analysis

The account presented highlights a number of important aspects of peasant farming enterprises in Kapepa. It shows for instance what types of essential resources the farmer needs to set up his farm. He needs access to land and natural resources; access to certain farming implements and oxen for ploughing; access to a reliable pool of labour and access to a fund of technical knowledge and experience. Moreover to acquire such items as plough and oxen he needs capital.

I described in Chapter II how, despite the development of a more settled form of agriculture, land rights continue to be vested in the individual as a member of a particular chiefdom, the chief acting as custodian of land and natural resources. Thus any individual wishing to become a farmer outside the block scheme must first establish the right to utilize the natural resources of the chiefdom. This is generally automatic for persons like Saini, who were born and bred in the chiefdom and who have maintained contact with it during periods of residence elsewhere; but for others it may be more difficult unless they can exploit some existing kinship or affinal link with persons from the chiefdom. In 1964, all but four of the 25 registered peasant farmers living in Kapepa Parish were Chibale subjects by birth.

Though Saini had spent a major part of his life in urban employment, he had kept regular contact with kin and friends in Chibale. In addition, he was well connected to the local chief and his court clerk, and this do doubt facilitated his obtaining permission to establish his own farm there. His brother, Petro, was married to a daughter of the present chief and a classificatory sister was married to the court clerk. Both the clerk and the chief had made frequent visits to Broken Hill (Kabwe), where they had received hospitality from Saini and his two brothers.

Most returning labour migrants require the assistance of some kinsman or friend to find a site for their farm. Saini had been helped by Yotam, his classificatory mother's brother. In selecting a site a number of important criteria are used. The farm should be located within reasonable proximity to existing motor roads so that produce can be easily transported to the markets. There should be a range of different soil types suitable for the crops which the farmer wants to grow; there should be a plentiful supply of adjacent unoccupied land for expansion, as well as pasturage and good water supplies. Also, since it is not yet normal practice to mark out farm boundaries, it is important to make some assessment of the likelihood of nearby areas being taken over by other farmers, for one may later come into competition with them for scarce resources. In all these respects Saini Farm was suitably located.

Most farmers acquire some farming equipment by purchase (using their own savings or cash borrowed from kinsmen) but obtain additional items and livestock through a loan from the Agricultural Department. Few attempt to operate their farms entirely by borrowing equipment and oxen from nearby kinsmen or friends. Saini was fortunately placed in that he had his own savings to draw on and had he wished could have set himself up without a loan. However, he chose instead to spend a lot of money on consumer goods rather than on farming equipment.

He also spent a fair sum on hired labour. Although he was already in his mid-fifties at retirement from urban employment, his children by his present wife were all under 15 years old and too young to take a major part in farm work. Adult children from a previous marriage lived with their mother in town. Yotam and his family could offer little in the way of skilled labour for none of them had had any experience of plough cultivation. Thus Saini was forced to get assistance from outside the farm. At first, rather than call in his sister's son, Sakishi, who lived close by, he chose to use hired hands. Several farmers were taken on to plough for him and villagers were employed to stump and clear the fields. His reason for not wishing to rely on Sakishi derived from the fact that in his and Petro's estimation Sakishi was not only a bad manager but a scoundrel to boot; and this was why Saini had originally set up on his own. His reason for not making more use of Yotam's family for unskilled tasks is less clear, but it seems at this stage that Saini was intent on maintaining a fairly high degree of independence from kin of any kind.

At this phase in the development of the farm Saini tended to dissipate his capital resources and made little attempt to invest in farming equipment or to recruit permanently resident skilled workers. He saw the farm more as a place to retire than as a genuine economic enterprise. Thus he aimed at an income which would provide the basic subsistence requirements for his family rather than at maximizing his returns as a commercial farmer. Moreover, Saini himself comments that he was not very successful in providing for his family. Figure I represents in diagrammatic

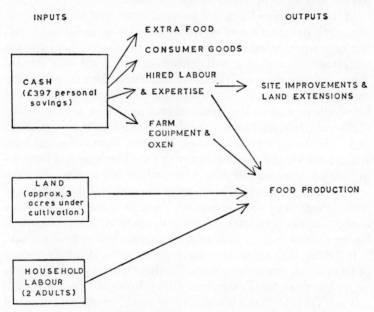

FIG. I. Saini Moloka Farm, establishment phase 1958–60

form the main types of resources available to Saini Moloka during the initial phase of establishing the farm, and their relative input levels, and indicates the kinds of production and non-production activities undertaken. From this it can be clearly seen that Saini was unable to replenish his capital resources and lacked the necessary expertise himself to develop the farm as a commercial enterprise.

As time wore on, however, Saini came to realize the importance of recruiting experienced men to work alongside him and the importance of acquiring additional farming equipment. The second phase in the development of the farm signified a change-over from what was essentially a food-producing unit to a cash income generating unit; and it is perhaps significant that this transformation occurred at a time when Saini was beginning to experience a certain amount of economic stress. By the end of 1960 Saini had little of his original savings left to meet his various needs. So in the last quarter of 1960 he obtained an agricultural loan for equipment and several head of cattle. Shortly after this Sakishi and his dependants joined the farm.

In the early years Saini had received some help from Manueli, his sister's daughter's son, who had been living at Sakishi Farm, but later when Sakishi and the others were evicted Saini saw the advantage of making a deal with Sakishi. Sakishi now needed Saini's help for the use of one ox to make up a team for ploughing and somewhere to stay. The latter responded by allowing him and his people to settle at the farm and promised them the use of one of his oxen. In return Saini was able to avail himself of their labour and expertise. After this, Sakishi, Manueli, Saini and other men at the farm assisted one another with the ploughing and harrow-ing of their gardens and their wives helped one another with the sowing and weeding. Unlike the earlier phase, the pattern of farm labour was now organized through a network of non-contractual ties between residents at the farm with a minimum of labour coming from outside to meet the demands of peak periods.

It is difficult to assess from the point of view of the economics of farm management how successful these working arrangements were, but from Saini's standpoint they brought reasonable cash returns. Table V gives a breakdown of Saini Moloka's income and expenditure for 1962–3. All but £4 of his gross income of £101 14s. was earned from farming. Others at the farm did less well. Sakishi and Musonda both grew tobacco but neither received more than £20 gross. They also sold a surplus of maize and beans and from this realized approximately £10 each. Buleni made about £6 on maize but the rest produced nothing of com-mercial value.

Figure II shows the main features of Saini's enterprise during the 1961–3 phase. Here it can be seen that although the level of cash available is less than his original sum he has increased his capital equipment and resident labour and expertise, and also has much more land under cultivation. He now relies less heavily

Table V: Income and expenditure for Saini Moloka: 1962-3

Income	£	s.	d.	Expenditure	£	s.	d.
Maize	22	19	–	Loan repayment	13	–	–
Beans	12	–	–	Labour on tobacco	8	–	–
Tobacco (after de-				2 chains for yoke	1	–	–
ducting service and				Purchase of goods			
transport costs)	22	15	–	(clothing, etc., for			
2 head of cattle to				mother, wives and			
butcher	33	–	–	children)	17	–	–
5 chickens	1	–	–	Gifts to kinsmen			
Gift from Petro	4	–	–	(estimated) (money			
Contract ploughing	6	–	–	and beer)	20	–	–
				Unaccounted for	42	14	–
	£101	14	–		£101	14	–

on hired labour and produces a surplus of crops for sale. But on the other hand his use of non-contractual kin labour involves him in a host of debt relationships with his resident kin. This tends to siphon off some of his cash earnings and requires him to make available to others his farming equipment and some of his own labour time.

In 1963 and 1964 several groups seceded from the farm to establish their own settlements or to join other kin. The reasons for their leaving were manifold, but chief among them was their growing dissatisfaction with the management of the farm. Without realizing it Saini had himself sown the seeds of discontent when he allowed Sakishi and the others to settle there. This move had the long-term effect of antagonizing Yotam's family and ultimately of others at the farm as well.

With the arrival of Sakishi, Saini was able to embark on a programme of fairly rapid expansion. He now had a body of skilled workers at his disposal and, providing he gave them free access to the equipment at the farm, could rely on them to assist him when needed. Earlier I described the network of work relationships that resulted. One significant aspect of this was the exclusion of the Yotam group. Yotam was an old man in his late sixties and not very strong physically. His sons and son-in-law were young men with no expertise in plough methods. The main

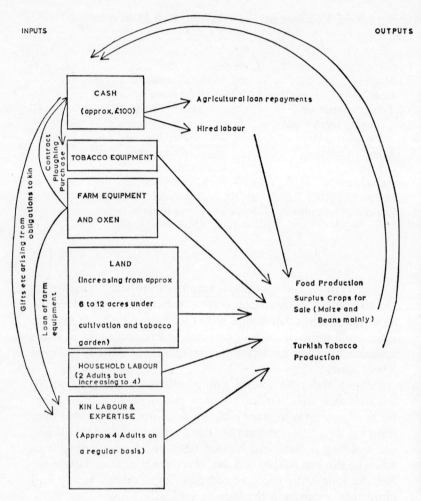

INPUTS

OUTPUTS

CASH
(approx. £100)

Agricultural loan repayments

Hired labour

Contract Ploughing Purchase

TOBACCO EQUIPMENT

FARM EQUIPMENT
AND OXEN

Gifts etc arising from obligations to kin

Loan of farm equipment

LAND
(Increasing from approx
6 to 12 acres under
cultivation and tobacco
garden)

HOUSEHOLD LABOUR
(2 Adults but
increasing to 4)

KIN LABOUR &
EXPERTISE
(Approx 4 Adults on
a regular basis)

Food Production
Surplus Crops for
Sale (Maize and
Beans mainly)

Turkish Tobacco
Production

FIG. II. Saini Moloka Farm, 1961–3 phase

teams for ploughing and harrowing consisted of Saini assisted by Sakishi and Manueli, and of Sakishi and his sons-in-law. Yotam and his son-in-law, Mambwe, were given the right to use the oxen and plough, and they received a certain amount of technical assistance, but with only one team of oxen available at any one time they often had to wait until Saini, Sakishi, Musonda, Buleni and the others had completed their gardens. This meant that they were not able to rely mainly on ploughed fields but had to cut a large *citeme* garden as well.

From Yotam's point of view this state of affairs ran counter to the expected pattern of behaviour that a sister's son should show to his mother's brother. He argued that as a sister's son Saini should have willingly undertaken to plough for him and should have provided him with food when necessary and with many gifts as a mark of respect. And if this argument did not hold for the modern situation, then Saini should have rewarded him anyway for his help in selecting a site and for the way in which he had kept Saini in touch with Chibale affairs during his urban employment. Saini, he claimed, had therefore neglected both his obligations to him as a senior kinsman and as a friend; and had finally repudiated these bonds by fixing a charge for ploughing.

Under the circumstances Yotam, Mambwe and the others found it difficult to remain at the farm. But before leaving they were involved in a number of disputes with others at the farm; Mambwe with Sakishi, Musonda and Saini over the grazing of crops by his cattle, and Yotam with NaMushili. At no time, it seems, did Yotam openly reproach Saini himself. Instead he attacked NaMushili, Saini's mother, and accused her of being a sorceress. The main reason why his anger was deflected towards NaMushili was because she enjoyed numerous economic benefits from staying at her son's farm and because she tended to align herself with Saini when quarrels broke out. Saini had built her a decent Kimberley-brick house and had provided her with food and clothing. Yotam felt that comparable treatment was due to him too and hoped that Saini would come to appreciate, through an understanding of the tense relations existing at the farm, that his grievances were well founded. Hence the conflict between Yotam and NaMushili reflected the underlying tensions which existed between Yotam and Saini over the question of economic assistance.

Mambwe's dispute with Sakishi and the others spread to include

Sakishi's wife, who used the episode to express her own feelings of discontent. Her hostility was directed mainly against Saini's wives and her own husband and centred once more on economic benefits. Why, she asked, should Saini's wives enjoy a higher standard of living than herself? Saini's wives did in fact enjoy a better standard of living and one of the reasons was because Saini had greater command over the labour of others and was able to cultivate larger acreages and sell a bigger surplus of crops. This was another point of tension at the farm, namely, the existence of asymmetrical work relationships whereby the labour input for Saini's gardens far exceeded that of anyone else.

The suggestion made by Musonda that she should pay for ploughing meant a change in the nature of these relationships. It transformed them from ties of mutual assistance expressed in terms of kinship to ties of a more commercial nature. To understand why it was that Saini so readily accepted this suggestion one needs to consider the development of the farm.

When a man like Saini returns from town to start a farm his major problem is that of skilled labour. He can operate on a system of hired labour if he has capital, but eventually he will need to recruit permanent workers. This is generally done by persuading certain kinsmen who have the necessary farming expertise to settle with him and assist in developing the farm. He may also wish to attract other kinsmen to help with the unskilled tasks. Many long-term urban workers have adult children who could assist with farm work but in most cases they remain behind in town, especially if they have secure jobs. During the early years of the farm, then, the most important single factor constraining its development as a commercial enterprise is the farmer's lack of expertise. Agricultural demonstrators may offer advice concerning crop rotation, animal husbandry, etc., and may even help him train his oxen and teach him how to plough, but they are no substitute for the assistance provided by kinsmen or friends who work regularly alongside the farmer. For Saini the opportunity for recruiting such persons came when Sakishi and his dependants were evicted from their farm. By this time of course Saini's freedom of choice was further restricted by the fact that he had little of his original savings left for hiring labour and yet needed a fairly large labour input to extend his fields. By the end of 1960 he still only had six acres cleared for cultivation.

The next phase in the development of the farm is reached when the maximum amount of land has been opened up for cultivation. By then the farmer and his wife are more skilled and his children older and better able to take a part in farm work. At this stage the farmer may feel that he can satisfactorily dispense with some of the labour from kinsmen or friends without seriously affecting the efficiency or output of his enterprise. Saini Farm is a case in point. The arrangements that Saini made with Sakishi and the others worked reasonably well for the first few years when he required their assistance for expanding his farm, but after this he found that, as his own experience grew and as his wives and teenage daughter were more able to assist with plough-ing and other skilled tasks, so he relied less and less on the help from Sakishi and the others. This process was accentuated by Saini's marrying a second wife in 1962 and introducing her to ploughing in the following season. At the same time, however, several of Saini's kin began to feel dissatisfied with working at a farm where they reckoned that they received little economic benefit. Once the opportunity presented itself, Saini did not hesitate to make clear to everyone, through his acceptance of Musonda's suggestion, that those who stayed on at the farm could no longer expect any special favours simply because they were related to him. And this was the major precipitating cause of the fission of the farm.

At this stage lack of farming expertise had ceased to be a critical factor and had been superseded by other sorts of constraints. It is clear from the data presented above that in order to recruit the necessary skilled labour Saini had to take a number of persons over and above the basic labour requirements of his farm. This resulted in the build-up of a network of work obligations among various residents and allowed a large number of persons to claim the use of Saini's oxen and equipment. There may also have been competition for the better soils close to the farm, though Saini never mentioned this as an issue nor was it brought up in any of the quarrels. In an effort to produce a viable farming unit Saini had in fact created a residential grouping which was far too large and unwieldy, and it could only be a matter of time before the component sections hived off to start their own settlements or to join other kin. Thus the network of work arrangements centr-ing on Saini himself, and the various demands made on him for

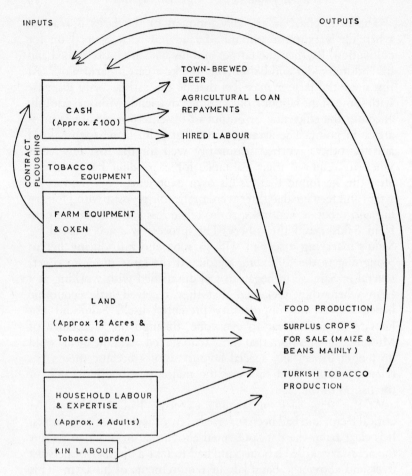

INPUTS
OUTPUTS

CONTRACT PLOUGHING

CASH
(Approx. £100)

TOBACCO
EQUIPMENT

FARM EQUIPMENT
& OXEN

LAND
(Approx 12 Acres &
Tobacco garden)

HOUSEHOLD LABOUR
& EXPERTISE
(Approx. 4 Adults)

KIN LABOUR

TOWN-BREWED
BEER

AGRICULTURAL LOAN
REPAYMENTS

HIRED LABOUR

FOOD PRODUCTION

SURPLUS CROPS
FOR SALE (MAIZE &
BEANS MAINLY)

TURKISH TOBACCO
PRODUCTION

FIG. III. Saini Moloka Farm, November 1963–4 phase

economic assistance, seem later to have threatened the economic viability of the farm itself. The way out of these difficulties was for Saini to repudiate some of these ties, otherwise they might effectively limit his choices concerning the future management and development of the farm. This he did. In this connection it is perhaps significant that it was Yotam's patrilaterally linked group which suffered most. Studies of matrilineal systems in central Africa have shown that male matrikin frequently provide points of fission in the system, as their children belong to a different descent group. This is especially the case for those with adult children who are collaterally related to the dominant descent group (Mitchell, 1956, Chapter 7).

Figure III shows the pattern of farm activities evolving during the 1963–4 phase. A prominent feature of this is the small contribution now made by kin and the corresponding increase in the regular labour supplied by Saini's own household. As a consequence he is no longer so committed to loaning out his equipment, giving of his time, or to dispensing largesse to members of other households. Yet he still maintains the same level of food and tobacco production, and takes on hired hands to meet peak requirements. He has also become a well-known beer seller in the parish. His link with his brother Petro, who has a motor-van, makes it possible for him to buy *chibuku* (a town-brewed beer) and to transport it to Kapepa for sale. The profits provide a valuable addition to the income from farming. Later he hopes to persuade his brother to invest money in a store which he thinks would be a good second line to farming.

I now describe the establishment of two other farming enterprises in the parish, giving prominence again to the question of the recruitment and organization of labour. Both farms differ from Saini Farm in that they were started by persons who left their villages to build independent settlements, and not by recently returned urban workers. Neither of them attracted a large body of resident kinsmen-workers as Saini did.

KATWISHI FARM

The owner of the farm, Katwishi (see Genealogy II, D35), lived originally in Lusefu Village, where he managed a store for his elder brother,

Bombwe (II, D25), who was working in Kitwe. Then in 1951, after a series of disputes with several of his matrikin in Lusefu, Katwishi persuaded Bombwe to give him the necessary financial support to leave the village and build a new store near to the motor road to Chibale Court. The site he chose was close to Kapepa Primary School and about 2½ miles from Lusefu Village. But four years later Katwishi left the store to start a farm some two miles from Lusefu Village. He had quarrelled with Bombwe over the profits from the business and had been forced to resign from his position as manager.[1]

His choice of farm site was influenced by his desire to remain in close proximity to Lusefu Village. Lusefu (II, C6) the headman, and Katwishi's mother's brother, had for many years acted as the custodian of a herd of cattle kept at the village and Katwishi wanted permission to castrate two of the young bulls and train them as oxen. He also thought that he might be able to utilize his links with the village to recruit labour for his farm.

The question of the ownership of the cattle at Lusefu Village had remained a vexed problem ever since the first beasts were acquired. The herd had been started in the mid-1940's from money received by Lusefu in payment of compensation for the death of Lusefu's classificatory mother (II, B1). Although Lusefu had been the recipient, Katwishi and other matrikin claimed that he had simply represented them as their senior kinsman and that therefore the ownership of the original cattle and their offspring should be distributed equally among all adults in the matrilineal kin group. Later, matters were further complicated by the addition to the herd of other cattle purchased by Bombwe and Lusefu out of their own personal savings. Thus various matrikin all claim that they have rights over the use, and possible disposal of the same set of animals. Moreover, the cattle are so interbred that it is impossible to say which cattle are individually owned by Bombwe and Lusefu. But for all intents and purposes most persons recognize that control of the herd is in the hands of Lusefu, under the patronage of Bombwe, a prosperous townsman. Katwishi exploited this situation to get Lusefu to agree to his training oxen for ploughing.

Even before leaving the store at Kapepa, Katwishi had become interested in the prospect of becoming a peasant farmer and hoped to combine this with storekeeping. He persuaded Bombwe to send him £5 with which to buy a plough and had got permission from Lusefu to castrate two bulls so that they might be used for ploughing. At the

[1] For details see pp. 100-6.

same time he established close links with several of the farmers at the farming block and visited their farms regularly to talk over farm matters. One of these was Godfrey, a boyhood friend with whom Katwishi had maintained contact over the years. Godfrey's brother Daiman (II, D16) was married to Katwishi's cross-cousin Chisenga (II, D15), one of Lusefu's daughters. Katwishi was able to use both this bond of friendship and his affinal link with Godfrey to get the latter to assist him with the training of the oxen. He was also favourably placed for receiving help from the local school teacher, who had recently taken to using a plough to cultivate the school gardens, and from agricultural demonstrators at the nearby agricultural camp. The teachers and agricultural demonstrators were regular customers at the store and obtained considerable quantities of goods on credit. Indeed, one of the major issues in the quarrels which developed between Bombwe and Katwishi was over this 'buying of friends' with store capital.

Having selected his farm site, Katwishi had a three-roomed brick house built at a cost of £9 9s. for labour and materials. The money for this, on Katwishi's own admission, was taken from the amount he collected for Bombwe for transporting persons to the Copperbelt towns in the latter's motor-van. There was insufficient cash left to hire people to help clear the site and stump the fields for cultivation, and so the bulk of this work was done by himself and his wife, with some additional help from his brother-in-law, Totwa (II, D33), and two classificatory sons-in-law from Lusefu Village. He was able to enlist their assistance on the understanding that he would plough some gardens for them.

At the time of his establishing the farm the labour input from Katwishi's nuclear family was insufficient to meet the demands of plough cultivation. Although Katwishi had had some previous experience in handling oxen and working the plough, his wife was untrained and his children too young to be of assistance. It was imperative therefore for him to recruit some extra help. He did this by arranging for his brother-in-law, Totwa, to help them each year during the ploughing season. Katwishi and his wife would alternate between holding the plough and goading on the oxen, whilst Totwa led the team. In return Katwishi each year ploughed a maize garden for Totwa. Similar arrangements were made with the two classificatory sons-in-law though on a less regular basis.

The sowing and weeding were done by Katwishi and his wife with no extra help, but for harvesting his wife enlisted the aid of her mother and sister, and Katwishi's widowed sister also occasionally assisted. Katwishi was married to his cross-cousin (II, D20), a daughter of Lusefu, and this no doubt facilitated his getting help from these kin as he could use both his own and his wife's links with them.

In 1956–7 Katwishi obtained an agricultural loan of £33 11s. 9d. for one scotch cart, one harrow and another, better-quality plough, which he agreed to pay off at the rate of £5 per year. His success in securing a loan was largely attributed to the favourable recommendations he received from his friends at the agricultural camp.

In 1959 he married a second wife and since then the farm work has been organized on the basis of co-operation between himself and his two wives. In 1963 each wife had her own gardens, consisting of two acres of millet, two acres of maize, one acre each of sorghum and beans, and Katwishi himself had a few acres of maize and beans which he said he grew entirely for marketing. The ploughing is done by Katwishi and his two wives, rotating between their respective gardens, with minimal assistance from Totwa and the young herdsboy at Lusefu, who are called in to help towards the end of the ploughing season. The sowing and weeding is done jointly by the two wives with occasional extra help from schoolboys whom Katwishi employs on a casual basis. Harvesting is the responsibility of each wife separately and each invites some of her own matrikin to assist her. In addition, Katwishi calls in some of his own sisters if they are available to harvest his own gardens and in return they receive some of the produce.

Throughout the history of the farm, Katwishi has never employed a herdsboy, as the oxen he uses graze with the herd at Lusefu Village, where they are looked after by one of Lusefu's maternal grandchildren.

In mid-1964, after a domestic tiff, Katwishi's first wife left the farm and returned to live at Lusefu Village. This move threatened to jeopardize the labour arrangements at the farm, for Katwishi had still not recruited any other permanent residents to assist with the farm work. The immediate outcome of this was that he ran into some difficulties with his tobacco crop which he had just started to harvest, and had to employ an outside helper to work with him and his other wife. The woman he took on at short notice was a young divorcee from a nearby village. The arrangement he made with her was that she would receive a proportion of the income made on this crop and would be provided with food and shelter during her stay at the farm. This had been the first time Katwishi had branched out into Turkish tobacco cultivation and already part of his crop had been ruined by his wife withdrawing her labour at a crucial stage in the processing of it. When I left the field in May 1964, there was no sign of there being a reconciliation between them.

Analysis
Katwishi contrasts markedly with Saini Moloka in that he had few capital assets of his own when establishing his farm. Thus he relied heavily on the assistance he could get from certain matrikin. His brother Bombwe provided him with money for the plough and Lusefu the oxen. Although Katwishi had recently quarrelled with Bombwe and Lusefu, and had been openly accused of practising sorcery by several of his matrikin at Lusefu Village, he nevertheless succeeded in getting them to supply him with the basic farming items. The reason for this was not only that they felt some moral obligation to him because he was their close uterine kinsman, albeit a somewhat wayward character, but also because they realized that his venture into farming might in the long run be to their own advantage. Later, for example, after Katwishi had trained the oxen and had started ploughing, Lusefu arranged for two more oxen to be trained by his son (II, D21) under the supervision of Katwishi and persuaded Bombwe to buy another plough for the use of Lusefu and others at the village.

Katwishi found it more difficult, however, to recruit labour from among his matrikin. This was partly because he needed male workers for clearing, stumping and ploughing at a time when many of his male matrikin were absent in urban employment, and partly because he had made himself generally unpopular with them for mismanaging Bombwe's store, and had acquired a reputation for sorcery. He was also unsuccessful in recruiting the help of Lusefu's sons, despite the fact that he had married their sister; and he had no close friends to whom he could turn. Up to about a year before he left the store at Kapepa, he had been a keen member of the local congregation of Jehovah's Witnesses and had been especially friendly with Zakeyo, the leader of the congregation, who was also the market supervisor at Kapepa and a very influential person in the parish. But Katwishi had destroyed his chances of recruiting assistance from this sector of his network by being expelled from the church for heavy drinking and for an alleged act of adultery with Zakeyo's sister. Even his friendship with Godfrey was adversely affected by his expulsion from the congregation, for Godfrey himself was a zealot of the movement and a brother-in-law of Zakeyo, the congregation leader. Thus it was that Katwishi had to enlist the help of three men related to him affinally, on the understanding that he would plough for them in return.

During the early years of the establishment of his farm Katwishi depended on the assistance he received from Totwa and the others to make up the team for ploughing, but later when he married a second wife he found that it was possible to manage the farm with only a minimum of help from them. Under the new arrangement he seemed to show some signs of producing a regular surplus of crops for sale. In 1963 he received an income of £26 6s. from the sale of grains and by then had a total of eight acres of land under cultivation. In previous years his acreages were much smaller and his crop surplus negligible. The reason for this increase in productivity was partly related to the fact that Katwishi had for the first time the beginnings of a permanent and reliable team of workers and had through his second wife been able to recruit additional help from affines outside the Lusefu group. His second wife's village was situated fairly close to the farm and had a relatively large number of teenage boys living there, who were prepared to work for Katwishi for a nominal sum so that they could learn the techniques of plough agriculture. From Katwishi's point of view, this was obviously a better arrangement than the deal he had made with Totwa and the others from Lusefu.

Then, in 1964, when he began growing Turkish tobacco, production was again seriously hampered by an insufficient labour supply. Tobacco cultivation demands a large labour input for approximately eight months of the year with especially heavy requirements during the picking and stringing stages. Since none of Katwishi's children were old enough to take any major part in this work, he had to rely on the hard work and co-operation of his two wives. The boys from his second wife's village were not able to give him assistance for they were similarly involved in processing tobacco for their own households. Quarrelling had broken out between Katwishi and his wives on several occasions and over many issues, but throughout all this was the constant theme of how much each would receive of the returns of the crop. Finally matters came to a head when his first wife left the farm and returned to Lusefu Village, and this created a labour crisis at the height of the harvesting season.

Throughout the history of Katwishi's farm, then, it emerges that whatever plans Katwishi may have had for developing his enterprise, these were continually restricted by three interconnected factors; his lack of capital, his difficulties in recruiting a permanent labour force to meet the demands of the various crops cultivated and the fact that he lacked an effective network of relationships with kinsmen and friends to whom he could turn for help, or whom he could persuade to join him at the farm. Unlike Saini, the question of farming expertise was never a critical factor, for during his days as Bombwe's store manager Katwishi utilized links with certain of his customer friends at the agricultural camp to acquire the basic skills. The dilemma which faced Katwishi was perhaps best summed up by Katwishi himself when he discussed with me what he would do if he won the state lottery. His plan, he said, was to build a 'compound' at the farm to house a group of permanently employed farm labourers, and a large barn in which to store his farming equipment, which among other things would include a tractor. He would then, he claimed, be free to assist whomsoever he wished from among his kin, and not just anyone who arrived at the farm. The irony of this last remark was, of course, that over the years it had been Katwishi himself who had constantly needed to seek help from kinsmen and not vice versa.

DAIMAN FARM

Daiman (II, D16) returned to Chibale Chiefdom in 1955 at the age of 26, after working for a few years in Luanshya, where he married the daughter of a Chibale headman. On his return he lived for about four years in his wife's village giving marriage service to his in-laws.

In 1959 Daiman's mother's brother, Mukwenda, who had been a farmer at the farming block for ten years, was killed in a car accident and a dispute arose between Daiman, who was supported by his elder brother Godfrey, and Amos, the deceased's classificatory brother, over the inheritance of Mukwenda's property. At the time of his death, Mukwenda's assets were considerable: 23 head of cattle, three ploughs, one harrow, one cultivator, one scotch cart and one hand grinding machine. Daiman managed to secure six of the cattle, one plough and the harrow and scotch cart. The rest went to his maternal uncle Amos. None of Mukwenda's sons were old enough to stake a claim to their father's farming equipment though they did receive some share of his household effects. The strongest argument in favour of Daiman's receiving some share of the property was that he had at one time worked as Mukwenda's herdsboy and later helped him in various agricultural tasks.

Daiman's elder brother Godfrey was already established as a farmer on the farming block and had recently paid off his agricultural loan. His farming assets in 1959 consisted of two ploughs, one planter, one harrow, one scotch cart and two oxen and two cows. Instead of attempting to acquire the property for himself, he chose to support his brother, who had no farming equipment of his own.

On receipt of the cattle and equipment Daiman decided to move out of the village, together with his wife and two young children, and start a farm. Godfrey had been considering setting up his own farm outside the block now that he had no obligations to the Agricultural Department. So the two of them agreed to join forces and establish adjacent farms. The plan was that Daiman would first obtain permission from the chief to have his own farm about two miles from the block and would later be joined by Godfrey, who would set up a farm immediately adjoining Daiman's. The two brothers would assist each other in putting up the farm buildings and in clearing the sites. Both were skilled bricklayers and carpenters. They also agreed to co-operate with various farming tasks.

The farm buildings and the clearing of the land were started in 1959, while they were still living at their respective settlements. Two large Kimberley-brick houses were begun, one of seven rooms and the other of four. When completed, Daiman had spent a total of £7 15s. on his for labour, mainly brickmaking, and materials. In the following year, he moved to the new site and hired villagers from nearby settlements to help with stumping. The money for this and for the labour on the house came from his earnings as a bricklayer and from what he received from contract ploughing for others. In 1959 he had built three houses for a total of £9 and had earned another £9 from ploughing.

Godfrey joined his brother at the new site in 1961 when his house was ready for habitation, and brought with him his wife and young children, and a teenage brother who was acting as herdsboy.

Although the farms were registered separately, Daiman and Godfrey have in fact always co-operated in farming duties. In 1963 each grew a basic seven and a half acres, consisting of two acres of maize, one of beans, one of cow peas, half of groundnuts and three acres of finger millet. These constitute the main plots and are ploughed and harrowed by Godfrey, Daiman and their young brother. Any acres above this amount are cultivated separately and usually ploughed with the help of hired labour. In 1963 both employed two additional workers for a period of two months to help cultivate a further four acres each, paying them at the rate of 30 shillings a month, plus board and lodging.

The planter, which is jointly operated by the men assisted by their wives, is used for sowing. Though again, they make their own arrangements if they wish to cultivate larger acreages. Weeding is undertaken by each couple separately with some extra assistance from hired schoolboy labour, and harvesting is similarly organized, with help this time from their wives' matrikin who live in nearby villages. They receive produce for their labour.

Daiman and Godfrey both cultivate Turkish tobacco, but only the initial ploughing of the tobacco field is carried out jointly. The rest of the production is left for them to organize individually. Contract labour is especially important during the picking and stringing stages, when both brothers need extra help, and workers are generally paid at the rate of 2s. 6d. a day and employed on a weekly basis. In 1963, in addition to casual labour, their father and a sister from Mkushi District stayed at Godfrey's farm during the season and took a major part in the production of his and Daiman's tobacco crop. At the end of the season they each received some proportion of the income derived from the crop.

In 1962 Daiman and Godfrey jointly financed the opening of a small store on the Chibale Road close to the farming block. Their business interests began in 1960 when they pooled their savings so that they could purchase £28 worth of goods, mainly clothing, which they hawked around the villages in Chibale. Though at first their profits from this were rather small they gradually built up a number of regular customers, and, being Jehovah's Witnesses, were able to reduce their transport costs by persuading a fellow Jehovah's Witness to bring goods from town for them.

Two years later they had saved enough money to build and stock a store. Their initial capital outlay was in the region of £120, most of which was earned from tobacco. £20 of this was spent on labour and materials for the store building—£15 on corrugated steel for the roof and £5 on brick making. The store was built by Daiman and Godfrey and their younger brother, who later assumed responsibility for running it. The remaining £100 was used to buy stock. By 1963–4 the store formed an integral part of their joint economic activities. Some of the income from the store was used to finance the hiring of labour and for purchasing new farming equipment, whilst each year some of the money derived from the sale of crops was used to replenish stock.

Table VI gives the total income and expenditure of Daiman during 1962–3. Since the store was treated strictly as a joint enterprise it was

Table VI: Income and expenditure for Daiman: 1962–3

Income	£	s.	d.	Expenditure	£	s.	d.
Maize	5	–	–	Sewing machine	23	–	–
Beans	2	8	–	Bed	3	–	–
Tobacco (after de-				Plough	6	15	–
ducting service and				Transport costs	3	–	–
transport costs)	76	–	–	Hired labour			
Potatoes	10	–		stumping	6	–	–
2 head of cattle to				ploughing	3	–	–
butcher	41	–	–	weeding	1	–	–
Earnings from store				harvesting	2	–	–
(calculated from				tobacco production			
store accounts book)	92	6	4	(paid to father)	10	–	–
				herding	1	2	6
				Clothing for family	23	–	–
				Gifts to kinsmen	1	10	–
				Stock for store	60	–	–
				Transport costs	9	9	–
				Unaccounted for	64	7	10
	£217	4	4		£217	4	4

not possible to deduce exactly how much of its income each brother received. To simplify matters I have therefore assumed that Daiman received exactly half of the total earnings and it is this figure which is shown in the table.

Analysis

Daiman was one of the youngest and most successful commercial farmers in the parish. He owed his success very largely to his having ready command over basic resources. He was fortunate in acquiring most of his farming equipment and cattle through inheritance and his expertise by having worked for some years on his mother's brother's farm and from the assistance given him by his elder brother. Any difficulties he might have met over farm labour were easily solved by taking on hired hands. This was made possible because his agricultural enterprise was subsidized from time to time by his earnings as a bricklayer and later by his income derived from the store. Thus Daiman's material assets were such that few major restrictions were placed on the development of the farm.

Right from the start of the farm there had been close co-operation between Daiman and his elder brother both in farm work and later in the financing of the store. But unlike Saini Moloka, Daiman was able to avoid becoming closely involved with other kinsmen. We saw earlier in the case of Saini how a large body of resident kinsmen can at one stage in the development of a farm be a significant asset to the farmer, whilst at another constitute a serious threat to the economic viability of the enterprise. Daiman staved off the possible effects of relying too heavily on kin by making no effort to recruit extra workers from among his kin on a non-contractual basis. Nor did he attempt to persuade kinsfolk to settle at the farm.

Several factors facilitated his maintaining this degree of independence from his kin. His bricklaying and later business activities provided him with a fairly regular source of additional capital which he could use to take on hired hands. Secondly, although Daiman could have sited his farm close to the border of Chibale and Kabamba Chiefdoms where most of his close matrikin were concentrated, he was persuaded by Godfrey to locate it instead in Kapepa Parish. Godfrey held the view that it was better to be as independent as possible from kin if one was intending to make an economic success of farming. Thirdly, it may be that even if Daiman had wanted to recruit other kinsmen he would not have found it easy, for many of his close matrikin (e.g. his classificatory mother and mother's brothers, and his young sister) were already well set up as farmers, or were married to men with substantial wealth of their own, and would not have wanted to join him at the farm. His wife's kin were also reasonably well provided for by their own male kinsmen and expressed no desire to settle with him. Finally, Daiman's close bonds with Godfrey tended to insure him against any possible attempts by other kin to latch themselves on to his farming enterprise. Godfrey said that they preferred to operate with contract labour and refused outright to assist kinsmen simply because they were kinsmen; 'we can only help those who bring in profits', he commented. Later their ties were strengthened by their financing the opening of the store. And in addition to the strong economic component in their relationship, they were both members of the local congregation of Jehovah's Witnesses. Thus they had a similar ideological viewpoint and cultivated the same network of friends. Their church membership was especially valuable for building up a regular clientele for the store and for getting contracts to build houses. Nearly half of their regular customers were Jehovah's Witnesses, who were allowed goods on credit up to about £5. Although Godfrey himself said explicitly that membership of the church did not entitle one to preferential treatment (he said he gave credit only to those in a position to pay off their debts at some later date), it turned out that most of those who were able to pay were in fact Jehovah's Witnesses with whom he was well acquainted.

Composition of labour force at 24 peasant farms

So far the discussion has centred around two main themes. In the first place I have documented the ways in which particular farmers gained access to certain essential resources; and secondly, I have indicated, through the exposition and analysis of selected case material, that differences in the pattern of farm organization are closely related to differences in the availability of resources and in farming objectives. Throughout I have stressed the importance of examining the specific sociological components of each farm situation. I want now to analyse the recruitment and deployment of labour in greater detail, using data from all 24 farms in Kapepa Parish, in order to show that some of the points made in the foregoing discussion of the cases are of more general significance.

A breakdown of the composition of regular labour units reveals that they fall into one of five distinct categories:

1. Those farms where the regular unit consists of the farmer, his wife and two or more adult children, and their spouses if they are married (six cases).

2. Those consisting of the farmer and two wives with no adult children (four cases).

3. Those made up of the farmer, his wife (or wives) and a group of resident kinsmen-workers (generally the farmer's matri-kin) and their nuclear families (five cases).

4. Those where the farm is jointly owned and worked by two uterine brothers and the labour unit consists of the two farmers and their wives (three cases).

5. Those where the farmer and his wife co-operate with a neighbouring farmer and his wife in all major agricultural tasks. Here the two farmers are uterine brothers and/or Jehovah's Witness friends (six cases).

Each of these five categories is exclusive in that only in category (1) are there adult children available to take a major part in farm work.

This indicates that, as is to be expected, the composition of labour at a farm can partly be explained by the number of adult members of the farmer's household available for farm work, which will vary according to the stage in the life cycle of the family. The average estimated acreage for the farmers in the parish was in the region of eight to ten acres per year, and four or five full-time workers were needed to cultivate an area of this size. Hence those farmers who have several sons and daughters old enough to assume an important part in farm work will probably not need to recruit other permanent workers, though they may take on a number of temporary hands to meet various peak requirements or to cultivate larger acreages. But if the farmer's children are still young then he will require the assistance of two or three additional workers, and possibly more if he en-visages producing a substantial surplus for sale.

In addition to differences in composition, there are also some differences in the deployment of labour. There is no strict division of labour according to sex in the case of categories (2), (4) and (5), all adults assisting jointly in all agricultural tasks and having interchangeable roles for ploughing. The same pattern emerges for category (1), with the exception of two farms where there are married children and their spouses available. Category (3), how-ever, stands out in sharp contrast. Here a reasonably strict sexual division is found, the men co-operating with ploughing, harrowing and handling the oxen, while the women do the weeding, harvesting and sowing. The same arrangement is made at the two farms in category (1) with married children. This suggests that only where there are at least three men and three women available as the regular labour force will the farmer be able to operate a system of different but complementary roles.

To explain further why variations in the composition of labour units exist one needs to examine other factors affecting the recruitment of labour. Why is it, for example, that some farmers recruit permanently resident kinsmen-workers whilst others do not?

Implicit in the case studies of farm organization is the contrast between the farmer who returns from town, having completed ten or more years in urban wage employment, and who uses his savings to establish a farm, and the farmer who has spent less time in urban employment, has little in the way of savings, and who has lived for a number of years at a village or individual settlement in the area before moving out to start his own farm. If we compare these two categories of farmers in terms of the composition of their labour units we find (excluding category (1) farms where there are adult children) that farmers of the latter type rely on the assistance of some nearby farmer and his family or work a farm jointly with their brother, while the former recruit permanently resident kinsmen-workers.

The reasons for this are more easily understood if one considers the problems facing an urban worker who returns to start a farm. During the establishment phase he often allows himself to be drawn into a series of debt relationships with certain of his matrikin: they help him in choosing a site, in training oxen and learning the techniques of plough cultivation, and in return he lets them and their dependants reside with him at the farm and receive some of the benefits of his accumulated wealth. This arrangement solves his labour difficulties and no doubt confers on him a certain degree of social prestige, though it frequently means also that he has living with him many more persons than he needs to run the farm. His choosing matrilineal kin rather than other types of kin or friends is probably because this is the most effective sector of his social network, for he has not yet had time to develop the necessary links to operate differently if he wished. More importantly, however, it is likely that he will be submitted to heavy pressure from his close matrikin when he arrives home, who will exploit their bonds of kinship and stress his obligations to them to their own personal advantage.

Hence, even when the farmer has sufficient capital to operate entirely with hired labour, in most cases he will find it expedient to take into his farm a number of kinsmen already skilled in plough methods in order that he may acquire the necessary expertise. If later he finds that such a large group of kinsmen-workers becomes a drain on the resources of the farm he may then attempt to get rid of some of them and organize his labour differently. One way of changing the pattern of work relationships, I suggested, was in fact to marry a second wife and to bring her into the team for ploughing. This was how Saini Moloka sought to handle the situation, and the evidence points to this being a general pattern among farmers of this type. Two out of the four farms where the regular labour unit now consists of the farmer and two wives had originally been composed of the farmer, his first wife and a group of matrikin. These kinsmen and their families had subsequently moved out following the arrival of the second wife. Moreover, three out of the five farms where there are several kinsmen-workers appear to be passing through a transitional stage in that the farmers have recently married second wives and there are signs at all three farms that some of the kin may shortly be leaving.

Unlike the farmer from town, the farmer who moves out of a village or settlement generally does not face the same kind of difficulties. Frequently he has already received some training in plough cultivation and has had some experience of the problems of farm management. Often he has previously lived and worked at a farm belonging to some close kinsman or has assisted some farmer friend or kinsman in the neighbourhood. Also the establishment of the farm tends to be a more gradual process, the clearing of the site and the construction of the buildings taking place over several years prior to the farmer moving to the new place. Frequently the farmer has relatively little capital and has to acquire his farming equipment gradually, unless he is fortunate enough to secure an early loan from the Agricultural Department.

This type of farmer is probably more able to make some appraisal of the problems associated with commercial production and may even have had first-hand experience of different forms of labour organization before embarking on his own enterprise. Yet why should farmers of this type apparently reject the advantages of having permanently resident kinsmen-workers?

An explanation of this seems to lie with four factors in the situation. Firstly, they have much less capital available when starting their farms, none had more than £50 and the majority much less. Perhaps therefore lack of funds acts to limit the number of close kinsmen who might be interested in settling at their farms for reasons of economic gain, or the farmer himself may not want kin with him lest they become too great an economic burden. Secondly, several of these farmers are somewhat younger than those who came from town and may have been less well placed for recruiting kinsmen-workers even if they had wanted. That is, they had fewer close matrikin willing to recognize their patronage by settling at the farm. Another constraining factor is the availability of close kin for recruitment. Four of the farmers came from outside Chibale Chiefdom where the bulk of their matrikin continue to reside and three others had recently been involved in serious disputes with their kin (one involving sorcery charges). It may therefore have been less easy for them to persuade kinsmen to join them, though they could of course activate some affinal or clanship links with persons in the vicinity if they so desired.

A fourth and probably more significant factor is that most of these farmers are Jehovah's Witnesses and operate a closely knit network of ties with members of the local church congregation which extends to include various extra-church activities. Thus, several of them have utilized links with some more established Jehovah's Witness farmer (or farmers) who has helped during the initial stage of establishing the farm by lending farming equipment and by assisting with ploughing, etc. Also several Jehovah's Witnesses have built farms within close proximity to one another so that they can assist each other jointly in farm work. This emerges most strikingly in the cases of farms U, V and W (see Table VII, p. 77) where the farmers co-operate for ploughing, harrowing, etc., and also borrow equipment and offer advice on crops and various techniques. Each of these farmers also possesses some non-farming skill—one is a sawyer, another a bricklayer and the third a tailor—which they place at one another's disposal. The same pattern holds for farmers who manage a farm in

Table VII: Differences in composition of labour force correlated with differences in social characteristics of 24 peasant farms in Kapepa Parish

Farms	Composition of labour unit	Type of peak labour	Present age of farmer	Returned labour migrant at least 10 years' urban experience +	Practises non-farming skill +	Religious affiliation JW = Jehovah's Witness
A	Farmer's wife and adult children	Hired non-resident affines	60	+	+	−
B		"	55	−	−	−
C		"	44	+	−	JW
D		"	53	−	−	JW
E		"	53	+	−	JW
F		Non-resident patrilateral kin	53	+	−	JW
G	Farmer and two wives	Hired non-resident affines	52	+	−	−
H			42	−	−	−
I			51	+	−	−
J			52	+	+	−
K	Farmer, wife/wives and group of resident kinsmen-workers	Resident matrikin	58	+	−	−
L			47	+	−	−
M			35	+	−	−
N			45	+	−	−
O			37		−	−
P	2 farmers and wives working joint farm	Hired	34	−	+	JW
Q		"	40	−	+	JW
R		Friends/matrikin	25		−	−
S	Farmer and wife co-operate with neighbouring farmer and wife	Friends/matrikin	23	−	+	JW
T		Affines	27	−	+	−
U		Friends/hired	49	−	+	JW
V		"	49	−	+	JW
W		"	36	−	+	JW
X		Affines	37	−	−	JW

partnership with a uterine brother or where the brothers jointly
assist each other in the running of two adjacently sited farms.
Moreover, in all but one case the brothers are also members of
the church. Those farmers who are Jehovah's Witnesses but who
only rely to a small extent on fellow churchmen have adult
children available for farm work and therefore depend to a much
lesser extent on outside labour.

I cannot here discuss in detail the content of the social ethic
preached by Jehovah's Witnesses in the parish and examine the
ways in which their ethic provides individual Witnesses with some
justification for certain modes of social action. But the ethic places
important emphasis on the nuclear family as a Christian grouping,
disapproves of matrilineal forms of descent and inheritance and
puts a ban on polygynous marriage. Such an ideology can serve
both to legitimize the repudiation of ties with matrilineal kin and
can sanction the furthering of close bonds with fellow Jehovah's
Witnesses. Hence several farmers who utilize links with fellow
churchmen to solve problems of farm management and labour
have a ready-made ideological justification for their actions.

The discussion of the reasons for differences in the composition
of labour units at farms in Kapepa Parish has led to a brief examination of the social characteristics of the farmers themselves. In the
first place I argued that the composition and deployment of
labour was directly related to the availability of labour from the
farmer's own household and to the kinds of opportunities that
exist for recruiting outside help. I finally looked at the kinds of
links utilized by farmers who do not recruit a large body of resident kinsmen-workers and showed how many of these relied on
the assistance of fellow Jehovah's Witnesses.

I now turn briefly to the question of peak labour requirements.
Those farmers (mostly Jehovah's Witnesses) who possess some
non-farming skill which provides them with an additional source
of income, or those who have their own savings or who can obtain cash from other sources, will tend to employ hired labour if
they have need. Those farmers without the necessary capital will
rely on casual, non-contractual kin labour recruited from among
their own matrikin or that of their wives, or in the case of Witnesses from among their church friends.

Table VII summarizes some of the arguments developed in this
section by tabulating the close association between differences in

labour organization and differences in the social characteristics of the 24 farms in the parish. The table presents an essentially synchronic view of farm organization, but one which substantiates several of the hypotheses put forward in the discussion of the cases.

In the first part of the chapter I examined the interplay of various social and economic factors in the establishment and development of three farming enterprises and discussed the constraints affecting the choices open to particular farmers. Here I have analysed the interrelationships between the same kinds of factors over a wider range of data and in so doing have isolated a series of intervening variables to be taken into account. Among these were the question of the urban experience, age, non-farming skills and religious affiliation of the farmers concerned. It was argued that all are of significance for understanding the patterns of labour recruitment and farm management.

CHAPTER IV

CHANGING SETTLEMENT PATTERNS

Historical background

We can best understand the present situation if we first sketch in its historical antecedents. Tradition holds that during the earlier phases of Lala history, when the plateau region was being settled, people lived in small scattered settlements, rather like the present-day *nkutu* (an *nkutu* is a small encampment of grass huts built nearby the *citeme* gardens). Nothing much is known about the composition of settlements during this period, except that close matrikin are said to have resided together.

Following this, in the early years of the nineteenth century, the Yeke peoples commenced raiding from the west.[1] At first, in the event of a raid, the Lala would desert their villages and seek refuge in the hills until the marauders had gone. But later, when external pressures increased as a result of Ngoni and Bemba raiding in the area, the form of settlements underwent a radical change. Many of the small, impermanent settlements were abandoned and large stockaded villages (*amalinga:* sing. *ilinga*) were built instead.

Each *ilinga* consisted of a huge concentration of huts, often numbering several hundreds, and was divided into administrative sections (*ifibansa*). Though sections were not always spatially discrete, old informants said that it was general for each to be mainly composed of a single large matrilineal descent group (*icikoto*) under the leadership of a section head (*mwine cibansa*). The section head was assisted by a group of elders from the section who together handled any disputes that might arise between members of their section.

Each section was held responsible for the maintenance of a portion of the palisade and it was the section head who organized such work. Above this level of organization was the 'owner' or head of the stockade (*mwine we linga*) and his councillors or ad-

[1] The Yeke later established a chiefdom on the west bank of the Luapula river. See Cunnison, 1959, p. 43.

visers (*mpemba*). The latter were chosen from the various sections of the village and would normally be section heads.

With the arrival of the British and the subjugation of the Ngoni and Bemba peoples in the 1890's, the stockaded villages began to break up quickly. A British South Africa Company report for 1904 records, for example, that, 'The natives are, now that they have no fear of war or raids, every where breaking up the larger villages into smaller settlements' (*Report on Native Affairs*); and Malcolm Moffatt, a Church of Scotland missionary, who arrived in Serenje to establish a new mission station in 1906, commented on the difficulties he faced when the bulk of the population was now scattered in many small settlements (*Chitambo Mission Records*, 1906).

In July 1906 attempts were made by the British South Africa Company to put into effect a policy of amalgamation. This met the approval of the missionaries and administrators in Serenje, who realized that administration and evangelization alike were seriously hampered by the dispersed nature of the population. Headmen of the district were instructed 'to give up the small villages and build proper villages under their chiefs' and were later also told (by a Company official who obviously had little understanding of the requirements of *citeme* cultivation) that 'they must not build or sleep in their gardens' (*Serenje District Notebook*, 1906). Finally, then, the Company undertook by force to re-group villages into units of about 100 huts each.

Table VIII shows the number and size of villages under Chief Chibale's jurisdiction in December 1914 when the Company made a census of the district. From this it can be seen that there were 18 villages varying in size from as few as 18 to as many as 160 huts. This gives a mean number of huts per village of 87 and a mean population of 244 persons. The population figures are estimates calculated by a Company official on the basis of 2·8 persons per hut.

There are no data relating to the composition of these villages, but they seem to have resembled the old *amalinga* in that each village contained several genealogically distinct matrilineal descent groups.

Often the Company regarded it more expedient to move groups into the nearest large village than to make detailed enquiries into their political allegiances. Thus it is not surprising that

Table VIII: De jure *Population and villages in Chibale Chiefdom: 1914*

Name of village	No. of huts	Population
Administrative District (a)		
Chintonkwa	97	
Kabamba	115	
Kanena	100	
Luusa	39	
Total	351	980
Administrative District (b)		
Lumwanshya	96	
Chiwati	93	
Mutonone	160	
Chililwa	59	
Chibale	110	
Total	518	1,450
Administrative District (c)		
Tai	70	
Wasa	94	
Chibuye Mwiembe	106	
Luombila	58	
Manjabila	18	
Total	346	970
Administrative District (d)		
Nchimishi	153	
Nalongo	61	
Kapenda	98	
Njikumbete	48	
Total	360	1,000
TOTALS	1,575	4,400
Mean size	87	244

they found it impossible to prevent the fission of these villages. Company records abound with examples of sections moving out to set up their own independent settlements. An important precipitating cause of the fission of these very large villages was, of course, sheer ecological pressure now that there was no need to stay together for protection. In a relatively short time the soils and woodlands within convenient walking distance of the village were in short supply and it was more practical for some groups to hive off and build their own settlements where natural resources were still plentiful.

By the time the Colonial Office assumed control of the territory in 1924, the break-up of the large villages in Serenje was already well under way. In Chibale Chiefdom, for example, there were already some 36 registered villages; and the official *de jure* population figure was 5,999 (2,861 males and 3,138 females), which gives a mean population per village of 166 (79 males and 87 females).

The coming of Colonial Office rule marked the end of attempts to keep people together in very large villages, though promulgation of the 'ten taxpayer' regulation meant that individuals were still required to live in villages of a defined minimum size. This regulation made it a condition for the formation of a new village that there be ten taxpaying males, i.e. able-bodied men over the age of 18, including the headman himself. The requirement for Serenje District was later reduced to eight taxpayers, 'of whom at least five must report to the District Commissioner when the village is registered' (*Native Authority Orders*, 1947). The latter clause was introduced to stop the registration of individuals who were away working in town, who might never in fact take up residence in the village. A similar rule was introduced requiring that all adult males obtain permission from the chief before moving to another village. However, neither ruling had much effect on either the mobility of individuals or on the fission of villages. Indeed villages became progressively smaller from 1924 onwards, until 1950 when the existence of small settlements without recognized headmen was made legal through the implementation of the parish system of local government.

Shortly before the new system was introduced, Peters made a detailed census of 26 villages in the district, two of which were located in Kapepa Parish. Peters found that the average resident village population comprised 12 families or households, with a total of seven men, 14 women and 34 children, making 55 persons in all. And, though he makes no mention of the existence of smaller non-registered settlements, he does suggest that the rate of village fission is on the increase (Peters, 1950, p. 17 & pp. 53–4). Later I shall discuss the reasons for the fission of villages and the emergence of smaller residential units. Let it suffice here to have drawn attention to the situation immediately prior to the introduction of the parish system and to have suggested that the new system simply legalized what was already afoot.

The aims of the parish system were first formulated in 1945 by the Native Land Tenure Committee:

> The essence of the parish system was that individuals were to be registered as belonging to an area, not a village, and that subject to the permission of the parish authority they might build and cultivate anywhere inside the area to which they belong.

It was envisaged therefore that within each chiefdom adjacent villages would be regarded as forming small administrative units or 'parishes' and that taxpayers would be registered by parish not village. The system also allowed for freer movement of individuals within the parish area and for the setting up of 'individual settlements', providing they fulfilled certain minimum building and agricultural requirements. The Administration felt that such reforms would pave the way to further social and economic development.

Parishes were demarcated in Serenje District in 1950. Each parish was named after a famous old village, or after some prominent topographical feature in the vicinity, and roughly represented the tract of territory originally associated with the village. In some cases the original village no longer existed, though some of the villages in the parish could claim historical connections with it. In Kapepa Parish eight out of 11 villages in 1963–4 were derived from the village of Kapepa, which predated the coming of Europeans, as is shown in Figure IV. Kapepa Village broke up in August 1962 on the death of the headman, but people continued to use it as a point of reference when discussing the historical links between villages in the parish. It appears then that some effort was made by administrators to ensure that parish

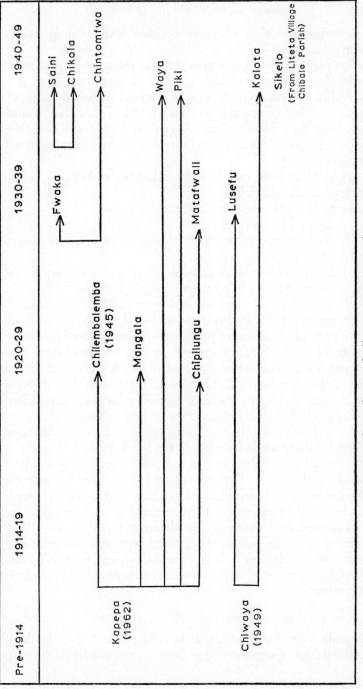

Fig. IV. The evolution of villages in Kapepa Parish 1914–50
Villages with a date beneath them were disbanded in the years mentioned

boundaries coincided wherever possible with existing neigh-
bourhoods.

The parish system made provision for the setting up of small
settlements without recognized headmen, and this meant that
individual settlers were no longer required to produce the requisite number of taxpaying males, though if they later wished
to register the settlement as a village then the rule still held. Yet
before a man could become an individual settler he was expected
to agree to,

(*a*) build a two-roomed house of Kimberley-brick or burnt-
brick or moulded-brick,

(*b*) build a pole-and-mud kitchen,

(*c*) dig a pit latrine,

(*d*) plant every year two acres of mounds or ridges of cassava
and 12 fruit trees,

(*e*) follow crop rotation as recommended by the Agricultural
Department and use cattle manure if cattle are kept,

(*f*) maintain cattle in a manner approved by the Veterinary
Department if cattle are kept; and all this should be done within
three years of his receiving permission to move out of his village
and build separately. Local chiefs were left to enforce these conditions, but as settlements increased in number it became more
difficult for them to do so. Thus by 1963-4, few of the individual
settlements in Kapepa Parish complied with these regulations
and many had been in existence for more than three years.

From 1958 onwards the Agricultural Department allowed
selected individuals living outside the block farms to register as
'peasant farmers'. I described in a previous chapter the kinds of
assistance that these farmers received from the Agricultural
Department. Like individual settlers, peasant farmers are expected
to observe the same rules of hygiene and good husbandry. By
1963-4 there had emerged two different types of non-village
settlements in the parish—the peasant farm and the individual
settlement—which, as I shall argue below, can readily be distinguished in terms of their size, social composition and economic
organization.

Present-day settlement types

Nowadays the Lala distinguish broadly between two kinds of
residential grouping: the village (*umushi*) and the farm (*ifwamu*).

A village is conceptualized both in terms of its physical character-istics—a relatively large, discrete cluster of houses, often laid out on a rectangular plan—and in terms of its social characteristics—a group of kinsfolk related in various ways to, and under the authority of, a senior kinsman, the headman (*mwine mushi* or *sulutani*). Every village has to be registered with the local chief and the names of at least eight taxpaying males entered into the Government Tax Register; and it is this act which people now see as constituting an important defining characteristic of the village. In contrast, the farm is seen as a small settlement where the residents are said to 'govern themselves' (*kuiteka bene*). Here the stress is on living outside the control and surveillance of a village headman, and local opinion has it that even where an individual remains attached to a particular village for taxpaying purposes this is no measure of his political allegiance.

The term *ifwamu*, however, is used to cover both types of non-village settlement. It can refer in the first place to those settlements registered as individual or peasant farms, or secondly, it can be used to describe those settlements which have been authorized by the chief only and which I have called 'individual settlements'. This distinction is recognized by the Lala themselves when they qualify which type of *ifwamu* they are talking about by using the phrase *ifwamu lya bakalakacha* (Agriculture) for the former and *ifwamu lya bamfumu* (farm of the chief) to describe the latter. The peasant farm and the individual settlement are distinct in that the farm is associated with small-scale commercial plough agriculture, whereas the individual settlement is associated with non-plough, subsistence agriculture, though at any point in time there may be a number of transitional types between these two extremes. Nevertheless, the Lala themselves operate in terms of these two ideal categories and argue that the farmer feeds himself and helps to develop the country, whilst the individual settler remains a poor man who must continue to beg for some of his food.

One other type of residential unit requires brief mention—the store (*ishitolo*). The store can be regarded as a separate category on the ground that all eight stores in the parish are clearly defined collocations of houses, sited at strategic points along the motor track passing through the parish, and have not been established within the village. They are also viewed by the people them-selves as being of quite a different order from farms or other settlement types. Stores are ideologically associated with an urban way of life, and the setting up of a store marks, as it were, an extension of 'town' values to Chibale Chiefdom. One feature frequently singled out for comment is the fact that most store buildings are built of burnt bricks, with corrugated steel roofing and cement floors, whereas other good-quality houses in the area are made of sun-dried bricks with thatch, the rural equivalents.

I want now, on the basis of these four categories of residential grouping recognized by the people in Kapepa, to isolate other criteria by which we may distinguish them.

A census of settlements which I made in March–April 1963 revealed that out of a total of 60 settlements in the parish, only 11 were villages. A majority of the *de facto* population, however, were residing in these villages, as Table IX shows. Out of a total of

Table IX: *Distribution of* de facto *population according to settlement types:* *1963–4*

Settlement type	Adults M	F	Children	Totals
Village	116	150	280	546 (53·4)
Individual settlement	46	60	113	219 (21·2)
Farm	44	65	112	221 (21·6)
Store	8	8	22	38 (3·8)
TOTALS	214	283	527	1,024 (100·0)

Percentages in brackets

1,024 persons, 546 or 53·4 per cent lived in villages, 38 or 3·8 per cent at stores and the remaining 440 or 42·8 per cent were fairly evenly distributed between the farms and individual settlements.

Table X compares the four types with respect to their size, as measured by the number of houses. Here I count as 'houses' only those dwellings used as sleeping quarters by adult residents and exclude all kitchens and the like which are not so used. The table shows that there is a marked difference in magnitude between villages and other settlements in the area. The total number of

Table X: Number of huts in settlements

Type of settlement	1	2	3	4	5	6	7	8	9	10	11	12	13	14	15	16	17	18	19	20	21	22	Total no. of settlements	Mean no. of huts
Village	—	—	—	—	—	1	—	—	—	—	1	—	—	2	2	1	—	—	1	1	1	1	11	15·7
Individual settlement	—	1	8	5	2	1	—	—	—	—	—	—	—	—	—	—	—	—	—	—	—	—	17	3·7
Farm	8	5	6	2	—	—	2	—	—	—	—	—	—	1	—	—	—	—	—	—	—	—	24	2·9
Store	7	1	—	—	—	—	—	—	—	—	—	—	—	—	—	—	—	—	—	—	—	—	8	1·1
TOTALS	15	7	14	7	2	2	2	—	—	—	1	—	—	3	2	1	—	—	1	1	1	1	60	5·2

houses in the 11 villages is 173, which gives a mean number per village of 15·7, 62 houses in 17 individual settlements gives a mean of 3·7 houses per settlement, and the total of 70 houses for the 24 farms a mean of 2·9. For the stores, seven have only one house and the eighth two. Thus with the exception of one farm which is a large unit of 14 houses, all farms, individual settlements and stores are small settlements of seven or less houses, whereas villages range mainly from 11 to 22 houses.

A similar pattern emerges if we take as our criterion the number of persons resident in each type of settlement. The average village of about 16 houses contains about 48 persons (10 men, 13 women and 25 children), the average individual settlement of 4 houses about 14 persons (3 men, 4 women and 7 children); the average farm of 3 houses about 11 persons (2 men, 3 women and 6 children); and the average store of one house about 5 persons (one man, one woman and 3 children).

The social composition of settlements

Gluckman has characterized the Central African village as 'a discrete group of people who reside in usually adjacent huts, who recognize allegiance to a headman and who have a corporate identity against other similar groups', and he goes on to stress that villages 'are formed crucially by common allegiance to the head-man. The kinship links between the headman and his followers may vary from tribe to tribe, or within a tribe, and within a single village there may be different kinds of kinsmen, but the headman is always regarded as the senior kinsman' (Gluckman, 1949, p. 90). Thus the composition of a village can be analysed by describing the various kinship, affinal and other links that residents have with the headman, and it becomes an easy task to quantify the results. Turner, for example, presents a detailed breakdown of hut owners and their relationships to the headman and shows that among the matrilineal Ndembu the headmen and their matrilineal kin account for nearly three-fifths of all hut owners in his sample, and that of the matrilineal kin, 33·7 per cent are women, 'an indication in a society practising virilocal marriage of the strong tendency of women to rejoin their male matrilineal kin' (Turner, 1957, p. 72).

The following analysis of the social composition of villages in Kapepa Parish adopts this view of village structure and gives a breakdown of the relationships of adult residents to headmen.[1]

Table XI shows the relationships of adult residents to their headmen in the 11 villages in the parish. I have chosen to include

Table XI: Relationships of adult residents to headmen in 11 villages in Kapepa

Category	Males	Females	Totals
Headmen	11		11
Spouses of headmen		14	14
Primary matrilineal kin	16	54	70
Classificatory matrilineal kin	8	19	27
Own descendants of headmen	5	11	16
Children of male matrilineal kin	2	4	6
Patrilaterally related	5	2	7
Affinally related	60	35	95
Unrelated	9	11	20
TOTALS	116	150	266

all adult residents rather than just hut owners because, unlike the Ndembu, the Lala do not equate hut ownership with having a primary link with the village; thus, in the case of married couples it is always the husband who is described as the hut owner, whether he is a close matrilineal kinsman of the headman or an affine, or someone who can trace no link of consanguinity or affinity with him. Where an individual has more than one link with the headman I have classified him by the relationship which the people regarded as the primary one for his membership of the village. Consequently the table grossly over-simplifies the network of relationships and takes no account of the fairly high incidence of cross-cousin marriage. Despite such inadequacies, the table brings out a number of interesting points about Lala village structure.

Firstly, it shows that of those related to the headman by kinship, 97 (76·9%) are primary or classificatory matrilineal kin, and this

[1] Alternatively, village structure may be seen in terms of a series of interlocking households or extended families. See, for example, Richards, 1939; and Gluckman, 1950.

testifies to the importance of matrilineal kinship as a principle of residential affiliation. Secondly, the preponderance of real over classificatory matrilineal kin emphasizes the importance of close uterine kin and their descendants; and thirdly, the fact that female matrikin outnumber male matrikin indicates a residential bias in favour of uxorilocality. Table XII gives a full breakdown accord-

Table XII: Breakdown of matrikin of headmen in 11 villages

Category	Primary			Classificatory		
	M	F	Totals	M	F	Totals
Headmen	11	—	11	—	—	—
Mother's mother	—	—	—	—	—	—
Mother	—	4	4	—	2	2
Mother's sibling	—	3	3	1	2	3
Sibling	5	13	18	3	9	12
Sister's child	10	24	34	4	5	9
Sister's daughter's child	1	9	10	0	1	1
Sister's daughter's daughter's child	—	1	1	—	—	—
TOTALS	27	54	70	8	19	27

ing to matrilineal kinship categories. From this it is clear that there is a strong tendency for female matrikin to be sisters or sister's daughters of the headman. 51 (69·8%) of female matrikin are sisters or sister's daughters. Male matrikin form a small minority and are either sister's sons or siblings of the headman.

We can now describe the main features of the village in Kapepa. It is a relatively small unit of about 16 houses, whose core consists of the headman together with his female uterine siblings and their immediate matrilineal descendants. Other groups of kinsmen in the village are small in size and may be attached to the headman's descent group in a variety of ways: patrilaterally, by distant matrilateral kinship, or by some clan affiliation. But one needs to be somewhat cautious about inferring from this that in the past the composition of villages was the same. For instance it may be that the figures relating to the numbers of female as against male matrikin show too marked a bias towards uxorilocality, for men who formerly would have returned to their natal villages after spending some years in their wives' villages may now prefer to establish their own independent settlements. Support for this interpretation is provided by Munday, who in 1940 observed that 'although marriage is by custom matrilocal, after being married for some years couples tend to move to a village whose headman is a member of the husband's clan, and who is usually his close relation' (Munday, 1940, p. 438). Another factor to consider is the pattern of labour migration. I estimated that just over half of the taxable males in Kapepa Parish were absent working in town. Moreover, during first and second trips to town it was common for wives to remain behind in their own natal village, and this may in part explain the preponderance of female over male matrikin.

A similar problem concerns the genealogical depth of the headman's descent group as against that of the village genealogy as a whole. Frequently one finds that the headman's own matrilineal descent group is rather shallow, seldom being more than three generations deep, whereas the genealogy for the village spans an extra two or three generations, and is often made up of a number of small groups of individuals linked to the headman's descent group through a complex series of relationships which stretch back to some apical ancestress in the distant past. Hence it is probably more realistic to regard these villages in the parish as the remnants of former large villages which had a number of well-developed secondary descent groups attached to the main one, rather than as examples of the earlier stages in the life cycle of the Lala village. Of these villages the most recently established was founded in 1947 and the oldest before 1914. Later when I examine the patterns of growth of the farm and individual settlement and compare these with the village it will also become clear that, because of the greater pressures towards fission, few localized descent groups remain intact for a depth of more than three generations. Thus several of the present-day villages in Kapepa are little more than depleted descent groups and not very different from some of the larger individual settlements in the area.

The social composition of the 49 smaller settlements is summarized in Table XIII. Each settlement is classified according to its social core and each core group described in relation to the owner or founder of the settlement. Hence I distinguish 'extended family' from 'sibling group' by reference to the genealogical

H

Table XIII: Structure of 49 smaller settlements

Type of structure	Farm	Individual settlement	Store	Totals
Nuclear family	10	1	8	19
Polygynous family	4	1	—	5
3-generation uxorilocal extended family	1	3	—	4
3-generation bilateral extended family	1	1	—	2
Polygynous 3-generation uxorilocal extended family	—	1	—	1
Uterine or classificatory sibling group	6	10	—	16
4–6-generation matrilineal descent group	2	—	—	2
TOTALS	24	17	8	49

position of the owner and not by generation depth alone. In my terms, an extended family consists of the owner, his wife and children, together with their married children, spouses and children (if any); whereas a sibling group is composed of the owner, his wife and children (married or unmarried), together with his or her real or classificatory siblings and their spouses and children.

The table shows that of the 49 settlements, 31 (or 63·2 per cent) are based on the nuclear, polygynous or three-generation extended family, 16 (or 32·6 per cent) fall into the group of siblings category and the remaining two have four- to six-generation matrilineal descent groups. Thus a majority of these settlements are relatively small and simple in composition. Furthermore, comparing the distributions for the various settlement types we see that size and composition are a function of whether the unit is a farm or store, or an individual settlement. Of the 24 settlements consisting of a single nuclear or polygynous family, 22 are farms or stores; and of the 16 based on a group of siblings, 10 are individual settlements. Two of the farms are rather atypical in that they have a descent group structure.

Let us now look more closely at those settlements which are based on a sibling group or have a clearly distinguishable descent group structure. There are 18 settlements which fall into this category. Table XIV shows the relationships of adult residents to owners of the settlements.

Table XIV: Relationships of adult residents to owners in 18 settlements of more complex structure

Category	Primary		Classificatory	
	M	F	M	F
Owner	18	—	—	—
Spouse of owner	—	27	—	—
Matrilineal kin				
Mother	—	6	—	—
Mother's sibling	—	3	2	—
Sibling	8	11	—	2
Sister's child	1	10	—	—
Descendants of matrilineal kin	—	3	—	2
Own descendants	1	—	—	—
Affines unspecified	27	14	—	—
TOTALS	55	74	2	4

The first point to note is that out of a total of 43 matrilineally related persons, 30 (or just over two-thirds) fall into the uterine sibling or sister's children categories, which emphasizes the importance of close matrilineal ties. Secondly, the total number of uterine or classificatory siblings of the 18 settlements is 21, which shows that in most cases the sibling group is of minimal size only, though there are also a few settlements where the owner's wife has in addition recruited her own siblings. This latter feature is of course not evident in Table XIV. Nevertheless, there are in fact only five settlements where the sibling group consists of more than two adults, including the headman or his wife. Thirdly, the ratio of female to male matrilineal kin is 3·7 females to every one male, which compares closely with the ratio of 3·1 females to every male for the registered villages. This suggests that close matrilineal kinship ties and uxorilocality remain important principles of residential affiliation among this group of larger non-village settlements. And like the villages, it is a group of uterine siblings and their immediate descendants which form the core of these settlements. Though somewhat smaller in size, many of these settlements resemble villages in terms of composition and some may eventually become registered as such. However, for reasons I shall elaborate later, it seems unlikely that many will in fact do so.

Factors promoting village fragmentation

Earlier I described the gradual breakdown of the village into successively smaller units, starting with the large amalgamated villages in the British South Africa Company days and leading up to the introduction of the parish system in 1950. It was suggested at one point in the discussion that an important factor was the changing ecological situation. Peters, for example, commented in 1946 that, 'The present lack of any large contiguous areas of woodland suitable for *fiteme* probably increases the tendency to fission, as does the lessening of the need for complete fencing of the *fiteme*' (Peters, 1950, p. 53). The ecological argument, however, can only provide a partial explanation, for it is still possible, even under deteriorating ecological conditions, for individuals to live in fairly large, compact settlements, providing they travel out to different areas in search of suitable woodland. In fact as suitable woodland becomes scarcer and more scattered in locality and as greater reliance is placed on hoed gardens, the advantages of remaining together in one spot where there are good soils for secondary gardens and plentiful water supplies, may outweigh the advantages of hiving off to establish smaller settlements within close proximity to good woodland, but where living conditions are less hospitable. The spread of cassava cultivation is especially important, as it allows for a more settled community. Anyway, it is quite clear that we need to look for other factors which may help to explain the enormous proliferation of small settlements in recent decades.

In an analysis of settlement history among the Ushi of Fort Rosebery District, Kay argues that the recent growth of small settlements may be 'not so much a feature of modern times as a resurgence of the traditional territorial unit that prevailed prior to colonial rule' (Kay, 1964, p. 256). Certainly the rate at which villages split up in Kapepa once the administration had begun to relax its attitude towards the maintenance of units of a defined minimum size gives some validity to this view. Also I have recorded the Lala tradition that, prior to the days of the stockaded villages, people resided in small impermanent settlements. But we should be careful not to ignore, or play down, the important differences that exist between present-day settlements and those of former times. Many of these contemporary settlements differ markedly from previous residential forms not only in terms of their social composition but also in their mode of economic organization. This is most strikingly the case with peasant farms and stores but may also apply, to some degree, to some of the individual settlements. We should also note that although the genealogical composition of some settlements may be said to resemble closely some past form, they have arisen in response to a totally new social, economic and political milieu.

Chapter II outlined the process of agricultural change and the development of small-scale business enterprises in Kapepa Parish. I argued that although the change-over to plough cultivation and Turkish tobacco as a cash crop did not in themselves make certain existing forms of social organization redundant—the nuclear or three-generation extended family remained the major unit for production and consumption, and various categories of matrilineal kin might continue to assist the farmer—the tendency has been for individuals practising these new forms of agriculture to detach themselves from the village and set up on their own. And the same is true of storekeepers in the parish. Thus, as Turner comments for the Ndembu, 'if a man wishes to accumulate capital to set up as a trader or tailor, or to acquire a higher standard of living for himself and his elementary family, he must break away from his circle of village kin towards which he has traditional obligations'. Hence, 'we see the spectacle of corporate groups of kin disintegrating and the emergence of smaller residential units based on the elementary family' (Turner, 1957, p. 43). The same argument holds for Kapepa. Many commercially oriented farmers, for instance, try to limit the number of kinsmen residing at their farms in an attempt to conserve their slender capital resources, though later they may find that they have to utilize these same ties to recruit labour for peak periods. Moreover, many individual settlers see their establishing an independent settlement as a move towards entering the commercial sector of the economy, rather than as the first step towards recruiting a large body of kinsmen which will later enable them to claim recognition as village headmen.

In addition to changing ecological and economic circumstances, we need also to take account of the emergence of new forms of power and social status. In Chapter VI I shall show how the position of the village headman in Kapepa Parish has steadily declined over the past few decades and will argue that this has been yet another factor contributing to the breakdown of the village into smaller units. Similarly, the introduction of the parish system of local government, which sanctioned the setting up of settlements without registered village headmen, has accelerated the process.

CHAPTER V

SETTLEMENT GROWTH AND FISSION

Of the two villages analysed in this chapter, one has spawned mostly peasant farms and the other mostly individual settlements. My aim here is to discuss the underlying sociological causes for their fission and to identify the main units of secession. I shall then compare the pattern of village development with that of the farm, store and individual settlement, and examine the social characteristics of the founders of these new settlements.

LUSEFU VILLAGE

The present village headman, Lusefu (II, C6), who is now in his late sixties, grew up in Chombela Chiefdom in the Congo. During his teens he moved with his mother, who had recently been divorced, and his younger sister (II, C8) to Chibale Chiefdom where his elder sister (II, C3) was living. The latter had married into Chiwaya Village. Lusefu's mother's sister (II, B1) and her daughter (II, C2) joined them later.

Lusefu was married shortly after the First World War and went to live in Kasuko Village to work for his parents-in-law. During his stay there a serious dispute broke out in Chiwaya Village over the death of his classificatory mother (II, B1), whose daughter had married Lemon (II, C1), a classificatory son of the headman Chiwaya. It is reputed that a domestic quarrel arose between Lemon and his wife and that his wife's mother had tried to prevent Lemon from beating her daughter with a hefty stick and was herself struck. She died shortly afterwards. The Lusefu kin group were angered by this and, after a period of bitter dispute, they left the village and established their own new settlement under Lusefu's leadership close to Kasuko Village. Extended negotiations followed concerning the payment of compensation 'to clear the death', but it was finally agreed that Lemon should pay them the sum of £30 and a muzzle-loader gun. The gun was handed over immediately but the money was not paid in full until some years later.

Any hopes that Lusefu may have had for the expansion of the settlement, however, were soon dashed, for after several years of incessant

raiding of their crops by a troop of monkeys it was decided to abandon
the settlement and join the nearby village of Matafwali, where Lusefu
had married a second wife. They moved into Matafwali Village somewhere towards the beginning of the 1930's.

Lusefu's second chance came in 1938. By this time several of his
sisters' children were already mature adults. The occasion for the split
with Matafwali came when Lusefu's first wife died suddenly and this
was followed by a series of accusations and counter-accusations of
sorcery between Lusefu's group of matrikin and the Matafwali family.
Lusefu claims that it was really Matafwali's sister who caused his wife's
death, but states that there had previously been a good deal of strife
between his wife and other women at Matafwali. Finally then, Lusefu
persuaded his mother and two sisters, and their husbands and children,
to leave the village and build a separate settlement. The group was
later joined by Kalikeka (II, C11) and his nuclear family when the
village they had been living in disintegrated on the death of the
headman.

Genealogy II[1] shows the composition of Lusefu Village in about
1950, immediately prior to the first breakaway. The village
consisted of a single matrilineal descent group, within which there
were a number of smaller groups, two descended from the headman's uterine sisters, one from a deceased classificatory mother,
and the headman's own sons and daughters from his two wives.
The dotted lines on the genealogy indicate the groups which have
since moved out to form their own settlements. The first group
to hive off was composed of Katwishi (II, D35), Lusefu's sister's
son, and his wife (II, Group 6).

Earlier I described the establishment of Katwishi Farm and how
Katwishi had previously managed a store for his elder brother
Bombwe (II, D25).[2] I now outline in more detail the events
leading up to his leaving the store and starting a farm.

Katwishi had worked in Kitwe with Bombwe for a number of
years. He returned to the village in 1949. Later in that year Bombwe
sent £30 to his mother's brother, Lusefu, so that he might open a store
in the village. Katwishi, the only resident sister's son, quickly assumed
responsibility for the running of the business. Katwishi was a very
ambitious manager and wished to see the business prosper, even if it

---

[1] See folder at end of book.   [2] See pp. 61–4.

meant denying some of his matrikin the right to preferential treatment. Thus, during the early years, there appears to have been considerable conflict between Katwishi and others over the profits derived from the store.

The store was heavily subsidized by Bombwe and another brother, Timoti (II, D34), and it was only through their good graces that it survived at all. After a while, however, Katwishi began to make it more of a paying concern and constantly boasted of his achievements and of his plans for future development. Then tragedy struck. Katwishi's mother (II, C8) suddenly fell ill and died, and this was followed in the same year by the death of Lameck's mother (II, C9). Many people in the village interpreted these deaths as an indication that Katwishi was dabbling in sorcery. It was argued, for instance, that a recent visit he made to Broken Hill (Kabwe) was really to obtain potent medicines (*fishimba*) with which to practise the craft. It was also said that he received help from a man from Matafwali Village who was a specialist in medicines for bringing prosperity to business enterprises. The deaths of his own mother and of his classificatory mother were, it was claimed, part of Katwishi's plan to captivate the spirits of some close matrilineal kinsmen so that he might send them out at night to steal the money and crops of others. (Such spirits operate as witch-familiars and are called *utumbuma*. People liken them to some small rodent and say that if they are not cared for properly then they can turn against their owners and devour them.)

When Lameck and Katwishi's classificatory sister's son, Kefas (II, E5), returned from town to mourn the dead the accusations against Katwishi were openly declared. This led on one occasion to fighting between them and Katwishi. When the two of them returned to resume urban employment they called in to see Bombwe and told him of the troubles. But all that he advised was for them not to provoke Katwishi for 'he obviously had strong medicines' and for them to set up their own independent settlements on retirement rather than go back to live in the village. Bombwe though, while admitting that Katwishi was probably indulging in sorcery, did not wish to condemn his brother completely for he had proved himself to be a capable store manager. Thus it was that Bombwe and Timoti the other brother continued to invest money in the store.

Eventually, however, Katwishi decided to leave the village with his wife and build a new store building close to the motor track leading to Chief Chibale Court. The spot he chose was close to Kapepa Primary

School. He at first constructed a pole-and-mud building but had this replaced in 1951 by a Kimberley-brick one with a corrugated steel roof. Bombwe supplied the roofing materials. Being near to the school and on the road to Chibale, Katwishi could count among his clientele the teachers and other government employees who stopped on their way to the court, and there were also a number of villages within easy reach. Kapepa school was the collection centre for local produce during the harvesting period. A number of markets had been set up throughout the district where farmers could sell their surplus crops, and supervisors had been appointed to organize the buying. Katwishi's choice of site was influenced by the fact that he hoped to net some of the money paid out to local farmers and he felt that he could do this more effectively if his store was close at hand. Later he had aspirations to become the market supervisor at Kapepa, but never managed to get himself appointed.

During his early years at Kapepa, Katwishi apparently made quite a lot of money, which he mainly used to extend his network of friends and to buy a few head of cattle. Later he rather overspent himself and was on the verge of bankruptcy when Bombwe called him to Kitwe to present a statement of the store's financial position. Bombwe was annoyed to learn that he had wasted much of the profits and refused to assist him any further, telling him to quit the store and return to the village. At the same time, Katwishi had also quarrelled with a local teacher over the grazing of the school gardens by his cattle. The case was taken before the Chief and Katwishi was ordered to pay £3 10s. compensation for the damage incurred. The outcome of all this was that Katwishi made plans to leave the store and establish his own farm about two miles from Lusefu Village. He moved to the new farm in 1955 and has remained there since.

After Katwishi left the store, Bombwe placed his divorced sister and her son in charge of it (II, Group 5). Chiboli (II, D29), the sister, and Patrick (II, E17), her son, had been living in Lusefu Village. Under the new regime Bombwe has expanded his business a good deal. In 1957, he purchased a lorry for transporting goods and people to and from the Copperbelt towns and Broken Hill (Kabwe) and, with the help of his brother, Timoti, acquired a second vehicle in 1962. The store building has been rebuilt and there are now Kimberley-brick houses for the sister and her son. Patrick normally travels with one of the vehicles and collects the fares, whilst his mother serves in the store. Now that Bombwe has vehicles at his disposal he can keep a much closer watch over the affairs of the store and often sends his wife to check up on things.

The next settlement to be formed from Lusefu Village was that started in 1956 by Lameck (II, D37), who had returned from the Copperbelt about a year before. He had spent a total of about 20 years working on the mines. In addition to being a classificatory sister's son of Lusefu, he is also married to one of his daughters (II, D19). While Lameck was in town he sent money home to Kalikeka (II, C11), his mother's brother, so that he could buy cattle in preparation for his retirement. He returned with about £250 in post office savings and a sum of £50 in cash. With this he bought a plough and various farming implements and in 1962 invested in a small motor-van. Lameck and his wife and children moved out of the village, accompanied by Kalikeka and his family (II, Group 7). Later he married a second wife and brought her to live at the farm as well. Then in October 1963 Kalikeka and his wife returned to the village, having quarrelled with Lameck over the question of farm labour. The latter argued that although each year he had regularly ploughed gardens for Kalikeka, his uncle had been very unwilling to assist him when he needed it. Kalikeka could not understand Lameck's attitude and felt that Lameck was neglecting his obligations to him as a sister's son.

Saulo (II, D2), who is married to Lusefu's sister's daughter (II, D1) and who owns a peasant farm about five miles from the village, returned from the Copperbelt in 1958 and within a few months had set himself up on his own farm (II, Group 1). Whilst in town he had saved a total of about £96 which he used to purchase the necessary equipment and oxen. Saulo and his wife and children were later joined by Saulo's two sisters from Matafwali Village, but they have since gone to town with their husbands. However, two sister's daughters remain at the farm with their husbands and children and take a major part in farm work.

Daiman (II, D16), who is married to Lusefu's daughter (II, D15), moved out of the village in 1959 (II, Group 3). In Chapter III I described how, with the help of his elder brother, he established his own farm. He has since become a very successful cash-crop farmer.

Kabichi (II, D18) is also married to one of Lusefu's daughters (II, D17). In 1961 he left the village with his wife to join his elder brother, who had become a farmer on the peasant farming block (II, Group 4). Both Kabichi and his brother are old hands at plough cultivation, having worked with their father, who had been a peasant farmer for something like ten years. When the father moved away from the block the elder brother took over his plot and worked the same fields. Kabichi joined him later. Both Kabichi and his brother are young men in their twenties. In 1963 they had one of the best crops of tobacco in the district.

The last group to leave Lusefu Village was Kefas (II, E5), his wife, and his mother (II, D9) (II, Group 2). Kefas is Lusefu's sister's daughter's son. He had worked for over ten years on the Copperbelt but had returned with little saved. In 1961 he arrived in Lusefu for three months' leave, and during his stay he got permission from the Chief to set up his own settlement on his return in 1962. Kefas states that he had two main reasons for wanting to leave the village. Firstly, he had for too long been embroiled in the troubles centring around Katwishi and the store, and was hated by both Katwishi and Lameck for being so friendly with Lusefu, the headman. Lusefu, he claims, had nominated him as the next headman but he had not wanted to take on the job. His second reason was that he felt that he had to provide for his parents-in-law, who were now rather old and ill cared for in their own village. Thus shortly after his return in 1962, Kefas and his wife moved out of Lusefu and were joined by his parents-in-law. His settlement is sited some five miles from Lusefu Village near to the village where the parents-in-law had been living. Kefas has seven head of cattle, no oxen and no farming implements. At present he practises mainly *citeme* cultivation but ploughs when he can borrow the necessary equipment.

Analysis

I have described the formation and fission of Lusefu Village at length for two main reasons. Firstly, it provides a convenient way of presenting essential background material for a later chapter which examines the struggles occurring among a group of Lusefu's kinsfolk for power and prestige. Secondly, the account enables one to appreciate more fully the sharp contrast which exists between the early period in the settlement's history when the village was formed and consolidated, and the later period characterized by a series of secessions from the village. This contrast is not merely one of different stages in the life cycle of a particular kind of residential unit, but one which signifies a fundamental change in the pattern of secession. Traditionally the establishment of a new residential grouping required considerable political skills on the part of the leader, who needed to canvas the support of a number of close kinsmen, usually uterine siblings and their descendants, and who might also have to compete with other male kinsmen for their allegiance. Sometimes, as was the case with Lusefu, an initial bid for independence was thwarted by various ecological, demographic and sociological factors. Nowadays the setting up of a new settlement generally requires little political manœuvring, and often the founder will consciously attempt to restrict the number of persons residing at his settlement. This is especially so with one category of farms described in Chapter III.

The first secession from Lusefu arose because of the struggles that occurred between Katwishi and his matrikin over the wealth deriving from the store which he was managing on behalf of his brother. Katwishi wished to keep much of the profits for himself and his own nuclear family, and, although some of the details of the particular quarrels that ensued escape us, it is clear that he refused to give financial assistance to his own matrilineal kinsmen. Later, when his own mother and a classificatory mother died, several of his classificatory matrikin attempted to rationalize the hostility between them by attributing these deaths to sorcery on Katwishi's part. His classificatory brother, Lameck, and his classificatory sister's son, Kefas, were his main antagonists. One of the reasons for this was that they saw Katwishi's attempt to seize control of the store as a direct threat to the position of Lusefu the headman, and feared that Katwishi might later use this wealth to win over the support of their own close female matrikin, and thus be in a strong position to take over the leadership of the village on the death of the headman. They were particularly concerned it seems because they had also had aspirations towards headmanship. Hence, although the accusations of sorcery did little to alter the relationship between Bombwe and Katwishi (he was allowed to continue as store manager), they did in the long run force Katwishi out of the village. After the sorcery charge, he became increasingly more alienated from his kinsmen and so finally decided to leave and build another store close to the Chibale Road. He was again subsidized by Bombwe. During this period Katwishi tried to gather round him a number of followers, this time on a non-kinship basis, but in doing so he misused the profits from the store and was eventually ousted by Bombwe. In a later chapter I shall discuss the more recent disputes which have arisen between Katwishi and Bombwe, and between

Bombwe and the rest of his kin over the store. Here I have simply shown that a principal cause of Katwishi's leaving Lusefu and the store at Kapepa were the quarrels that developed over his use of the economic benefits derived from the business.

Following Katwishi's removal as manager, Bombwe invited Chiboli his younger sister, and her son to take over, which they did in 1955. Later when Lameck returned from town he also hived off from the village to start his own farm, accompanied by Kalikeka, his mother's brother. Lameck was apprehensive about staying in the village, which he now believed was mystically dangerous as a result of Katwishi's activities. Another reason was that he had already witnessed Bombwe's and Katwishi's attempts to conserve their capital resources when surrounded by a group of matrikin and he sought to free himself from this restricting influence. Kefas, Katwishi's classificatory sister's son, did not retire from town until much later by which time the village had been further reduced in size by the splitting off of three men married into the village who established peasant farms. Kefas' stay in the village was short as the events over the past years had convinced him that headmanship nowadays was no longer a position worth competing for.

A striking feature of the break-up of Lusefu Village was the type of settlements established by the seceding groups. All but one of them started peasant farms, using either their own capital, or capital received from close kinsmen. Thus the break-up of Lusefu Village can be largely attributed to the introduction of new forms of wealth and to new socio-economic goals. The quarrels which arose in the village, and which some had given as a reason for leaving, had centred around the question of control over the assets of the store and the benefits enjoyed from them. Even the accusations of sorcery were a product of the competition between Katwishi and others in the village for economic resources rather than merely a reflection of the hostility between specific categories of kinsmen seeking to gain the allegiance of a group of female matrikin.

CHINTOMFWA VILLAGE

Chintomfwa Village was founded in 1945 when the old village of Chilembalemba fragmented on the death of the headman. The headman of Chilembalemba died as the result of an axe wound sustained while cutting his *citeme*. His death had quickly followed that of his predecessor. The residents of the village interpreted the deaths as an ill omen for the future prosperity of the village and some say that it was for this reason that they disbanded it and scattered. Some of the residents joined the villages of Saini and Chikola where they found distant matrikin, and some set up on their own. Chintomfwa (see Genealogy III, B5) led one group, consisting of his uterine siblings and their descendants. Their settlement was later registered as a village. Chintomfwa died in 1956 and was succeeded by his sister's son, Misheck Kasubika (III, C4).

Genealogy III shows the composition of Chintomfwa Village in 1957, just before the first breakaway, The village was made up of the headman's matrilineal descent group of four-generations depth, and a second matrilineal descent group linked to the first through a matrilateral clanship tie. The latter group had joined the village in 1955 with a view, it was said, to being closer to the Chibale Road and thus more within the orbit of agricultural extension work. They came from a village which was located some ten miles or so from the parish boundary. Their leader, Mwape (III, C28), aspired to be a peasant farmer.

Mwape's group (III, Group 9) did not remain for long in the village, for in 1958 they hived off to establish their own independent settlement, which subsequently became a registered peasant farm. The main precipitating reason for their leaving was that Mwape's mother (III, B6) and his classificatory mother's brother (III, B8), who were both aged dependants, had been accused by Misheck (III, C4) and others of bringing witchcraft into the village and causing the sickness of Machisa's wife (III, C12). Besides this, Mwape claims that Misheck had committed adultery with one of his two wives. Mwape has now purchased oxen and farming implements and operates his farm on a commercial basis.

The next group to leave the village was Nchepeshi (III, C16) and his two wives (III, Group 6). When Nchepeshi married Misheck's sister (III, C15) her parents were already deceased and so the former headman, Chintomfwa (III, B5), undertook to act as the father-in-law. However when Misheck succeeded to his maternal uncle's position it appears that the new 'father-in-law' began to demand too much from him. Nchepeshi claims that Misheck treated him like a slave (*umusha*), forcing him to collect and cut firewood, make axes and bellows for him and cultivate only in his gardens. He was not even allowed to cut his own *citeme* garden, when a son-in-law would normally be expected to cut his own *citeme* as a way of demonstrating to the girl's parents that he is capable of providing for his future family. He would assist Misheck in hunting but received little of the meat; and his children were expected to help in Misheck's household at a time when Nchepeshi's wife should have had her own household. Finally, in 1960, Nchepeshi and his two wives and children left the village to establish their own independent settlement. Later they were joined by Nchepeshi's old widowed mother and his blind brother. Nchepeshi possesses no oxen or farming implements but occasionally gets Kapepala (III, C19) to plough for him.

In the same year, another disgruntled 'son-in-law' Kapepala (III, C19) left with his wife (III, Group 7). He was also dissatisfied with the way in which Misheck treated him and claims that Misheck's younger brother, Machisa (III, C13), also tried to play the 'father-in-law' role. Machisa, he said, had tried to force him to cut *citeme* for him and, after he had refused, had offered Kapepala's wife to a friend for the night. Since leaving the village, Kapepala has acquired oxen and a plough and is now a registered farmer, though he prefers to make his money by contract ploughing rather than by cultivating a surplus for sale.

Tomo (III, D9) and his wife (III, Group 3) moved out in 1960 to join his father and a small group of matrikin who had asked him to assist them in building a new settlement nearby.

Chimbala (III, B2) and his nuclear family returned from urban employment in 1961, stayed for a short time in the village, and then set up on their own (III, Group 9).

Sopo (III, D1), who is an agricultural messenger for Chief Chibale and married to Misheck's sister's daughter (III, D2), built and moved into his own settlement in 1960 in anticipation of his retirement from Local Authority service (III, Group 1). At present he devotes little time to cultivation but later hopes to become a cash-crop farmer. In recent years a group of close matrikin from Mutonone Village have joined him at the settlement.

Maluben (III, D14) left the village in 1962 (III, Group 4). His mother-in-law (III, C6) claims that it was she who persuaded him to leave because of the petty quarrelling in the village. Maluben has taken over a recently built settlement which had been vacated by a man who had emigrated from the chiefdom, and lives there with his wife and mother-in-law. Like Sopo, Maluben is a messenger attached to Chief Chibale and does not spend much time on cultivation.

Mandala (III, C2), his wife and their married daughters and their husbands, split off from the village in 1962 (III, Group 2), following a series of disputes which arose between them and Nathan (III, C8) and the headman, Misheck. Nathan is a Bisa from Lundazi District. He married Misheck's sister (III, C7) on the Copperbelt and returned with her to live in the village in 1960. Nathan prides himself on being a townsman and on his arrival in Chibale lived a somewhat extravagant life, buying bottled beer instead of the local millet brew and smoking the better brands of cigarettes. He also had plenty of clothing and household effects. Nathan, wishing to win the favour of Misheck, the headman, bestowed on him many more gifts than he gave to others in the village, and from time to time quarrelling broke out over this. Mandala and his wife were major figures in this.

Then, in 1962, Nathan cut his foot on a stone when walking in the bush near to the village, and it went septic. After a while when there was no sign of the foot healing, Nathan consulted a diviner who confirmed what was already in his mind—that it was the result of sorcery by Mandala. Later at a beer drink Nathan became very inebriated and in the middle of the night decided to have the matter out with Mandala. The latter and his wife had already retired to bed. Nathan, however, was determined to see them and so he burst into the house. They were both naked. Fighting ensued until Nathan was finally dragged out of the house by other members of the village. The next day Mandala filed a case against Nathan with the local 'parish head'.[1] The parish head gave Mandala a letter to take to the court explaining the affair. On the face of it, the charge was a fairly serious one, for Nathan had invaded the privacy of his sister-in-law, who, it was said, claimed also to be his 'mother-in-law' because the real mother-in-law was deceased and she had taken over her role, being the eldest woman in the sibling group. Yet before the case reached the court, Nathan had approached Misheck to ask him to intercede on his behalf. Misheck agreed to do this and went to see the chief to request him to dismiss the case on the grounds that it was a simple domestic quarrel which could best be settled among themselves. The chief accepted the headman's argument and refused to hear the case. When Mandala learnt of this he interpreted it as an indication that Misheck had been bribed by Nathan. His wife was also dismayed and regarded Misheck's move as a direct

[1] See Chapter VI for an account of the duties of the parish head.

rebuff to her seniority in the sibling group, as she was the firstborn, not Misheck. Moreover, Misheck, she argued, should recognize the fact that if it had not been for her and her husband's support Chintomfwa could never have started the village, nor would it have grown to the size that it was now. She had three married daughters living in the village and that was more than anybody else.

As a result of these quarrels Mandala, his wife and their daughters and families moved away from the village and established their own separate settlement about two miles away. But the bitterness continues. Nathan still suffers from his foot which seems now to have gone gangrenous and has consulted several diviners who have all confirmed that it is Mandala who is the sorcerer. Mandala's settlement is registered as an 'individual settlement': he is a relatively poor man who cuts *citeme* and has no cattle.

The last group to leave Chintomfwa Village consisted of Edward's polygynous extended family (III, Group 5). Edward (III, C10) is a younger brother to the headman. He gives as his main reason for leaving that his brother, Misheck, committed adultery with one of his wives. But during the previous year he had suffered from chest trouble and attributed this to the deteriorating social relationships in the village which had caused some of the residents to resort to sorcery. Edward's new settlement is sited two miles from the village. He has few capital assets and as yet has no means of becoming a peasant farmer.

Analysis

Unlike Lusefu Village, the break-up of Chintomfwa Village was not ostensibly related to economic factors and, significantly, most of the settlements established were individual settlements not peasant farms. Most of the seceding groups left after a series of quarrels and hostilities, which were rife in the village and which frequently revolved around the headman, concerning the extent of his authority in the domestic and political fields and the nature of his rights and obligations to various resident kinsmen and affines. Many of the disputes stemmed from his taking on a new role-set on succession to headmanship.

The Lala, as also reported for several other central African peoples, practise 'positional succession' whereby the successor inherits the name (or title of the village), the 'spirit guardian' (*umupashi*) and the genealogical position of the deceased (see Mitchell, 1956; Richards, 1950; Cunnison, 1956; Stefaniszyn, 1954;

and Munday, 1948). He also frequently takes over the property of the dead man, his clothes and material goods, and may inherit his wife (or wives) without further marriage payment. On succession to the headmanship the new man will normally be addressed by the same kinship terms as his predecessor. Those eligible for succession must be close matrilineal kinsmen of the former headman and preference is usually given to a uterine (or sometimes even a classificatory) brother before it drops to the sister's son's generation.

A major aspect of positional succession which I wish to discuss in reference to Chintomfwa Village, and one which has received little attention in the literature, is the question of the adjustments which must take place in the personal relationships of the successor when he takes over the role-set of the former headman.

Cunnison has shown for the Luapula peoples that in a majority of cases a successor is found from either the men of the deceased's own generation or from among those of the grandson's generation. The reason for this, he suggests, is because far greater personal adjustments have to be made by the successor if he is a sister's son. A sister's son moves into what was his own parental generation and this implies a radical change in the content of his relationships with both his own matrikin and with affines of various categories. Cunnison argues that if a man succeeds to his mother's brother's position then his uncle's wife's mother, his 'grandmother', suddenly becomes his mother-in-law who commands respectful treatment. And similarly, if a man is married to his mother's brother's daughter and succeeds to his uncle's position then this makes 'mother' and 'daughter' co-wives. Yet despite these difficulties inherent in the succession of someone of an adjacent generation, the peoples of the Luapula region do in fact allow sister's sons to succeed to their mother's brothers' positions and normally talk of succession in these terms (Cunnison, 1956, pp. 36–7). The same rule is true of the Lala, and Misheck Kasubika was such a sister's son.

Although Cunnison points to the re-ordering of role-relationships which are necessitated by positional succession and sketches in some of the difficulties associated with taking over a new role-set, especially if the sister's son succeeds, he provides no detailed illustration of the kinds of problems which beset particular successors. Nor does he examine changing role-relationships from the point of view of residents of the village other than the headman. The discussion that follows then focuses on the crisis that developed in Chintomfwa Village following the succession of Misheck Kasubika to the genealogical position of his mother's brother, and shows how the succession gave rise to conflicts between residents of the village which were expressed in terms of role expectations. I shall not have space to examine in full the implications of the changes wrought by Misheck Kasubika's succession for I am primarily interested in relating this to the process of village fission.

Normally when a man succeeds to the headmanship of a village a short ceremony of installation is performed during which the weapons (*ifyenso*) of the deceased are handed on to his successor and his name (the title of the village) officially conferred on the new incumbent. Thereafter the successor is generally addressed by this name or by kinship terms appropriate to his new genealogical position. He may also inherit the wife or wives of the former headman. The main feature of the succession ceremony is that the change in roles and status position of the new headman is formally recognized by the members of the village.

Misheck Kasubika underwent this installation ceremony though he did not inherit the widow. The reason for this was that it was considered unwise for him to inherit her as he had previously inherited another mother's brother's widow and could not be expected to care for another dependant. Thus, after the woman had paid the necessary death dues (*mpango shamfwa*) to release her from the spirit (*umupashi*) of her deceased husband, she left the village together with her children to remarry elsewhere.

At the time of the succession, there were no males of the former headman's generation available for consideration. The only surviving uterine brother, Chimbala (III, B2), had lived and worked most of his life on the Copperbelt and was not expected to return to Chibale; and none of the classificatory brothers laid claim to the headmanship. The succession fell then to Chintomfwa's eldest sister's son, Misheck Kasubika, who had been the assistant headman for a number of years. Misheck had two younger brothers, Edward and Machisa, resident in the village at the time but neither of them attempted to stand as a rival claimant.

Succession to headmanship meant a re-ordering of Misheck's

relationships with both his uterine siblings and their descendants, and with his affines in the village.

It meant a radical change in his relationship with his brothers, Edward and Machisa, for he now became their 'mother's brother' (*munshyo*). Whereas uterine siblings (*bakwesu*; sing. *mukwesu*) share common interests and a common identity, expressed in the Lala phrases *tuli bamo* ('we are one'), *tulibamunda imo* ('we come from one womb'), the relationship between sister's son and mother's brother is characterized by a strict code of respectful command on behalf of the sister's son who must fear (*kotina*) his mother's brother. Thus, although Misheck had been the eldest brother and commanded some extra prestige on this count, his move into the adjacent ascending generation brought with it an increase in his jural authority over his real brothers and also his sisters, who became his 'sister's daughters'. At least that was the theory. In practice, Edward and Machisa by their subsequent behaviour obviously refused to accept his elevation in status. They continued to refer to him as 'brother' (*mukwesu*) and tried to maintain as familiar a relationship with him as previously. This was illustrated most strikingly by the way in which they begged beer (*kulomba ubwalwa*) from him at beer drinks and by the fact that they expected Misheck to continue assisting them in such tasks as thatching their houses and hunting. Neither of them felt that Misheck's new status required of them any special etiquette, nor any additional obligations. One of the reasons for this was that Misheck, Edward and Machisa, had, prior to the succession, entered into a number of reciprocal obligations based on a certain equality of status. They had, for instance, pooled their capital resources in order to purchase two head of cattle, and regularly assisted one another financially. Edward and Machisa reasoned that to have recognized Misheck's new superior status without question might have later led to a situation where their elder brother was able to claim major control over their joint property, and to an increase in the demand for services of various kinds because they were now his 'sister's sons'. On the other hand, Misheck himself felt he had no effective way of enforcing his new-found authority over them, 'lest they break up the village' (*bangatoba mushi*).

Yet Machisa was not beyond acknowledging his brother's change in status if he could use it to his own advantage. This is exemplified by the way in which he tried to force his brother-in-law Kapepala into cutting *citeme* for him. The argument he employed was that since Misheck was now Kapepala's 'father-in-law' and Machisa himself Misheck's brother, so was Machisa also Kapepala's 'father-in-law'. And if this was the case, then Kapepala should also show respect (*mucinshi*) towards Machisa by undertaking to assist with *citeme* cutting.

When Kapepala refused his request, Machisa attempted to assert his right to authority over Kapepala's wife, who, in terms of his argument, was now his 'daughter'. It is alleged that he did this by offering her sexual services to a friend when at a beer drink.

Both arguments were falsely grounded. In the first place, even if the woman was his 'daughter' he clearly had no right to try and control her sexual activities. These had been made the responsibility of the husband from the time of her marriage. Secondly, a 'father-in-law' other than the one with whom the marriage contract has been made (or his successor in the case of death) cannot demand services from his 'son-in-law'. And finally, and most interestingly, Machisa's whole argument rested on the assumption that Misheck and himself still remained 'brothers': if the latter had moved into the parental generation then Machisa must also have moved. Quite clearly Machisa was not prepared to make the necessary adjustments in his relationship with Misheck and continued to regard him as his uterine brother.

Misheck also had difficulty in getting his elder sister, Linesi, to acknowledge his senior status. This emerged clearly in the dispute which developed between Linesi and her husband, Mandala, and Nathan and Misheck. The quarrel with Nathan arose because Nathan curried favour with Misheck by successive gifts of various sorts. Nathan, it seems, saw this as a way of increasing his status within the village, but in doing so he effectively alienated himself from Mandala and his wife and family. The latter were founder-members of the village and expected Nathan to bestow some gifts on them too. Thus when Nathan fell sick he attributed this to sorcery by Mandala and the dispute between them took a more serious turn. The final affront to Linesi and Mandala came when Nathan burst into their house at night to have the matter out with them. At this point in the quarrel Linesi raised the question of Nathan's relationship to her. Nathan, she argued, should have shown greater respect towards her than is normal for a brother-in-law because, on the death of her mother, she had taken over the role of 'mother-in-law' towards him. Though a certain degree of propriety is normally expected between a man and his wife's sister, his relationship with the mother-in-law is typically of a stricter avoidance kind.

The basis for Linesi's claim was more legitimate than Machisa's case against Kapepala for, according to Lala custom, the eldest female of a sibling group will generally assume her mother's role of 'mother-in-law' when the mother dies. However, by the time this takes place the 'sons-in-law' are often already middle-aged men with children of their own and thus are not expected to conform so strictly to avoidance rules or to give service as they had done in the earlier years of their marriage. In singling out this aspect of her relationship with Nathan, Linesi was in fact manipulating the formal norms in her favour to give additional weight to her case against him. She had not stressed her position as 'mother-in-law' on previous occasions.

Later when Misheck took sides with Nathan she further emphasized her position as the firstborn (*umubele*) in the sibling group and accused Misheck of not showing her the respect appropriate to her seniority. She introduced this argument to suggest that Misheck had no right to make decisions affecting domestic and kinship affairs without first consulting her. Hence she chose to regard the sibling tie as being the primary component in their relationship and not Misheck's new genealogical position as mother's brother.

The tension between Linesi and Misheck found expression on another occasion when the latter took her to court for flouting his authority as village headman. The incident occurred when Linesi commenced burning the bush near to the village without first seeking his permission. As headman, Misheck had the responsibility of organizing the systematic burning of a fire-break around the village to protect it and the gardens from bush fires. During the scuffle which developed, Misheck is alleged to have struck his sister, but at the court it was decided that each was equally responsible for the fracas and that they should pay a fine of ten shillings each.

This provides the background to the secession of Mandala and his wife, Linesi, who left the village in 1962. In later years, Edward the brother of Misheck, moved out to start his own settlement and when I left the field, Machisa was also intending to leave. Edward and Machisa both found it rather intolerable living in the village as they were continually caught between the cross-fire which erupted between their elder brother and other residents. Even Mandala's leaving had not really solved the difficulties for he had established his settlement within close proximity and still had a reputation for sorcery. Shortly before Edward left, his daughter suddenly fell sick. Her sickness was attributed to the work of Mandala who had been put up to it by his wife. The wife, it was said, was trying to 'get even with' her uterine brothers for the way in which she had been treated by them. Edward interpreted this as a bad omen for his future if he remained in the village, and so he obtained permission from the chief to establish his own settlement. He moved there with his wives and married daughters in 1964.

Through positional succession Misheck's relationships with his affines were also affected. The relationship between brothers-in-law is generally an easy-going and familiar one. They are frequent companions in work and leisure time pursuits and they will talk over any marital troubles they have. In theory, Misheck's succession transformed these brother-in-law relationships into a father-in-law/son-in-law pattern. A son-in-law (*mukweni*) is expected, especially during the early years of marriage, to perform a number of services for his father-in-law (*batafyala*). These include the cutting of *citeme* and the cultivation of hoed gardens. The son-in-law becomes part of his father-in-law's household and is under his authority in most matters. Only later when his wife acquires her own independent household does he obtain exclusive right to the produce resulting from his own labours. Yet even then he is expected to continue to show respect towards his parents-in-law and to assist them from time to time as required. Misheck's move into his own parental generation gave him the right to demand certain services from persons who were formerly his brothers-in-law, and he exploited this situation to get Nchepeshi and Kapepala to work for him.

Both Nchepeshi and Kapepala were young men in their late twenties at the time of his succession. Nchepeshi's real father-in-law was deceased and so he had worked instead for Chintomfwa, the previous headman, who had assumed the role of father-in-law towards him. Kapepala's real father-in-law was Chimbala who was away working in town, and so again Chintomfwa took his place. On succession Misheck insisted that they should now cut *citeme* for him. It appears that at first they made little objection to this, but as time wore on they felt that Misheck's demands were becoming excessive and began to question his authority over them. By this time Nchepeshi had two children and wished to have his own independent household, but Misheck refused to allow him. So finally Nchepeshi and Kapepala both repudiated his claim to be their 'father-in-law' and moved out of the village to establish their own settlements. In this they had the full support of their wives. One of the several arguments they advanced was that if Misheck had truly taken over the father-in-law's role there was little evidence that he appreciated the full nature of his obligations to them. A proper father-in-law, they said, would for instance have rewarded them for their labours by brewing beer in their honour (*ubwalwa bwabako*). Since Misheck had not done this, the relationship was one-sided.

Following this other affines left the village with their nuclear families. From the evidence available we cannot say definitely whether similar issues were involved, but it may be that they too had experienced difficulties in their new relationships with Misheck.

Then, in 1961, Chimbala returned from town, having been sacked from his job. He had been too old to get other employment. Chimbala is Misheck's mother's brother, and the elder brother of Chintomfwa, the former headman. Chimbala's arrival created something of a stir in the village as he was not expected to return to Chibale. He did not, however, remain long in the village, having learnt from his daughter (III, C18) of the way in which Misheck had treated her and her husband, Kapepala.

Chimbala found some difficulty in accepting Misheck's new status. The latter was now his 'younger brother' and headman of the village, whereas before he had been his sister's son. The dilemma which faced Chimbala was made clear on several occasions during my stay in Kapepa Parish. For example, one day Nathan's wife wished to open her millet grain bin and invited Misheck to perform the task for her. Chimbala felt that it should have been his right to do this for them, for custom requires that the most senior member of the matrilineal kin group should undertake this duty. By extending the invitation to Misheck, Nathan's wife was giving public expression to the fact that Misheck was now the senior kinsman, not Chimbala; and Chimbala, like some of the others, found this unacceptable.

Another major breakaway occurred two years after Misheck's succession to the headmanship. This was the splitting off of Mwape and his group of matrikin. Although there is no indication that this particular secession was directly related to the problem of positional succession, it seems likely that the accusation of sorcery against Mwape's aged dependants stemmed from the tensions which existed in the village between Misheck and his various matrilineally related kinsmen. Mwape's group were linked to Misheck's descent group through a matrilateral clanship tie and were therefore not directly involved in the struggles taking place. Their position as 'strangers' provided the means by which blame could be shifted on to some other party. But in the process, of course, Misheck lost the support of a fairly large group of persons.

The foregoing discussion of the break-up of Chintomfwa Village has been primarily anchored to an analysis of the structural implications of positional succession, and has examined the ways in which particular individuals attempted to manipulate other persons in their own interests through an appeal to different and often conflicting criteria of status. Much of the discord which arose within the village, and which in many cases led to fission, concerned the question of how far positional succession entailed a radical re-ordering of role-relationships in the village. The difficulties here partly developed from the inherent ambiguities of the situation, for any particular succession will inevitably raise a number of issues which cannot simply be handled in terms of a set of well-defined norms. Misheck Kasubika had been the most senior matrilineal kinsman resident in the area on the death of the former headman, Chintomfwa, and had been groomed by the latter for the job. He therefore seemed the obvious choice. But subsequently several people felt that he was abusing his new social position for purely selfish reasons; and this implicitly questioned the legitimacy of his succession, especially after the unexpected return of Chimbala, who had a stronger genealogical claim to the title.

Yet equally important for a fuller understanding of the situation was the fact that the quarrels and hostilities occurred at a time when a number of significant changes were taking place in the economic and social organization of the people of the parish as a whole. For reasons suggested in the previous chapter, the village was no longer the major residential unit. This was reflected in the fact that none of the seceding groups from Chintomfwa Village were composed of a reasonably large group of matrikin. None of the leaders, it seems, were able to gain the allegiance of persons outside their own nuclear or three-generation extended families. Thus, though Misheck had difficulties with his male uterine siblings, neither one of them emerged as a rival claimant to the headmanship. Part of the explanation for this lies in the fact that neither of them seemed to regard village headmanship as carrying high social prestige. They were more concerned to safeguard their joint economic interests with Misheck and to exploit existing kinship relations for short-term economic and social advantage than to build up a political following.

Another factor to consider was the question of economic differentiation in the village. The quarrels between Nathan and Mandala and his wife were sparked off by the way in which the former had distributed his urban savings, and this was undoubtedly a factor influencing Misheck's decision to terminate the court proceedings. As for Misheck himself, he too attempted to make use of his position in the village—as headman, 'mother's brother' and 'father-in-law'—to gain certain economic rewards; and it was this which made for difficulties with his kin and affines, and which allowed for the expression of widely different views on the role adjustments entailed in his succession to headmanship.

Patterns of growth

Lusefu and Chintomfwa villages were both founded by a group of uterine siblings and their immediate descendants, and this seems to have been the typical unit of secession in the past. All 11 villages in the parish were established by such a group, though one headman also took with him a group linked patrilaterally to the main one. In time, however, Lusefu and Chintomfwa expanded in size as their residents' children grew up, married and had children, and each headman attracted to him some other more distantly related persons. The next phase in their history was marked by a series of breakaways which left both villages on the brink of disintegration. In Lusefu Village, plans were made shortly before I left the field in May 1964 for several of the remaining households to go their own separate ways: Kalota (II, D14), Kapianga (II, D24), Chisenga (II, D5) and Laban (II, E7) had already commenced building new settlements and it was expected that Kalikeka (II, C11) would follow suit. This would leave Lusefu and his wife, and only three other households. Lusefu had shown some concern about this by writing to his sister's son, Bombwe (II, D25). Bombwe replied that Lusefu should not worry unduly about this and should re-register his village as a 'farm'. The empty brick houses could then be used to accommodate visitors from town.

A similar situation existed in Chintomfwa Village where the headman lived with his younger brother Machisa (III, C13) and a sister (III, C7) and their nuclear families. Since the brother was now looking for a suitable site for his own settlement, it seemed that Misheck would soon be left with the sister and her incapacitated husband Nathan (III, C8).

Most of the other villages in the parish exhibit similar processes of growth and recent rapid decline. The two largest villages in April 1963 had, by the time I left the area, suffered a whole number of secessions as people moved out to start small settlements. One of the reasons for this sudden fission was the opening of a portion of the Protected Forest Area along the Lukusashi River which had been unavailable for cultivation for something like 30 or more years. Chief Chibale was placed in charge of the allocation of land rights in the area and he received a flood of applications from both established peasant farmers and from villagers wishing to have their own settlements. Several of the villagers were granted rights there. Another village in the parish, though still a village in name, was by May 1964 nothing more than a very small settlement consisting of the headman and some of his wife's matrikin. In recognition of the fact that the settlement had undergone the qualitative transformation from a village to a 'farm', the headman had painted in red ochre on the outside walls of his house his own personal name (not the name of the village) and, in English, the words 'Own Farm'.

Lusefu and Chintomfwa villages are also alike in that many of their seceding groups were composed of single nuclear family units. In Lusefu all seven groups and in Chintomfwa five out of eight were of this composition. Of the remaining three groups from Chintomfwa, two were made up of three-generation uxori-local extended families and one was composed of a small matri-lineal descent group. Hence, the process of village fission tends now to take the pattern of individual household units moving out to start their own small settlements rather than of uterine sibling groups hiving off to establish embryonic villages; and data on the fission of other villages in the parish confirm this view.

In Chapter IV I compared peasant farms, stores and individual settlements and found that, whereas farms and stores are generally small in size and simple in genealogical composition, individual settlements are larger and are often made up of a group of siblings and their families. The case material suggests, however, that some individual settlements start off in much the same way as farms: they are initially composed of a single nuclear or small extended family. But having moved out of their parent village the settlers are joined by kinsmen from other villages or returning from town. This was the case with Sopo, Tomo and Chimbala settle-ments which split off from Chintomfwa Village. The reasons for this are not altogether clear but it seems that a crucial factor is the mode of economic organization practised. Most individual settlers are essentially subsistence cultivators using *citeme* methods: they see their farms as non-commercial enterprises and aim at pro-viding for the basic needs of their families. Thus they see no reason why they should restrict the number of persons resident at their settlements for such persons do not threaten the viability of their production unit (they do not need to conserve their re-sources in the same way as peasant farmers) and, indeed, may constitute a valuable labour pool to meet the peak requirements of *citeme* cultivation. In addition, of course, the presence of resident kinsmen may enhance their social prestige which, in terms of 'traditional' values, would be measured by the number of adher-ents an individual gathers around him.

Occasionally a peasant farmer is joined by some of his kin, often matrilineally related, as was the case with Saulo and Lameck from Lusefu Village. This I suggested was a particular feature of farms established by recently returned urban wage-earners with savings of their own, and was related to the problem of their lack of farming expertise, to the need for a large labour input during the initial stages of establishment, when the land has to be stumped and the site cleared, and to the pressures that operate from their close matrikin. One farmer, Saini Moloka, whose farm development I analysed in Chapter III, was eventually joined by an enormous group of matrilineal kinsmen so that in terms of size and genealogical composition his settlement was indistinguishable from many of the villages in the area. Later, several groups seceded from the farm because of difficulties arising over economic assistance and labour deployment. This indicates that various socio-economic factors operate which cause farmers of this type to shed some of their residents during later phases in the development of their farms.

Other types of farmers never in fact recruit resident kinsmen and instead utilize other links to meet any extra labour demands they may have. In Chapter III I argued that this category of farmers tends to rely on the assistance of some neighbouring farmer and his wife or on hired hands, and that many of these farmers are Jehovah's Witnesses. Jehovah's Witness farms are established by a single nuclear (or, in a few cases, a three-generation extended) family and do not later expand in size through the accretion of new households.

Another aspect of the growth of farms is that if the farmer has married sons he generally sets them up on their own farm. This was the case with Kabichi from Lusefu Village who had spent a short time working for his father-in-law before joining his elder brother at the farm which their father had provided. In most instances, the son's farm is located in close proximity to the father's and they continue to assist one another with farm work. In addition, the father transfers some of his farming equipment and possibly also some oxen to his sons with the promise that they will inherit a major share of the remaining property when he dies. The establishment of a separate farm by a son must be seen more in terms of the father wishing to ensure that his son receives a handsome share of the property before he dies, than as merely an attempt by the son to become independent. The dilemma facing the farmer is that under the customary matrilineal system of inheritance all major property items should go to sisters' sons and not to his own sons; and yet the farmer may feel that his sons should be rewarded for the important part they have played in the development of the farm. Some farmers attempt to solve this through a form of 'anticipatory inheritance', hoping thus to avoid the bitterness that is likely to arise between sons and sisters' sons on their death, and reasoning that by giving their sons a certain degree of autonomy they are making it possible for them to establish unambiguous ownership rights over some of the property at the farm.[1]

We can now summarize the differences that emerge from this comparison of the growth patterns for the different types of residential grouping.

It is somewhat difficult to speak of 'growth cycles', for the past 50 years or so have been characterized by a series of radical changes in residential patterns. But if we take the period from the beginning of the break-up of the large amalgamated villages of the British South Africa Company days until the emergence, in about 1950, of very small settlements without recognized village headmen, we can attempt some generalized statement about the pattern of village development.

During this period, most villages passed through several distinct phases of growth. The first was the initial establishment phase when the headman, generally accompanied by some of his uterine siblings and their families, moved out of their parent village to build an independent settlement. This was followed by a phase of expansion and consolidation when other groups of kinsmen, or unrelated persons, joined the original settlers, and during which the headman's own children and those of his various kin married and had children and, in the case of female matrikin anyway, remained in the village. It was during this stage of development that distinct matrilineal descent groups linked to the headman's own descent group in a variety of ways (e.g. patrilaterally or through clanship bonds) emerged as significant groupings within the village. Several of these might be linked to one another through patrilateral or matrilateral cross-cousin marriage-alliances, or through other affinal relationships. The final phase was reached when a number of secessions took place. Each seceding group would normally be composed of a small group of uterine siblings and their descendants, though sometimes persons linked in other ways might also join together to

[1] For a similar practice among the Plateau Tonga of Zambia, see Colson, 1962, pp. 129–30.

form a new settlement. Thus the original village would as a result be reduced considerably in size, if not completely broken asunder. Each of the seceding groups would, in theory, form the core of new villages and would undergo the same development cycle.

This, of course, is an ideal cycle of development and was frequently modified by various contingent factors, such as the particular demographic, ecological and sociological circumstances of the village in question. Nevertheless, the cycle has been well documented for a number of culturally similar peoples in central Africa and I see no reason why the Lala should have been fundamentally different in this respect. Moreover, the case material I collected relating to this period indicates that the growth and fission of Lala villages was essentially similar to that of the Cewa or Yao, though the special ecological situation on the Serenje Plateau probably increased the rate of fission and prevented villages from attaining the large size that certain Yao and Cewa villages did (see Mitchell, 1956; and Marwick, 1965).

During the late 1940's the rapidly deteriorating ecological situation led to increased fragmentation of villages and then, with the other economic and administrative changes which took place, to a proliferation of much smaller settlements during the 1950's and 1960's. Today it seems extremely unlikely that any of the existing villages in Kapepa Parish will survive the next five years or so, though it is possible that one or two of the individual settlements may be re-registered as villages if their owners recruit sufficient taxpayers. It was suggested earlier that of these new settlement forms, individual settlements are somewhat larger in size and in terms of genealogical composition resemble villages during their early developmental phase, whereas farms and stores are typically much smaller and more often based on a nuclear or extended family pattern. Furthermore, individual settlements tend to increase in size with the incorporation of additional kinsmen, whereas farms shed many of the kin who have settled there as they become more established and as their children mature. Also several farms and all eight stores have, since their inception, remained single nuclear family units and show no signs of recruiting any new residents.

Social characteristics of founders of new settlements

The data on Lusefu and Chintomfwa villages show that over half the seceding groups were led by men who were affinally related to the headman and who had been living uxorilocally. The same general pattern emerges in Table XV, which gives the relation-

Table XV: Relationships of the leaders of seceding groups to previous village headmen

Categories	Settlement type				Totals for non-movers
	Individual settlement	Farm	Store	Totals	
Owner	—	I	—	I	II
Matrilineal kin					
Sister	I	—	—	I	13
Sister's son	2	4	—	6	10
Younger brother	I	I	2	4	5
Classificatory brother	—	2	—	2	3
Mother's brother	I	—	—	I	I
Son	—	I	—	I	5
Patrilaterally related males	I	—	—	I	5
Male affines	10	6	—	16	60
TOTALS	16	15	2	33	113

NOTE: The last column gives the figures for the same kinship categories for non-movers (i.e. those who, at the time of fieldwork, had not yet hived off to start their own independent settlements). This provides some way of assessing the significance of the figures for leaders of seceding groups, but does not take account of those who have left their villages to join other kin living at individual settlements, farms or stores.

ships of the leaders of 33 seceding groups to their previous headmen. 16 of these were affinally related and 14 matrilineal kin. This suggests that many individuals are now choosing to establish their own independent settlements rather than return to their

K

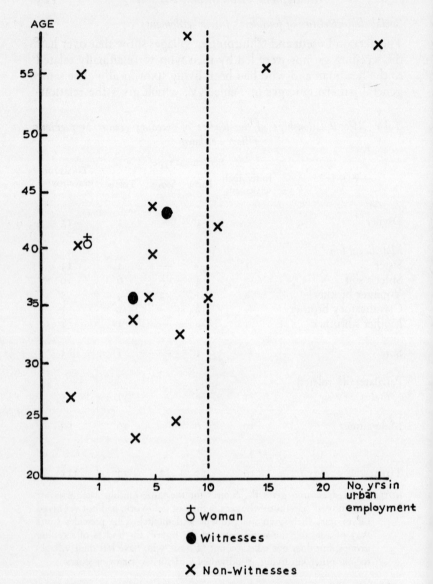

FIG. V. Age, urban experience and religious affiliation of founders of
individual settlements

own villages or stay on in those of their wives. The table also shows that headmen's sister's sons and uterine or classificatory brothers tend to leave, though nowadays it is rather unusual for them to be joined by a large group of matrikin.

Another important aspect of settlement formation is that of the 49 small settlements in the parish, 16 were established by recently returned labour migrants. Of these 16, ten were peasant farms, five were stores and the remaining one an individual settlement.

Further comparisons can be made of individual settlements as against farms and stores on the basis of the age, urban experience and religious affiliation of their founders. Figures V and VI present the results in the form of scatter-grams. The most important point to note is that there appears to be a direct relationship between urban experience and age with the farmers and storekeepers, but no such relationship with the individual settlers. Also proportionately more farmers and storekeepers have had ten or more years in urban employment than individual settlers: 21 out of the 33 farmers and storekeepers as against four out of 16 individual settlers. This suggests that the longer one spends in town the more likelihood there is of one having the capital available for starting either a peasant farm or some business enterprise, though if one is already 55 or over on retirement then one is probably less motivated to do so.

Furthermore, if we now compare founders in terms of their religious affiliation, we find that of 18 founders who were Jehovah's Witnesses at the time of establishing their settlements, 16 set up farms or stores; whereas the non-Jehovah's Witness founders are fairly evenly distributed between the various types of settlements. Moreover, proportionately more Jehovah's Witness farmers and storekeepers fall into the younger age categories. Ten out of the 16 were under 40 years old, as against six out of 15 for the non-Jehovah's Witnesses. And consistent with this is the fact that fewer of them have had ten or more years' urban experience: six out of 16 Jehovah's Witnesses as against all of the non-Witnesses. Hence we can conclude that within the farmer-storekeeper group we have two somewhat distinct categories of individuals. There are those who are somewhat older and have more urban experience, and who are not Jehovah's Witnesses; and there are those who are rather younger, who have

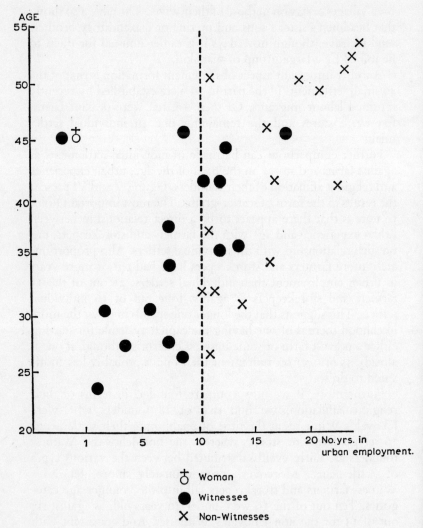

AGE

FIG. VI. Age, urban experience and religious affiliation of founders
of farms and stores

spent much less time in urban employment, but who are Witnesses.

In an earlier chapter I gave reasons for some of the marked differences which exist between Jehovah's Witness and non-Jehovah's Witness farmers, arguing that the former frequently practise some additional non-farming skill, such as carpentry or bricklaying, from which they derive some cash income, and that they utilize their links with fellow Witnesses to gain access to essential resources. In contrast, those farmers who are not Witnesses are mostly recently returned, long-term urban workers with savings of their own and individuals who, for various reasons, find it expedient to operate their farms through the assistance of resident kinsmen-workers. The same kind of pattern pertains for Jehovah's Witness storekeepers as against other storekeepers. The former tend to graduate to storekeeping through running a hawker business or through cash-crop farming, whereas the latter are generally persons who return from town with urban savings which they invest in the setting up of a small store.

Later I shall examine more closely the relationship which exists between religious commitment and socio-economic action. Suffice it here to have indicated that religious affiliation appears to be an important factor motivating individuals towards the setting up of a farm or store, though, as I shall argue, there are also a number of important intervening variables to be taken into account. In connection with this, it is significant that I recorded few cases where a family or household split off from a village or settlement primarily because of the hostilities existing between them and the rest of the residents over religious differences. For example, although Bombwe, Timoti and, at one time, Katwishi and Chiboli were Jehovah's Witnesses this does not appear to have been a factor of importance for understanding the quarrels that developed in Lusefu Village over the store; nor does it account for the re-building of the store at Kapepa school away from the village. Similarly, although Lusefu's sons-in-law are both Jehovah's Witnesses this does not seem to have made for difficulties between them and their in-laws and was only indirectly a factor influencing their moving out of the village. Yet despite this, many Jehovah's Witnesses do use their religious commitment as a way of explaining or of legitimizing their leaving the village; and this is an especially useful device for young men wishing to bring to an end their period of service towards in-laws.

This chapter has explored several themes relating to the growth and fission of residential groupings in Kapepa Parish. The exposition and analysis of case data on Lusefu and Chintomfwa villages was primarily aimed at discussing the precipitating sociological causes for the fission of these two villages. In the first case study I argued that the breakaways were connected with the struggles which occurred between various residents for control of certain economic resources and to the question of the development of new socio-economic goals. In the second, I showed that a primary factor was the difficulties that arose from the particular form that positional succession took in Chintomfwa Village, but I also examined the impact of various modernizing influences.

In both villages it emerged that several of the secessions which took place were preceded by periods of dissent between various kinsmen and affines, sometimes leading to accusations of sorcery. Similar observations have been made by Mitchell (1956), Marwick (1965) and Turner (1957) for central African peoples, and by other anthropologists for other areas (see, for example, Middleton, 1960; Middleton & Winter, 1963). Here, however, instead of casting the analysis mainly in terms of the difficulties that can arise between specific categories of kinsmen and affines, I have tried to isolate those underlying factors which made for conflict between the residents and which in the long run led to settlement fission. I have shown how new types of socio-economic inducements operated to persuade people to leave the village and set up independent settlements, and have analysed the ways in which increased economic differentiation within a village can lead to hostilities among its residents. In addition to this, of course, I have had to explore the idiom in which the conflicts were expressed and this involved me in some discussion of the ideology of kinship as presented by particular actors. Later in Chapter VII I shall return to analyse further quarrels within the Lusefu kin group and argue that in certain situations one has also to take account of new types of status ideology relating to forms of social categorization outside the kinship frame of reference.

Another theme which I have developed has been the question

of the differences which exist in the growth patterns of the
various types of residential units and in the social characteristics
of the founders of new settlement forms. Throughout I have
touched on the question of changing concepts of power and
social status and have suggested that few men these days aspire
to village headmanship. In the next chapter, then, I focus on the
changing role and position of the village headman, and present
a generalized view of the patterns of social prestige emerging in
the community.

CHAPTER VI

CHANGING PATTERNS OF SOCIAL STATUS

The Village Headman

The symposium on *The Village Headman in British Central Africa* by Gluckman, Mitchell and Barnes (1949), provides a useful basis for discussing the changing position of the village headman in Kapepa, for much of their argument can be extended to include the Lala village headman in the period before 1950. Gluckman argues that the headman occupies an intercalary position between two distinct systems of social relations, the domestic-kinship and the political fields. He is, at one and the same time, the senior kinsman in a group of kinsmen interrelated in various ways and also a key figure in the politico-administrative hierarchy. Thus inherent in his position is the likelihood of role conflict: at times he is torn between his loyalty to his kinsfolk and his loyalty to his chief and the administration, and this places him in a particularly difficult and ambivalent situation. Later I shall return to discuss this theme when I examine the creation of the new administrative post of parish head and the effects that this has had on the village headman's position *vis-à-vis* both his followers and the chief. But before doing so, I shall describe the position of the Lala village headman prior to the important changes wrought by the coming of British administration. The description will inevitably fall short in that one can only present an idealized picture, but it is nevertheless an essential one for understanding the contemporary situation, for it is largely in terms of such a model that the people themselves evaluate the changes that have occurred.

Earlier I showed that the core of most Lala villages consists of a group of matrilineally related men and women with the headman as senior kinsman. His seniority in this context rested customarily on the fact that he had certain jural and ritual responsibilities towards the group, though the nature and extent of these duties varied somewhat with the degree of kinship involved and the availability of other male kinsmen to assume leadership of different uterine sibling groups. In a large village, for example, authority might be divided among several senior men, of whom one would be designated village headman (*mwine mushi* or *sulutani*). Each would act as warden (*inkoswe*) to a particular set of matrilineal kinsmen. Like Yao sorority group organization, the central link was that of the warden to a group of uterine sisters and their matrilineal descendants, residence being predominantly uxorilocal (Mitchell, 1956). But unlike the Yao the Lala have no term commonly used to describe such a group. Hence it seems better to conceptualize the relationship between the warden and his wards in terms of a network of individual relationships clustering around a senior kinsman (*inkoswe*) rather than as a corporate kin group.[1]

The warden represented his wards in court cases, helped them to pay fines or compensation, offered advice on matrimonial affairs and vetted prospective brothers-in-law. When one of them fell sick it was his duty to consult a diviner, procure a herbal remedy or, if necessary, propitiate the aggrieved ancestor spirit at a small shrine on the outskirts of the village. He also exercised a fair degree of direct authority over his wards. He had the right, it was said, to hand over a sister or her child into slavery to clear a debt, or to act as security for payment of compensation; and all axes, spears and weapons of the group were placed in his safe keeping.

Few enduring economic ties existed between the warden and his kin as the main unit for production was the individual household, not a group of uterine siblings and their families. However, the warden by virtue of his senior status stood at the centre of a network of ties based on mutual assistance and hospitality. Exchange of agricultural labour occurred among close matrikin towards the end of the *citeme* cutting season when additional labour was required for the piling of branches, and during the harvesting period when crops needed to be reaped and stored with a minimum of delay. Though he could apply no direct sanctions on his kinsmen to secure their assistance and might well be required to reciprocate at some later date, the warden was obviously more favourably placed than others for receiving help. Similarly, wardenship carried with it no specific rights to any portion of the food obtained by his wards, but in practice he frequently received

[1] The Lala word *ibumba* (which is presumably from the same root as the Yao *mbumba* for 'sorority group') has a wide usage, being the general term used for any kind of social group (e.g. a beer-drinking group or a group of co-religionists).

gifts of food and beer and was normally presented with one of the hind legs of any game killed. Thus the village headman as leader of a particular group of matrilineal kin acted as *inkoswe* to his uterine siblings and their descendants, and might also be treated as such by more distantly related matrikin, especially if they had no male kinsman available to represent them.

In addition to the matrilineal core, there were usually other groups living in the village who were related to the headman in a variety of ways. The wife of the headman may have attracted some of her own matrikin to the village, or there might be some other patrilaterally related descent group, or a group linked through a common clanship bond, living there. Any authority that the headman had over individuals in these groups was necessarily of a more tenuous kind and lacked the moral sanctions associated with matrilineal kinship. Indeed some of the larger groups of more distantly related persons would have their own wardens residing in the village to represent their own specific interests. But nevertheless, the headman was still called upon to act for them in particular situations. He was frequently asked to speak on their behalf in inter-village disputes and in cases heard before the chief; and he might also be consulted over marriage or sickness. In return, arrangements were made by the village as a whole to provide the headman with additional agricultural labour during peak periods and when beer was brewed he normally received one calabash as a gift.

Any bonds of mutual assistance that existed between the headman and his non-matrilineal followers, however, were morally less binding than those between close matrikin. They were based on the tie of common residence rather than on the ideologically more powerful one of matrilineal kinship. Moreover, because headmanship was largely evaluated within a kinship frame of reference, the headman was first and foremost seen as the *inkoswe* or leader of a group of close matrikin and it was to them that he owed his greatest loyalty. Only after having demonstrated his skill and acumen in handling kinship affairs as warden of a small group of matrikin could he confidently look forward to attracting other dependants. Other individuals might then choose to live under his leadership, in preference to joining some other village where they might find closer kinsmen but a less favourable regime. On his part, the headman served their interests by helping them to find good land for gardens and by offering them his protection. In return, of course, he gained their allegiance and so increased his own social status.

The same argument applies to the headman's relationship to his matrikin: the more of them he could bring under his wing, the more prestige he derived from his wardenship, though the difficulties of maintaining their allegiance tended to multiply as numbers increased. In a large village the headman's following could be drastically reduced by the secession of one or more of the linked descent groups, and the bigger these became, the more likelihood there was of fission. Likewise, he was constantly threatened by his own younger brothers and maternal nephews who might persuade some of their matrikin to join them in a bid for independence and thus undermine the headman's own position in the village. Yet, despite these difficulties, the headman did manage, for limited periods anyway, to preserve the unity of the village.

He had a number of ritual duties to perform on behalf of the village as a whole. At the building of a new village or at the moving of an existing one to a new site he was required to carry out special divination ritual to assess whether the site was a propitious one. Before the building of huts took place the headman would sprinkle millet flour on the ground and return the next morning to see whether the flour had been scattered or remained in a heap. If the heap remained intact then this was taken as a good omen and plans would be made to build the village there. Sometimes also a small pole of the type used for constructing the wooden framework of a hut would be placed on the ground to see whether in the morning it had been eaten by termites. If it had not, then this too was evidence of the site being an auspicious place. In doing this the headman was approaching the spirits (*imipashi*) of the former occupants of the area to see whether they sanctioned the building of the new settlement.

Before the villagers moved to the new site the headman and his wife would spend a night at the settlement to perform the marital act which was part of the ritual of inauguration. In the morning careful note would be made of whether they had experienced any unfavourable dreams, and if none had occurred people would begin to take up residence. The move to the new settlement was further marked by a ritual of fire-making performed by the *cishikamulilo* or 'firemaker' who made fire by rubbing two sticks together. The firemaker was appointed by the headman and would normally be a sister's husband. Thus both the main descent group and the 'stranger' element were represented in the founding of the new village. Each household took cinders from the new fire to light their own hearths, the headman's being the first to be kindled, and this symbolized the new life to be enjoyed by them.

The headman was also responsible for rituals (*kusunga*) designed to protect the village from lions, leopards, hyenas, snakes and malignant spirits (*ifibanda*) and to promote harmonious relations both within the village and in its affairs with other villages. One such ritual involved the tying of branches of the *mutaba* tree[1] on to trees situated at strategic points around the perimeter of the village. This, it is claimed, would prevent any spirit or beast with evil intent from entering the village. Similar rituals were performed to protect crops from wild animals. It was the headman's duty to renew these rituals periodically and to perform a special cleansing ritual, if, for example, a lion or leopard had marauded there. In addition, the village maintained a series of small shrines or spirit huts (*inanda yamipashi*) on the outskirts of the village where offerings of millet and sorghum flour were made and where libations of beer were poured to various spirits of the dead members of the main matrilineal descent group and to the spirits of famous former inhabitants of the neighbourhood. Other alien spirits were also honoured from time to time if there were good reasons to do so (e.g. in times of famine or sickness). Most rituals of this kind were performed or directed by the headman, assisted by the firemaker and other elders, but members of the village would gather to witness the ceremonies and the women to ululate. The headman also represented the village at the chief's headquarters (*ipanga*) during the yearly first-fruits thanksgiving ceremony and in times of serious drought when the chief made appeals to the spirits of his predecessors.

A common theme throughout the rituals was the maintenance of the physical and spiritual well-being of the village as a whole. The headman was commissioned to act on behalf of the entire village community and not just his own matrikin. Thus he

---

[1] A tree belonging to the *ficus* family and planted in the village. Its bark was used for making cloth.

symbolized the community of interest that the village had as a residential grouping.

He also represented their interests in political situations, especially in their relations with other villages. For example, it was usual for the village *citeme* gardens to be located in a block and occasionally a dispute would arise between villages as to the boundaries between their respective gardens. It was the headman's duty to try and effect an amicable solution in consultation with the other headmen, and if unsuccessful then he was expected to put their case before the chief.

Writing in 1939, Munday noted that the Lala headman 'is not appointed by the chief but by the villagers with the chief's consent' and that 'the subjects of any ruling-chief seem always to have been free to move as individuals or as village groups from the jurisdiction of one chief to that of another' (Munday, 1939, p. 439 & p. 436). It seems reasonable therefore to assume that at any one point in time a chief's area of jurisdiction was somewhat ill defined and subject to phases of expansion and contraction, and this, I suggest, was one index of the rather ineffective control that the chief exercised over groups within his chieftaincy. Thus the extent of the chief's authority over headmen and villagers might vary considerably from village to village according to its geographical position and the general social standing of the headman.

In theory, however, the chief had certain specific judicial and administrative powers over all villages within his chieftaincy. All cases of homicide had to be brought to him for judgement, and inter-village disputes for arbitration. He also had the right to call for tribute labour when, for example, he wished to repair his dwelling houses or to open up new gardens. His order would be circulated among the headmen and they were made responsible for sending some of their followers to work for him. In return, the chief was expected to provide the workers with food and beer. The chief could also ask for grain or beer when his stocks were running short, and certain game and trophies were to be handed over to him. The hunter of eland or buffalo was expected to make a present of the hind legs, breast, intestines and liver of the animal. These portions were tied together in bundles and placed just outside the chief's village where they were collected by one of his councillors. Skins of lions and leopards and one of the tusks of any elephant killed were the property of the chief and had to be handed over to him. It was the headman's duty to see that such trophies were in fact delivered.

The title 'owner of the land' (*mwine mpanga*) was mainly applied to the chief though this expression was used to emphasize his political position in the chieftaincy and did not mean that he had full control over the allocation of land to individuals. Most of the time he was called in *ex post facto* to ratify land rights and not to allocate them. Thus land that was not under cultivation was held in trust by the chief for the people until they had need of it. As Stefaniszyn notes for the Ambo, the chief had no right to prevent a man from obtaining land and if he did, it 'would be resented as an irresponsible and tyrannical act' (Stefaniszyn, 1964, p. 66). It is said that the chief could also grant to a hunter who had distinguished himself the right to exclusive use of a particular tract of bush. The hunter would then be known as 'the owner of that land', usually identified by the name of a stream or some topographical feature, and those who wished to hunt there would first have to obtain permission from him. In return he might ask them for help with *citeme* cutting or with harvesting. How far such a man was able to maintain his rights over the tract is uncertain, but assuming he was the headman or a man of senior status in the village this honour might be an added advantage to him when seeking followers.

Unlike the Bemba situation, the Lala chief could not mobilize men for military service except from among his own band of followers, nor had he the right to appoint headmen. Headmen either achieved their position by succeeding to the position of a senior male kinsman, normally an elder brother or a mother's brother, or by hiving off with a group of their own matrikin. Thus the chief had only limited control over the actions of his headmen and no way of enforcing his orders save by sending a force of his own followers or by manipulating his own network of allies over and against those of other leaders in the chieftaincy. Hence the extent to which a particular headman acted as the chief's representative—he was sometimes described as 'the eyes of the chief'—was partly dependent on the extent to which the headman felt that close association with the chief would bring him increased power and social status.

Status was largely measured by the number of adherents a man could claim. Brother competed with brother and nephew with maternal uncle for wardenship of a group of matrikin and ultimately for headmanship of a village. Success was judged by the number of matrilineal kinsmen and other dependants one could muster at critical points in the power struggle. The key to political success lay in the control of a group of female matrikin, for given the ideology of matrilineal descent and uxorilocal residence, women constituted the points of growth in the descent system. Only later could a man hope to attract the allegiance of unrelated persons. Some headmen, by engaging in trading activities (e.g. the export of iron hoes and axes in return for salt or such commodities), by acquiring domestic slaves and receiving substantial prestations from their followers, could achieve higher economic status, but most redistributed this wealth to their followers or used it to attract more dependants. Wealth in itself did not confer high social prestige but was more a by-product of, and a way of maintaining, a position of leadership in the society.

The power of the chief was probably not very different from that of headmen of large, long-established villages, though he claimed somewhat higher social status on account of his being the direct matrilineal descendant of the original settler of the region. Here his ritual status was of primary significance for he had direct access to the spirits of his dead ancestors, whom it was believed controlled the health, harmony and general prosperity of all those living within their domain.

The advent of British administration brought additional administrative duties to the incumbents of positions of authority. The chief became recognized as a Native Authority, receiving a small annual stipend and commanding his own retinue of paid councillors and officials to act as executives, and was made directly responsible to the District Commissioner. Below him were the unpaid village headmen. Thus the village became the smallest unit of administration and every effort was made to keep it so, by compelling Africans to live in villages of defined minimum size and by issuing orders concerning the administrative duties required of headmen. Village headmen were made responsible for village hygiene, for the clearing of paths, the construction of latrines, and for the implementation of a host of agricultural and veterinary regulations. They were expected to see to it that all taxable males residing in their village paid their taxes regularly, though they were not required to collect the taxes themselves. They also had to report 'violent or unnatural deaths' and strange illnesses, and were held responsible for the enforcement of any new orders put out by the chief or administration. Headmen were permitted to handle minor disputes arising in their villages, but they had no authority to levy fines. Most people, however, continued to take cases to their headmen for advice if not for settlement before going to the chief's court. The chief's court was empowered to judge most of the more usual types of dispute (e.g. marital troubles and land disputes, etc.), and could levy fines and assess the amount of compensation to be paid over to the injured party, but was not authorized to handle any of the more serious cases (e.g. those involving serious bodily harm or death or an accusation of witchcraft). These had to go before the District Commissioner, who acted as local magistrate and who would perhaps send them on to the High Court sessions.

The net result of these changes was that the headman and chief were incorporated into a formal administrative hierarchy with the District Commissioner representing the apex at district level. Thus the areas of jurisdiction of all chiefs in Serenje were formally demarcated, such that it was no longer possible (theoretically anyway) for a headman to change his political allegiance, or for a man to establish a new village, without the permission of the chief and District Commissioner. On the other hand, the chief relinquished his monopoly over ivory and certain game hunted in his chieftaincy, and the right to demand tribute either in the form of goods or labour. Yet, within the limits defined by his new administrative role, the chief clearly assumed stricter control over his headmen.

I have previously described how parishes were demarcated in Serenje in 1950 and how one of the aims of this new system of local government was to build up a parish framework within the existing Native Authority structure. It was originally hoped that parish councils would be formed to take over all the administrative duties normally carried out by village headmen. However, the plan did not materialize and each parish now has as its official leader a parish head or *cilolo* (pl. *filolo*).

When the administration first appointed parish heads it chose either the headman of the village from which the parish derived its name, or, if that village no longer existed, a prominent local headman, usually of the same clan. Nowadays, the following procedure is adopted. A special meeting is held at a convenient place and all men and women residing in the parish are invited to attend. The chief's court clerk and one of his messengers are sent to represent the chief, and another parish head is asked to chair the meeting. Nominations take place and people vote by a show of hands. Any man living in the parish can be elected, whether a village headman or not, and he does not necessarily have to be related in any way to the previous incumbent, though preference is still often shown for someone of the same clan as the original headman of the village from which the parish derived its name.

Under the new system, the village headman assumes a lesser role administratively, for the parish head has taken over several of the duties formerly his. The most important single duty that the parish head has, and the one most associated with his office, is the hearing of cases. Before a case is dealt with by the chief's court the litigants must first have been to their parish head. Sometimes a solution will be reached and the case ends there, but, like the village headman, the parish head cannot fine or assess the amount of compensation to be paid. As one man put it: 'The parish head hasn't got a receipt book like the clerk of court.'

It is not often these days that the village headman is called in to arbitrate in a dispute. Cases are normally, in the first instance, brought before the parish head, and then taken to the chief's court. When persons arrive at the court they are required to produce a letter from the parish head giving a brief summary of the case and containing his assessment of it. It is said that whatever the parish head writes in his letter it is treated as 'the chief's eye' and judgement is largely based on his recommendations. Any person who fails to bring the letter with him will be turned away without his case being heard. Moreover, if for some reason a person refuses to go before the parish head, this is regarded as contempt of court. Recently a Jehovah's Witness, charged with permitting his cattle to graze another man's crops, refused to see the parish head, stating that 'he is not God and therefore cannot pass judgement on me'. Later the court clerk and senior court assessor, commenting on this, said, 'We take this as very abusive towards the chief because the parish head is the chief's representative.' They added that the man would now receive a summons to appear before them for contempt of court on two counts; one, for refusing to go before the parish head, and the other for being disrespectful to the chief.

The parish head is also expected to visit regularly all villages and settlements in his parish to check that government regulations are being observed. Theoretically, Local Authority Rules and Orders still make each village headman responsible for his village, but it is the parish head who is usually accredited to be the local watchdog, by the chief and people alike. Furthermore, since in Serenje taxpayers continue to be registered by village not parish, many individual settlers are still legally linked to their villages of origin. Yet few village headmen feel that this entitles them to interfere in their affairs by enforcing government regulations, and prefer to leave this to the parish head. New instructions from the chief or District Commissioner are now received by the parish heads, who in turn circulate the news around the villages and settlements, and the local political party also uses this channel for communication.

In the Introduction to the village headman article, Gluckman argues that the headman is 'the personality in whom the domestic-kinship and political systems intersect'. He is 'entangled in the web of kinship links and yet has power of another kind, either from the chief or as an autonomous political leader, in relation to the same set of people', and this creates a situation of potential role conflict (Gluckman, 1949, p. 93). Moreover, under colonial rule his position becomes subject to still greater strains due to his now being a key figure in the new administrative system. My description of the role of the 'traditional' Lala headman and of his position under British administration up to 1950 substantiates Gluckman's argument; but how far does the same hypothesis apply to the Serenje situation in 1963–4?

The parish system in Serenje District has had two main consequences. Firstly, it has legitimized the growth of smaller settlements without recognized headmen, in an attempt to make the parish, not the village, the basic unit of administration. Secondly, through the institution of parish headship it has directly and indirectly reduced the administrative functions of the village headman. Thus, although the village headman remains head of a localized kinship group, he is no longer so ambivalently placed.

It is the parish head who has taken over many of the administrative duties formerly his, and it is he who is now directly responsible to the local chief, and ultimately to the Lala Local Authority and District Commissioner. *A priori*, therefore, one might expect parish headship rather than village headmanship to bring with it difficulties of the kind suggested by Gluckman.

Yet many parish heads do not represent a group of kinsmen in the same way that the village headman does. Indeed, six out of 11 parish heads in Chibale Chiefdom either live at their own individual settlements, or are living uxorilocally in villages *under* village headmen. Thus, these six, at least, cannot from the structural point of view be said, in terms of the domestic-kinship and political systems, to occupy an intercalary position similar to that occupied by the village headman prior to 1950: though they are key figures in the administrative hierarchy and represent both the people of the parish, their electorate, and the chief and administration.

Furthermore, the fact that persons prefer these days to take cases to their parish head without first consulting the village headman, is, I suggest, an index of the greater receptivity that notions of modern bureaucratic administration now have. Ideally, bureaucratic authority pertains to the office not the person. As Weber puts it, 'the dominant norms are concepts of straightforward duty without regard to personal considerations. Everyone is subject to formal equality of treatment; that is, everyone in the same empirical situation' (Weber, 1947, p. 340). Thus a tentative hypothesis suggests itself, namely, that the election principle enables the community to select for office those persons who, on the face of it, have few obtrusive sectional loyalties, are qualified in their knowledge of parish affairs and have a modicum of literacy. Since village headmen represent specific kin group interests and are generally illiterate they are regarded as unsuitable. This is not to say, however, that parish heads do not experience 'in the daily exercise of authority . . . conflict between particularistic loyalties and the norm of disinterested and impartial administration' (Fallers, 1956, p. 239), but only that some attempt seems to be made by the people of the parish to keep local administration separate from local politics.

With the creation of the new post of parish head, the village headman's politico-administrative role has been substantially circumscribed and this has had the effect of reducing the potentiality of role conflict which was inherent in his position during the earlier phases of British administration. But what of his position as senior kinsman and ritual head, has this too been eroded away?

In Chapter IV I discussed the growth of smaller settlements and argued that an explanation for this can be sought in the various ecological and economic changes taking place in the parish, and that the process seems also to have been facilitated by the introduction of the parish system which has sanctioned the setting up of small independent units outside the control of existing headmen. These developments have led to an overall decrease in the size of villages as more and more persons have moved out to set up farms and individual settlements, and for many headmen this has meant a considerable loss of followers and a consequent drop in their power and status.

Nowadays headmanship in itself offers no discernible economic privileges. The headman does not advise or control the selection of the village *citeme* area or of its secondary gardens; nor does he in any way organize agricultural activities. Moreover, only occasionally does he receive gifts of beer and meat, and only then from his very close matrikin. Ritually too he has lost most of his authority. He does not appoint a *cishikamulilo* or any other ritual specialist, for the spirit huts outside the village are no longer kept up. As far as I was able to ascertain, the last ritual associated with the founding of a new settlement took place towards the end of the 1940's. *Kusunga* rituals may occasionally be performed to protect gardens from predatory game, or as some informants told me, to prevent arrests being made in the village by administrative officers on tour, but these are no longer regarded as the sole prerogative of village headmen, as farmers and individual settlers may sometimes undertake them themselves.

The headman's role as senior kinsman and warden of a group of matrikin has also been modified. Whilst he may deem it necessary to assist financially his own uterine siblings (though often he is not in a position to do so) he would not normally be expected to extend this to other kinsfolk except where the arrangement is strictly on a loan basis or is part of a contract. Similarly, although he may accompany his uterine sibling to the chief's court and speak on his or her behalf, he would not usually

do this for any other member of the village. His advice on matrimonial matters is frequently valued but he is not generally asked
to approve of a prospective brother- or sister-in-law. Again, he
may consult a diviner on behalf of a close kinsman but more
usually the person concerned or his son will do this themselves.
Frequently, of course, the headman's close matrikin will be dispersed throughout town and country and, because of the dis-
tances involved, will not look to him for advice or assistance;
indeed there may be some younger kinsman who is in a better
position to help in times of crisis.

All this has tended to undermine the status of the headman in
Serenje. At best he is seen simply as a senior kinsman, commanding some respect because of his age and experience, but possessing
few powers and responsibilities, and often precious little in the
way of resources, either human or material. Perhaps one of the
clearest indications of the headman's and thus also the warden's
reduced status position, is the fact that the word for warden,
inkoswe, is now extended to cover any member of a group of
matrikin who is given the responsibility of acting as banker for
the family. Often this devolves on a senior kinsman, who may
or may not be a village headman, but it may also be given to
some junior member who displays good business sense and can
be trusted. The role of the modern *inkoswe* is to safeguard the
money, property and interests of all those close relatives who are
away working in town. The *inkoswe* acts as their adviser and
trustee.

Further discussion of the position of the village headman requires closer attention to the question of the evaluation of social
status in general, for alongside the changes occurring in the role
of the headman have come the emergence of other non-indigenous forms of leadership and new criteria for assessing status.
It is important therefore to examine the present-day position of
the village headman *vis-à-vis* other social personalities in the
community.

One technique for doing this is through a prestige rating study
of the kind used by Mitchell and Epstein in their studies of
occupational prestige and social status among urban Africans
(Mitchell and Epstein, 1959). Such a study attempts to achieve a
generalized view of the patterns of prestige operating in a given
community, and takes the following form. Each subject is asked

to indicate the degree of respect he thinks is accorded persons holding certain social positions in the community. From this it is possible to compute the mean scores for each of the positions and to construct a scale of relative status. Providing the positions chosen are roughly representative of the range of occupations or social positions open to individuals in the community, then the results should enable one to arrive at some understanding of the overall patterns of prestige and should also give some clue as to the importance of particular status criteria. As an experiment, it was decided to adopt a similar approach among the rural Lala.

Prestige rating study

A schedule was designed to be administered verbally in the vernacular. Each of the subjects was asked to say what degree of respect they thought each of ten positions held by persons living in the area were accorded by the local people. The positions selected were: Chief, Village headman, Parish head, Court clerk, United National Independence Party branch chairman, Overseer of the local congregation of Jehovah's Witnesses, Primary school teacher, Agricultural demonstrator, Peasant farmer and Storekeeper. It was intended that the degree of respect should be indicated by placing each of the positions on a five-point scale (i.e. into one of five categories, Very high, High, Neither high nor low, Low, and Very low). But in the pilot study it was found that five categories were too many for most people to handle and so they were reduced to four: High, Neither high nor low, Low, and Very low. Four categories seemed to elicit a better response from the subjects, and so these were used in the final study. Each subject was also asked a number of supplementary questions in which he had to state reasons for his ratings, and was encouraged to extemporize on the theme of social status in general.

There are many vernacular terms for respect and one of the aims of the pilot study was to determine which term had the widest meaning and could confidently be used to cover the kinds of respect associated with all ten social positions. The three most commonly used terms were *bucindami*, *mucinshi*, and *bukankala*. It became apparent that the latter two terms were more associated with the kind of respect given to those holding positions of 'traditional' status, whereas the first term, *bucindami*, seemed to be used more widely to refer both to traditional and to new forms of social status. This was the term used in the questionnaire.

It was originally intended to interview a random sample of 100 out of the 497 adult residents in the parish. However, only a handful of questionnaires given to the women were satisfactorily answered and so it was decided to process only those interviews completed by the men. 65 questionnaires made up the adult male sample but of these only 50 were properly completed. These 50,

Table XVI: Prestige rating results

Positions	High respect		Medium		Low respect		Very low		Don't know	
	(a)	(b)	(a)	(b)	(a)	(b)	(a)	(b)	(a)	(b)
Chief	42	29	5	5	3	1				
	(84)	(82·8)	(10)	(14·3)	(6)	(2·8)				
Teacher	33	19	14	14	3	0	0	1	0	1
	(66)	(54·3)	(28)	(40)	(6)			(2·8)		(2.8)
Local religious leader	21	22	11	4	15	3	2	0	1	6
	(42)	(62·9)	(22)	(11·4)	(30)	(8·5)	(4)		(2)	(17·1)
Agricultural demonstrator	27	13	15	19	5	2	3	0	0	1
	(54)	(37·1)	(30)	(54·3)	(10)	(5·7)	(6)			(2·8)
Peasant farmer	25	15	18	11	6	9	1	0		
	(50)	(42·9)	(36)	(31·4)	(12)	(25·4)	(2)			
UNIP branch chairman	22	9	11	10	11	8	1	0	5	8
	(44)	(25·4)	(22)	(28·5)	(22)	(22·9)	(2)		(10)	(22·9)
Village headman	18	11	19	7	11	14	2	1	0	2
	(36)	(31·4)	(38)	(20)	(22)	(40)	(4)	(2·8)		(5·7)
Storekeeper	13	10	19	13	12	6	5	3	1	3
	(26)	(28·5)	(38)	(37·1)	(24)	(17·1)	(10)	(8·5)	(2)	(8·5)
Court Clerk	11	6	21	13	14	13	3	2	1	1
	(22)	(17·1)	(42)	(37·1)	(28)	(37·1)	(6)	(5·7)	(2)	(2·8)
Parish head	12	5	16	12	18	12	3	5	1	1
	(24)	(14·3)	(32)	(34·3)	(36)	(34·3)	(6)	(14·3)	(2)	(2·8)

Percentages in brackets
Total sample: 50 Adults ⎫
               35 Schoolboys ⎬ 85 subjects
(a) Adults
(b) Boys

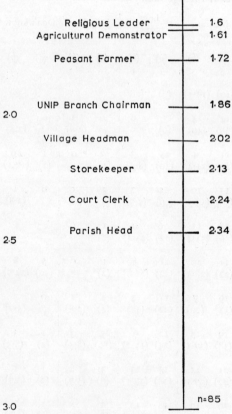
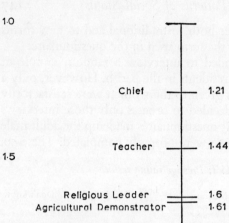

1.0	
Chief	— 1.21
Teacher	— 1.44
1.5	
Religious Leader	— 1.6
Agricultural Demonstrator	— 1.61
Peasant Farmer	— 1.72
UNIP Branch Chairman	— 1.86
2.0	
Village Headman	— 2.02
Storekeeper	— 2.13
Court Clerk	— 2.24
Parish Head	— 2.34
2.5	
3.0	n=85

FIG. VII
Mean Scores
on a
linear scale

Mean scores derived from averaging the
proportion in each prestige category.
Arbitrary weighting given: 1 for High,
2 for Medium, 3 for Low and 4 for Very Low.

together with a further 35, answered by a group of Standard V schoolboys, made up the final sample for analysis. The schoolboys had all completed a minimum of seven years schooling and their average age was 16 years. The ages of the men ranged from the mid-twenties up to the late fifties, the mean age being 39 years.

Table XVI sets out the numbers and percentages of the sample placing the positions into each of the four categories or into a residual 'don't know' category. Figure VII shows the mean ratings on a linear scale; and Figure VIII presents a comparison of the mean ratings for the adults and schoolboys. No significant difference was found between the overall ratings of the two groups, with the notable exception of the religious leader who was placed much higher by the schoolboys. Figure IX gives a breakdown of the adult sample into four occupational categories, subsistence cultivators, peasant farmers, storekeepers, and those educated persons in government employment (e.g. teachers, court clerk and agricultural demonstrator), showing the mean ratings for each category.

A convenient way of discussing the results is to regard the ten positions as falling into one of five associated pairs:

1. The Chief and Village headman because both hold positions of leadership in the 'traditional' political system.

2. The Parish head and Court clerk because both are officials in the modern administrative hierarchy.

3. The U.N.I.P. branch chairman and the Overseer of the Jehovah's Witness congregation because both occupy important positions in the two voluntary associations in the area.

4. The Primary school teacher and Agricultural demonstrator because both are government employees practising specialist skills and are educated.

5. The Peasant farmer and Storekeeper because they both have high economic status.

The discussion that follows is interspersed with textual material extracted from comments made by the respondents themselves. This has helped to identify the main lines of interpretation and makes the results themselves more meaningful.

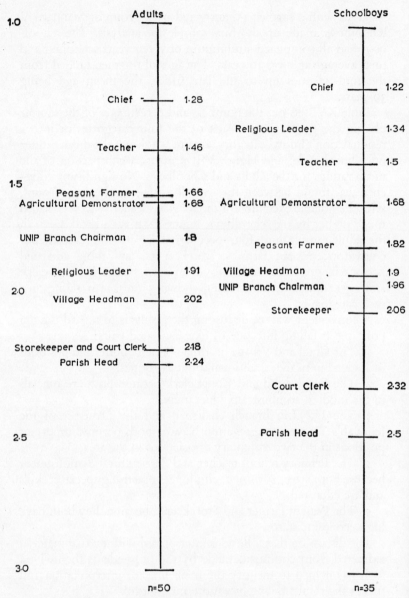

1·0
Adults   Schoolboys

                                    Chief ———— 1·22

                         Religious Leader ———— 1·34

Chief ·———— 1·28

Teacher ———— 1·46   Teacher ———— 1·5

1·5
Peasant Farmer ———— 1·66
Agricultural Demonstrator———— 1·68   Agricultural Demonstrator ———— 1·68

UNIP Branch Chairman ———— 1·8
                                    Peasant Farmer ———— 1·82

Religious Leader ———— 1·91   Village Headman ———— 1·9
2·0   UNIP Branch Chairman ———— 1·96
Village Headman ———— 2·02

                                    Storekeeper ———— 2·06

Storekeeper and Court Clerk ———— 2·18
Parish Head ———— 2·24

                                    Court Clerk ———— 2·32

2·5   Parish Head ———— 2·5

3·0
n=50   n=35

FIG. VIII. Comparison of mean scores for
adults and schoolboys

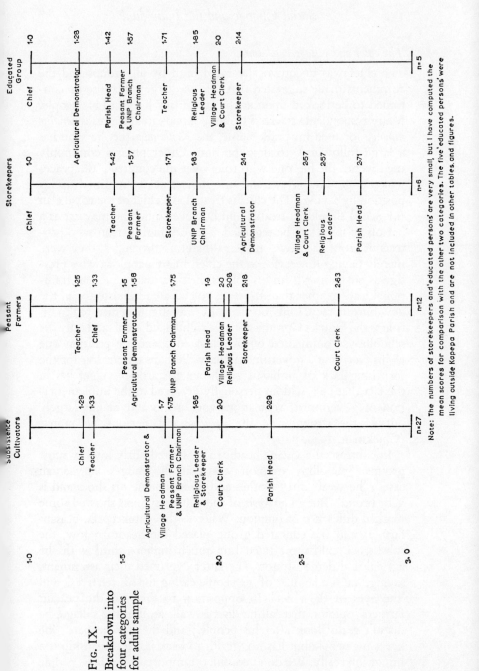

Fig. IX.
Breakdown into
four categories
for adult sample

Subsistence Cultivators

1·29	Chief
1·33	Teacher
	Agricultural Demonstrator &
	Village Headman
1·7	Peasant Farmer & UNIP Branch Chairman
1·75	
1·85	Religious Leader & Storekeeper
2·0	Court Clerk
2·29	Parish Head

n=27

Peasant Farmers

1·25	Teacher
1·33	Chief
1·5	Peasant Farmer
1·58	Agricultural Demonstrator
1·75	UNIP Branch Chairman
1·9	Parish Head
2·0	Village Headman
2·08	Religious Leader
2·18	Storekeeper
2·63	Court Clerk

n=12

Storekeepers

1·0	Chief
1·42	Teacher
1·57	Peasant Farmer
1·71	Storekeeper
1·83	UNIP Branch Chairman
2·14	Agricultural Demonstrator
2·57	Village Headman & Court Clerk
2·57	Religious Leader
2·71	Parish Head

n=6

Educated Group

1·0	Chief
1·28	Agricultural Demonstrator
1·42	Parish Head
1·57	Peasant Farmer & UNIP Branch Chairman
1·71	Teacher
1·85	Religious Leader
2·0	Village Headman & Court Clerk
2·14	Storekeeper

n=5

1·0
1·5
2·0
2·5
3·0

Note: The numbers of storekeepers and 'educated persons' are very small, but I have computed the mean scores for comparison with the other two categories. The five 'educated persons' were living outside Kapepa Parish and are not included in other tables and figures.

The chief and village headman

The chief was unequivocally rated high by all groups and the comments made suggested that this was largely because he continued to be looked upon as the customary leader of his people. Many respondents referred to his politico-ritual status as *'mwine mpanga'* or used his praise name, the *Kankomba* (i.e. he who has a large following), to describe him. Other phrases commonly used were: 'the big one who rules over the country', 'the peacemaker', 'the law giver'; and one subject neatly summed up his position by saying, 'The chief is treated as a chief of the royal clan (*nyendwa*) should be treated and however much he may err as a person he must still be regarded as a very high person who protects us from bad laws.' It seems therefore that unless they were merely paying lip-service to the chief, many people saw his prestige as emanating from his role as their representative and traditional leader rather than from his role as an administrator in the new bureaucracy. Only occasionally was attention directed to his role as the District Commissioner's 'right-hand man' and only the schoolboys commented on his elevated economic position due to his receiving a government salary. Perhaps one reason for the surprising lack of ambivalence shown towards the chief lies in the fact that he is seldom personally involved in the implementation of government regulations and orders and 'stands largely outside the struggles of the groups and persons he unites' (Gluckman, 1949, p. 93).

In contrast, the village headman was rated fairly low by most groups. Schoolboy opinion was that 'he judges very small cases', 'he wears dirty clothes and doesn't shine his shoes and is very proud'. But an analysis of the adult responses showed some marked difference of opinion. Whereas the storekeepers, peasant farmers and the educated group placed the headman low, the subsistence cultivators rated him much higher—third with the agricultural demonstrator. The latter explained their assessment, saying, 'he is a kapitao of his people caring for his relatives', and 'the eyes of the chief'. In opposition to this was the peasant farmers' opinion that 'all he does is walk around the village, he doesn't really look after his people'; and the storekeepers', 'he keeps his people but has no wealth to back it. Headmanship is a minor job really. We don't consider it important, for *those* people are not educated. He implements rules which each individual family can best carry out for themselves.' The teachers concurred with this, one of them adding that 'a person only wants to be headman so that he can be "boss" over his brothers and sisters'. Thus we find that persons of different socio-economic standing in the community differed as to how far they thought the village headman still functioned effectively as senior kinsman, and as an administrative official. They also gave a different weighting to prestige criteria, the storekeepers and teachers emphasizing, for example, the importance of wealth and education as against leadership of a kin group.

Even though as a group the subsistence cultivators rated the headman high, only 37·5 per cent of those interviewed said they would like to become village headman if they had the opportunity, and other groups showed even more disdain for the position. None of the storekeepers or educated people said they would like to become one and only 20 per cent of the peasant farmers. Moreover, many of the peasant farmers said they were their own village headmen anyway. Thus only a minority of individuals aspired to village headmanship and only those subsistence cultivators directly under the authority of the headman felt that the post carried a fair amount of social prestige. Such attitudes correlate with the various social, economic and administrative changes taking place in the community which are tending to undermine much of the village headman's power and prestige.

Parish head and court clerk

I have already provided a sketch of the parish head's responsibilities and so here I consider only those of the clerk's. Briefly, the court clerk is a paid official attached to the chief's court whose duties consist in recording court cases, and issuing receipts for taxes, court fees, fines, and for licences of various kinds. He normally accompanies the chief when out on tour. He is usually required to be of Standard VI (i.e. eight years of schooling), or above. Table XVI shows that both positions were placed at the bottom of the prestige scale by adults and schoolboys, though the parish head received better ratings from the peasant farmer and the educated group. The schoolboys, subsistence cultivators and storekeepers, commenting on their extremely low appraisal of the parish head, gave as their reasons that 'he only receives messages from the chief and passes them on. If no cases are brought to him then he sits idle, for he is parish head only when he is hearing a case and at other times just an ordinary citizen.' Another frequent remark was that he 'trails behind the chief when the latter is on tour and is not paid for the job'. The peasant farmers gave him a slightly higher rating, placing him number six, though it is difficult to see why, unless it is because they attach somewhat more importance to the part he plays in local administration. They would know, for example, that he sometimes is asked by the chief to act as referee for a man wishing to set up as an independent farmer and that he submits regular reports on agricultural progress in his parish. The educated group placed him number three. Here a typical explanation given was that 'he acts in place of the chief, keeps his eye on all things in the country and thus becomes the eyes of the chief and the Boma'. Apparently then educated persons also attach more value to this kind of administrative post than do most other people, or it may be that because of their own social position they have had only slight contact with parish heads and found it rather difficult to assess his position other than in a very generalized form as 'second-in-command' to the chief. Living as they do near to the chief's court and interacting with the chief and the various government officials stationed there, the teachers would take any disputes they might have straight to the court rather than go through a parish head as required for other residents.

The court clerk was consistently rated low by all groups with such comments as, 'There is nothing he does to help the people. He only gets his salary and sits quietly whilst cases are judged. The Europeans wanted things written down so they created the office. But even if the case is relatively straightforward you can count on the clerk writing it down inaccurately and confusing things at a later hearing.'

U.N.I.P. branch chairman and overseer of the Jehovah's Witness congregation

The United National Independence Party first opened a branch office in Chibale Chiefdom in 1962, but since then the number of branches has multiplied and the chiefdom has been granted constituency status. By April 1964, there were six branches distributed throughout the chiefdom and a constituency office at Chief

Chibale Court with its own staff. There were six main officials attached to the Kapepa Branch: a chairman who had overall responsibility for the running of the office, a treasurer, a secretary, a publicity officer, a leader of the Youth Brigade and several junior officials attached to him, and a leader of the Women's Brigade and her officials. None of these officials received a salary or any kind of allowance. The chairman and his officers had been elected by the people of the parish with the one requirement that the chairman be literate and capable of handling correspondence with both the Regional and National headquarters. Most of the branch chairmen in Chibale were young men in their twenties who had received a minimum of about six years' formal schooling.

The other major voluntary association in the parish in 1963–4 was the religious congregation of Jehovah's Witnesses. Jehovah's Witnesses started proselytizing in Chibale Chiefdom towards the end of the 1930's and had since then steadily increased their membership, until in 1963–4 they numbered 11 congregations in the chiefdom, each consisting of between 50 and 100 regular adherents. Each congregation is part of a highly bureaucratized religious organization whose international headquarters is in Brooklyn, New York, with branches scattered throughout the world. The branch office for Zambia is located in Kitwe. At the local congregation level, there are seven officials appointed to manage local congregation affairs. None are paid or receive subsistence money. The overseer is the elder or leader of the congregation and, in the final analysis, it is he who is held responsible for the overall running of the congregation. He must be literate and well versed in the scriptures and is generally required to have held some more junior post in the organization.

In the rating study, the U.N.I.P. branch chairman was placed in the middle range by all groups, with 13 out of the 85 subjects refusing to rate him at all. This, I think, reflected the fact that many people were rather uncertain as to his status position in the community. Some expressed it, saying that, 'U.N.I.P. is a new thing and we haven't yet seen it work. I can't rate the branch chairman for I can't predict the future.' Or again, 'He is part of the new government but we don't know yet whether we shall be made slaves or gain benefits from it.' Others had greater confidence in the party and thought leadership within it conferred high prestige: 'The branch chairman is acting like a lion. He taught people politics in this area and if things get difficult he is prepared to suffer imprisonment. He leads the people whom he represents and is fighting for freedom and independence.' Clearly, however, his position as the leader of a particularly active interest group was picked out by a majority of respondents as commanding some respect though they were as yet unable to say how much.

Except for the schoolboys, all groups gave a fairly low rating to the religious leader. His mean score for the adults placed him sixth. Typical comments were: 'we are in doubt whether he prays to God or not, whether he is wasting his time or not. Christianity is a new thing, Chieftaincy is not.' 'What he preaches is not always true and sooner or later people will find out.' 'He doesn't wish to live with the people, he lives in isolation.' This latter comment refers to the tendency for Jehovah's Witness leaders and their members to live outside the village in small settlements and possibly also to the rather endogamous group life that members of the sect are said to lead. Only five Jehovah's Witnesses agreed to answer the questionnaire. They all placed the overseer in the high respect category. Of the rest of the adults, a few claimed to be Presbyterians of the United Church of Central Africa, but most were non-Christians. All but the Jehovah's Witnesses were nominally members of U.N.I.P. Recent fierce antagonism between U.N.I.P. and Jehovah's Witnesses had arisen over the latters' refusal to buy U.N.I.P. membership cards and to register as voters in government elections. Thus the low rating of the religious leader could be explained in terms of the hostility which existed between U.N.I.P. and Jehovah's Witnesses, though one U.N.I.P. official spoke favourably of the religious leader saying, 'He teaches us to know God and saves us from sin. He wipes away ignorance from the people and looks brightly to the future, and he is respected because he is the leader of his group.'

In contrast, the schoolboys rated the religious leader very high, second to the chief. Their explanation for this took the following form: 'He teaches us to know God. He teaches the people how to read the Bible. He is an expert in the knowledge of God and teaches people how to lead a decent life.' It is not at all clear why they placed the religious leader so high. One possible reason is that the schoolboys tended to see him as belonging to a category of educated experts rather than merely the leader of a religious sect. Within Jehovah's Witness congregations great stress is laid on private Bible study and going out to preach. In order to advance himself spiritually every member must be well versed in the Bible and must acquire the ability to teach others, and to do this he has to be able to read the scriptures. Hence all congregations run literacy classes and special Bible study sessions. The overseer is in charge of all instruction which takes place within the congregation, and makes out reports and gives public lectures. Moreover, when preaching from house-to-house, he dons his best clothes and usually carries a briefcase of books. Perhaps it was these aspects of his role which the schoolboys felt qualified him for high social prestige. When asked the question 'which of the ten positions would you choose to be?', the religious leader was the boys' first choice. Eight of them chose to be a religious leader, seven a chief, six an agricultural demonstrator, five a teacher, three a court clerk, two a storekeeper, two a peasant farmer and two a U.N.I.P. branch chairman. None aspired to village or parish headship.

The teacher and agricultural demonstrator

There is one primary school in Kapepa Parish, with two teachers, and a somewhat larger one in an adjacent parish where there are six teachers working. Of these teachers several are from other Lala chiefdoms in Serenje and two are non-Lala by tribe. There is also an agricultural station situated in the parish where about six agricultural demonstrators work. From there they tour the area offering technical assistance to farmers and Turkish tobacco growers. Several of them are also strangers to the chiefdom and non-Lala by tribe.

All groups, except the teachers themselves, agreed that the school teacher commanded high respect. It was said of him, that 'he is wisdom itself, his authority derives from book knowledge, and he is helping the people to advance. He teaches the children to speak English so that they can converse with Europeans and so that they can write letters for those villagers who cannot write.' Other comments were, 'The teachers are our real leaders for they teach us things of which we are ignorant. They are the mothers of this country. They have good jobs and keep their families well.' The teachers placed themselves in the middle range. The

M

reason for this may be that they tended to regard themselves as being rather apart from the local status system, though felt that their job in itself had some general prestige value.

The mean ranking for the agricultural demonstrator for both adults and schoolboys placed him in number four and three positions respectively. Typical comments were, 'He is playing an important role in the development of the country. He is respected for doing a European job because he is trained and shares his knowledge with people so that they may become *basambashi* (i.e. people who are reasonably wealthy and who show this by dressing well, eating good food and owning major items of property, like cattle, farming implements, cars, sewing machines, etc.). He is the brains of the country, and teaching new methods of agriculture means development (*buyantashi*).'

Of the adult sample, the only group that did not rate the agricultural demonstrator fairly high was the storekeepers. This was largely, I think, because storekeepers do not depend on his advice in the same way that the farmers and villagers do. Storekeepers are interested in commerce, not agriculture. As one storekeeper put it, 'I can't see what great work the agricultural demonstrator does around here!'

Peasant farmer and storekeeper

In Chapter II, I described the recent development of cash-crop farming and the rise of stores in the parish, and gave some account of the general economic position of farmers and businessmen resident in the parish. The farmer and storekeeper stand out from the rest of the population as men who have achieved notable success through exploiting the new opportunities available in a developing money economy.

The general consensus of opinion about the peasant farmer was that he commanded medium to high respect, though the schoolboys' rating was slightly lower, probably because they attached a higher value to the educated person. The peasant farmer was described by many respondents as 'an independent person who gets a lot of money from his sale of crops and is able to live a decent life as a *basambashi*. He does not beg from others. The country cannot function without him for he provides food for the masses. Even the storekeepers cannot operate without him.' A dominant theme in most of the replies was that the peasant farmer had learnt to exploit the natural environment more effectively through the use of the plough and improved farming techniques, and as a result had amassed a certain amount of wealth. Yet all that he had gained in the way of material goods had been achieved legitimately for he remained closely linked to the land and to the customary mode of livelihood. He therefore could claim some degree of respect from his fellow countrymen whose common aim was to grow enough food for their families and to have enough money to care adequately for their families' other needs.

In contrast, and despite the fact that the storekeeper is generally more prosperous than others in the community, he was rated fairly low. Here the main reason given was that he had achieved a position of economic dominance through the direct exploitation of ordinary people, and had severed his links with the land. 'It is we, the people, who make him rich. He is a money-monger stealing money from his friends and not caring about anyone other than himself. He is a hard man because he charges high prices for his goods. Stores have suddenly sprung up but it is not the kind of wealth I consider proper.' In Kapepa then there is as yet no generally recognized 'business' ethic which allocates high prestige to the role of the entrepreneur.

The storekeepers' assessment of themselves took a different line: 'We made the villages look like town by bringing town goods to the rural area, nobody else!' They placed themselves number four in the scale of prestige.

The results for these two positions raise an interesting problem which I take up again in the next chapter, the question of the relation between, and interpenetration of, town and country values. In some respects the farmer and storekeeper display similar styles of life and in some contexts they are both described as 'townsmen' (*bena tauni*). Yet whilst the farmer is frequently praised for his achievements, the storekeeper is despised.

The general pattern of prestige that emerges from the study can now be summarized. Figure VII shows the mean ratings for the total sample. The chief heads the list, but is followed by a group of educated persons, the teacher, the religious leader and the agricultural demonstrator. Thus education and specialist knowledge are seen to be important criteria for determining prestige and status in Kapepa. Next comes the peasant farmer whom 58 per cent of the adults said they would like to be if they had the opportunity. He is respected for his independence, his wealth and his attachment to land. The United National Independence Party branch chairman in 1963-4 was in an uncertain position and was placed in the middle of the scale, but may well have been accorded higher prestige since then, following the changes which have taken place in the system of local government subsequent to Zambia acquiring full independent status.

The village headman was rated fairly low. Some of the reasons for this rating have been discussed earlier in the chapter, where I argued that his changing status position can be related to a complex of factors: the breakdown of the village as a major residential grouping and the development of new settlement forms, the transfer of many of the headman's administrative duties to the parish head following the implementation of the parish system of local government, the general erosion of his politico-ritual role and the emergence of new criteria for evaluating status which offer alternative ways of achieving status within the community. Thus today the desire to attain headmanship of a village seems very largely outweighed by the desire to gain status in some other spheres, in a political party or religious organization, or through acquiring wealth or education. The present dilemma of the village headman in Kapepa is perhaps best summed up by a text taken from an interview I had with one such Lala headman:

In the old days hunters honoured the headman by presenting him with a leg of any game animal killed. If beer was brewed in the village one big calabash was sent over to the headman, and sometimes men of the village would assist the headman by cutting his *citeme* garden, finishing the job in a day or two. They did all this because the headman cared for his people (*kusunga bantu bakwe*), kept them free from wild animals and disease (i.e. he had ritual responsibilities towards them). Nowadays, the Europeans have changed all this. Today a hunter gives small pieces of meat to his close kin and sells the rest. The headman no longer receives a special calabash of beer, he buys his own. These are the reasons why I do not like being a village headman. There are few benefits attached to it. I shall hand over the headmanship to my younger brother and move out to establish my own farm. Village headmanship is a name only (*busulutani buli isina yenka*).

At the bottom of the prestige scale come the parish head and court clerk who are both closely identified with the colonial administration and for that reason seem to be given little respect. In the pilot questionnaire the Boma or District messenger, who acts as a kind of local policeman, was also included and he too was rated very low.

The low rating for the parish head raises an intriguing analytical problem. This is the relation between social power (i.e. having some degree of command over the actions of others) and social prestige. Earlier I outlined the kinds of administrative duties undertaken by the parish head and suggested that this is a social position which indirectly carries with it a fair degree of social power. Yet despite this, parish headship was accorded very low respect in the prestige study. The main reason for this apparent discrepancy was, I think, that in the rating questionnaire people tended to see parish headship as an administrative post of the same type as that of the chief or village headman but possessing none of the latters' 'traditional' status. Unlike the chief, and to a lesser extent the village headman, the parish head has no easily identifiable political following. He was therefore evaluated merely as a very minor officer in the modern administrative bureaucracy, on a par with the court clerk and district messenger. The fact that people preferred to take their disputes to the parish head without consulting their village headman never emerged from the prestige rating.

Within this general pattern of prestige there were some slight divergences of opinion among the subjects interviewed and it has been shown that these varied according to socio-economic status. The most striking difference of opinion was over the rating of the religious leader, and this I related to the different criteria used to evaluate him. The schoolboys saw him primarily as an educated person displaying a style of life to which they themselves apparently aspired, whilst the adults regarded him as the leader of a somewhat fanatical sect whose sights were fixed on the attainment of status in Jehovah's New World Kingdom rather than on status in this. It is of some significance that out of some 20 adult Jehovah's Witnesses interviewed only five agreed to answer the questionnaire. There was an interesting uniformity in the reasons given for refusing. In general they argued that since all men suffer in their human condition no one stands out as commanding higher respect, except the religious leader who represents Jehovah's New World Society and who, together with his fellow believers, preaches 'the good news of the everlasting life' (*iliyashi ilisuma muyayaya*). All other positions are 'useless' (*cabecabe*) and part of the Old World order of things. Despite their response to the questionnaire, however, Jehovah's Witnesses do have a highly consistent ideology of social status, with an emphasis placed on becoming a *basambashi*, which as I shall later show, bears some relation to their pattern of social action.

I wish to stress that my aim here has been simply to isolate those factors in the situation which seem important nowadays for the evaluation of social status, and my discussion of the changing position of the village headman has had this end in view. I do not claim to have shown that, either in the past or during the present time, there exists a single hierarchy of prestige. For more than anything else this rating study has demonstrated that obviously there exist several dimensions of social prestige, which may or may not be hierarchically organized and may or may not overlap. Moreover I accept the criticism often made of studies of this kind that it may not be very meaningful to compare the respect accorded different social positions by plotting the results on a single scale of status.

Nevertheless the study does, I think, yield results in that it has helped to identify the more important criteria used by the people themselves when evaluating status, and has provided some useful information as to which social positions are more highly prized and why.

CHAPTER VII

THE DYNAMICS OF POWER AND PRESTIGE

Before describing the social situation which forms the core of this chapter, it is necessary to outline briefly the verbal categories commonly used to conceptualize status differences as they are relevant for understanding some of the details of the case itself.

Categories of social status

As I indicated earlier, several vernacular words are used to mean 'respect' or 'social prestige', but the three most commonly used are *bucindami*, *mucinshi* and *bukankala*. Each of these words, however, tends to have a slightly different referent. *Mucinshi* is normally used to refer to the kind of respect that exists between specific categories of kinsmen and affines (e.g. the respect that a son-in-law should show towards his parents-in-law, or a sister's son should show towards his maternal uncle), *bukankala* to the kind associated with holding office within the politico-administrative system and is the term most frequently used when speaking of the prestige of chiefs or headmen. The third term, *bucindami*, appears to have a somewhat wider meaning and is used to cover both ascribed and achieved status. Hence, though the term may be used to describe the status of a chief, it may also be meaningfully applied to the kind of respect that a successful peasant farmer or storekeeper commands.

Other words are used to specify status achieved through wealth, education or style of life. Most of these terms are used in the proper noun form and describe the attributes of a particular category of individual. A wealthy man is described as *bawina*, which apparently derives from the English verb 'to win' and could perhaps be translated as someone who has achieved notable financial success. A *bawina* is most typically described as a person 'who has money, cattle, guns or who owns a store or tearoom'. Most of the storekeepers in Kapepa are regarded as *bawina* and some of the more successful farmers too. Thus to be a *bawina* a person must show evidence of considerable capital investment and would not be judged one, for example, simply on the basis of how much beer he buys at beer drinks, for this might be a very temporary affluence.

Another concept, one which tends to be associated with *bawina*, is *basambashi*. This word is used generally to describe someone who enjoys a reasonably high standard of living. He dresses well, eats well and possesses plenty of furniture and other items of property and is said 'to govern himself' (*kuiteka mwine*). Successful farmers and storekeepers are given as examples. The essence of this concept is that it focuses on style of life attributes rather than merely on financial resources. Whereas *bawina* singles out wealth as a distinguishing characteristic, *basambashi* tends to place emphasis on the patterns of consumption and on the types of consumer goods purchased. Thus, for example, one wealthy farmer in the parish owning about 30 head of cattle was often referred to as *bawina* but never as *basambashi* because in appearance and general standards of eating and housing (he did not build a brick house or acquire Western-type furniture) he could not easily be distinguished from the rest of the village population. Whilst, on the other hand, a school teacher who, when compared with many of the farmers and storekeepers in the parish could not be considered their equal in material possessions, was nevertheless regarded as a *basambashi* because of the way he conducted himself. He had suits, drank tea and ate European-type foods and was economically independent of his kinsfolk. Similarly, a retired medical orderly who lived with his two wives (one of whom was from South Africa) was called *basambashi* but did not qualify as a *bawina*. The criteria used here were that he always purchased bread, tea and sugar at the local store and had good furniture at home, but he possessed no cattle or major items of property and was only able to maintain this standard of living because he received a small monthly pension from the government for his long service with the Health Department. In general, however, a person who is regarded as a *basambashi* will tend also to be a *bawina*, and this is most clearly the case with the storekeepers in the parish.

An educated man is described as *basambilila* (from the verb *kusambilila* to learn, to acquire knowledge) and is said to possess wisdom (*balimano*) and to look like a *bwana*. The term *bwana* comes from the Swahili for master and until recently has been applied only to European males. Nowadays it tends to be used towards anyone considered of high status and has been popularized as a more general term of address by the United National Independence Party who often use it towards party officials, or sometimes even to ordinary party members. In this context, the term *bwana* is mainly used to indicate that the educated person is well acquainted with modern ways of life and commands respect because of it. The real mark of an educated man is that he can read and write in the vernacular (one man suggested that one could recognize an educated man by the pencil he carries in his top pocket) and displays a certain cunning or ingenuity (*kucenjela*) in arguments. Though teachers and clerks are most frequently given as examples of the educated man, some persons also suggested that some Jehovah's Witnesses, because of their literacy and training in debate, might also be described as *basambilila*.

Implicit in this discussion has been the contrast between the *bawina, basambashi* and *basambilila*, and the rest of the population who command little respect for their wealth, style of life or educational achievements. These people are the villagers (*nshimishi*). Some of them may be accorded some prestige either as the headman of a village (*basulutani*), or as the warden (*inkoswe*) or senior of a group of matrikin, but few will be wealthy or sufficiently well educated to read and write in the vernacular, and they will be typically described as leading a village or country way of life (*kukonka mibele ya calo*). Conversely, *basambashi* are frequently referred to as 'townsmen' (*bena tauni; mwina tauni*, sing.). Hence differences in wealth, education and style of life are often expressed in terms of a dichotomy between town and country. This emerges most strikingly in the case of the storekeeper, who is the *bawina* and *basambashi par excellence*, and who is reckoned by most persons to exhibit a townsman's way of life. I previously mentioned that as a residential unit the store symbolizes an extension of 'town' values to Kapepa; thus the storekeeper is seen as the exemplar of town values. Though he relies on the local people for their custom, he remains apart from them: he does not depend for his subsistence on the exploitation of the natural resources of the chiefdom, and his commercial interests orient him to maintaining strong links with the urban areas. Moreover his general standard of living and style of life are markedly different from that of villagers, and frequently he is also a stranger to the chiefdom or parish. In addition to the storekeeper, teachers, agricultural demonstrators and peasant farmers are often designated *bena tauni* as they too may display similar styles of life.

One of the more interesting aspects of the way in which the concept of *mwina tauni* is used is that a man does not necessarily have to have spent much time actually residing in town, so long as he exhibits the right attributes of the 'townsman' as perceived by the people of the parish. Thus, for example, a teacher may have only visited town to see friends and relatives and may not have lived or worked there for any lengthy period, but is still regarded as a 'townsman'; and the same may be true of an agricultural demonstrator or peasant farmer.

CASE STUDY: THE VISIT OF PATI, THE TOWNSMAN[1]

At the time of the events which I shall describe, Bombwe's store was being run by his sister, Chiboli (II, D29), assisted by her son, Patrick (II, E17). Bombwe himself was still working and living in town with his wife and children. Katwishi had been farming for about six years and Lusefu, his mother's brother (II, C6), remained headman of the village. Timoti, Bombwe's other brother (II, D34) and business partner, had recently died in a mine accident at Bancroft (Chililabombwe). Most other members of the Lusefu family lived either in the village or at their own settlements within close proximity to the store.

In April 1964, Bombwe wrote to Lusefu telling him that he planned to send his son-in-law, Pati (II, E13), on a visit to Lala country so that he might meet Bombwe's kin. Pati is Kaonde by tribe and works as a hospital clerk. His wife, Eliza (II, E12), Bombwe's eldest daughter, is a nurse in the same hospital. The young couple were to spend about two weeks at the store in Kapepa and would be accompanied by Pati's mother and Bombwe's wife, NaBombwe (II, D26).

Bombwe sent explicit instructions on what must be done to prepare for the visit. The store and surrounds were to be cleaned and the spare room behind the store got ready for the two older women to sleep in, and Pati and his wife were to take over Patrick's three-roomed brick house. Chiboli was instructed to take charge of the feeding arrange-

---

[1] On pp. 100–6 I described the fission of Lusefu Village, discussed why Katwishi (II, D35) left the village and opened a store near Kapepa school, and how he was eventually levered out of the store by his elder brother, Bombwe (II, D25), and set up his own farm. I return now to this same set of people and examine a further series of incidents involving them.

ments and to stock up with various Lala specialities. Pati, it was said, was very keen to taste finger millet *nshima* (porridge): being Kaonde his staple was sorghum and he had never eaten finger millet. Lusefu was told to slaughter one of the cattle in Pati's honour and to present the meat to him when he arrived. For his part Bombwe promised to send plenty of bread, sugar, tea and some crates of bottled beer and drums of *chibuku* beer. Bombwe emphasized that every effort should be made to give Pati a warm welcome and Lusefu should see to it that all the kin came along to greet him.

On the day before the visitors were due to arrive Chiboli was seen cleaning out the store and grinding large quantities of millet. She was helped by her classificatory sister's daughter, NaNason (II, E9), who lived at a nearby store. Chiboli also employed two young boys to slash the grass around the store dwellings and to clear the motor track leading to it. But throughout these cleaning operations Chiboli grumbled to herself, to NaNason and to people passing about 'these *basambilila* (educated types) who were coming and who must have everything so clean'.[1]

Day I

On the day of the visit, Bombwe's lorry drove in bringing *chibuku* beer, a hundred-pound bag of maize flour, a bag of charcoal and various items for the store. Later Pati arrived in his shiny saloon car with his mother, his mother-in-law, his wife and his younger teenage brother. Katwishi and Chiboli were there to meet them, and they were shortly joined by Lusefu and others from the village.

After the visitors had settled in it was decided to open the beer that Bombwe had sent. But just as Chiboli was about to serve it, NaBombwe stepped in to tell her it was to be sold as usual and not given out freely as everyone had thought. This created an immediate uproar amongst the gathering, but NaBombwe insisted and went on to deliver an attack on the Lusefu people present, saying that it was always them who benefited from her husband's wealth and never her own matrikin. Though fuming, none of Lusefu's people wished to make a scene in front of Pati's mother and so Chiboli undertook to sell the beer.

Two drinking groups formed. Pati and his wife were served with beer freely in the house, together with Katwishi, who had skilfully manœuvred his way into their group by arguing that as he was

[1] This was the background to their arrival. I now describe in chronological order the major events which took place during their visit.

standing in for Bombwe as Pati's 'father-in-law' he should be given the earliest opportunity of getting acquainted with him. The second group consisted of NaBombwe, Pati's mother and the Lusefu people and neighbours. This group gathered inside the store building and had to buy the beer at the normal price of a shilling per large mug.

For a while Chiboli served the beer without interruption. But soon NaBombwe sharply criticized her for not washing the returned mug before serving the next person. At first Chiboli ignored her comments but finally when NaBombwe collected together all the serving para-phernalia to wash them and brought in a dish of clean water so that the mug might be washed after each sale, Chiboli got very annoyed. She grabbed the dish of water and hurled it away, refusing outright to bring more drinking mugs when NaBombwe suggested this as an alternative. Chiboli then resumed serving beer in the same manner as before.

Chiboli and NaBombwe clashed once more before the evening was out. This time the issue was the sleeping arrangements. NaBombwe and Pati's mother refused to sleep in the old store, complaining that it was unclean and that Chiboli had not whitewashed it as Bombwe had instructed. They suggested instead that they should sleep in the new store where Chiboli normally slept. The latter replied that, as she was the one with the key to the building and had helped to build it, she was the one who was entitled to sleep in it. NaBombwe retorted, 'And who will sleep there when Bombwe retires from town?' 'I will,' answered Chiboli, 'and your husband will have to build a new house. Moreover I have not yet been paid for the work I have put into the store, either as manager or bricklayer!' The first round had been won by Chiboli and so Bombwe's wife and Pati's mother retired to the room in the old store building.

Day II

On the following morning NaBombwe altered the cooking arrange-ments. Although Chiboli had been asked by Bombwe to cook for Pati and his wife, NaBombwe effectively excluded her by producing her own charcoal burner and cooking utensils and her own maize flour which, she claimed, was the right sort of flour for porridge for a seasoned townsman like Pati, as it did not lie heavy in the stomach like the local millet *nshima*. She had brought her own burner, she argued, so that her pots would not be blackened on a wood fire. Other food-stuffs she required were taken from the store. Chiboli objected strongly to the way she was doing this, saying that in the past Bombwe had often accused her of taking things from the store without paying for them. And to register her complaint she drank two bottles of Coca-Cola in NaBombwe's presence while the latter was in the store collecting some sugar and tea.

NaBombwe also arranged for some local boys to take an empty 44-gallon drum to the stream to be filled with water because she said she had no wish to fetch water on her head. As a townswoman she was not used to it.

When the food was ready for serving, Pati and Eliza were served in their own house and the two mothers ate together in the forecourt of the kitchen. Chiboli and her sister Changwe (II, D32) were forced to prepare their own food and eat separately.

Later the same morning, Katwishi, who had slept at the store, hurried off to summon the Lusefu people to come and greet Pati and the others, and to organize the slaughtering of the beast. An hour or so afterwards, Lusefu, the village headman, accompanied by several women from the village, arrived at the store. As they approached, NaBombwe dashed over to Pati's house ordering her daughter Eliza to tell her husband to come out of the house 'for the people will dirty the floor when they enter'. Pati then had two chairs taken outside in readiness for the guests. When the party arrived, Pati offered Lusefu one of the chairs to sit on and insisted that he accept despite NaBombwe's attempt to get Pati himself to take it. The other chair was taken by Pati's younger brother. Throughout all this Pati was rather embarrassed by the situation and both parties quickly found some excuse to break up the gathering. No gifts were brought by Lusefu or the others on this first meeting.

Several other individuals came to meet the visitors during the day. Two primary school teachers living at the nearby school arrived bringing gifts of bread and sugar; as also did an agricultural demonstrator based at Kapepa. The parish head came to greet them and then assisted with the slaughtering and skinning of the beast which was to be presented to Pati. NaNason (II, E9), the young wife of a neighbouring storekeeper and classificatory daughter of Chiboli, came over to greet the young couple and stayed on to talk to Eliza about cosmetics. As she left the house she commented to a group of Lusefu people sitting close by that she was very pleased to see her 'sister' married to an educated and rich man (*abasambilila elyo abawina*), and went on to explain that she will also one day marry a rich man and enjoy the luxuries of good living, like travelling in a motor-car, eating good food, wearing fine dresses and powder on her skin every day as Eliza does.

Pati was also visited by the leader of the local congregation of Jehovah's Witnesses, Zakeyo, who lived nearby and who owned the diesel-engined grinding mill close to the store. Zakeyo spent a few minutes with Pati introducing himself. Pati, himself a Jehovah's Witness, seemed pleased to hear of the work of the local congregation, so Zakeyo promised to call in again some time.

Others who stopped by to greet the visitors were Sikelo, a local village headman, together with a man from his village, another agricultural demonstrator from the area, and Machisa (II, E15), sister's son to Bombwe, who had arrived from Mkushi where he had married. During his visit, Machisa got into conversation with his 'brother-in-law' Koda (II, E1) who suggested that 'the Lusefu people only honour a son-in-law if he is in paid employment because they are only interested in money. They never honour a man if he is only a villager.' Koda went on to state that they had never honoured him in this way 'and yet a Kaonde is honoured. This man we shall never meet again if Eliza divorces Pati.' Machisa agreed with Koda's sentiments but said he did not know what one could do about it. Similar comments were also made by other villagers like Sikelo and his friend.

Around midday Pati and Katwishi decided to travel to Broken Hill (Kabwe), some 150 miles away, to pick up more *chibuku* beer as the beer sent by Bombwe was already finished. They left in the lorry and did not return until after dark. They brought back with them several four-gallon drums of *chibuku* worth about £4. Pati privately instructed his mother-in-law to sell this as she had the first consignment from Bombwe, and told her not to put the money into the store. Instead she should keep it and enjoy the marriage of her daughter just as Bombwe and others had done, and he went on to say that the store was full of Bombwe's matrikin.

Later that evening quarrelling once more broke out between Chiboli and NaBombwe. As before, the initial issue was the question of taking items from the store, but this time it ranged more widely over the question of the control, ownership and inheritance of the store and of Bombwe's other property, and spread to include Katwishi, who had not yet recovered from the heavy drinking session he had had with Pati in Broken Hill (Kabwe). Katwishi was clearly ready for a show-down.

NaBombwe triggered off the affair by asserting that in future Chi-

boli would not work in the store because she regularly helped herself
to such items as cooking oil, candles, bread and coffee without paying
for them. In reply to this, Chiboli said that she had only taken things
from the store equal to what NaBombwe herself had taken for her
own use since her arrival, and argued further that NaBombwe had
never shared with her any of the foodstuffs she had taken. NaBombwe
then said, 'Do you realize that the *cikanda*[1] roots and groundnuts which
you buy here and send to Kitwe are sold by me at the market place?
Thus I also suffer like you do, selling things.' At this point Katwishi
intervened to deliver a lengthy attack on her. The nub of his extremely
vitriolic speech was that 'whether you sell *cikanda* roots or not does
not alter the fact that you are wasting your time and energy. We are
the owners of the wealth (*bene bafyuma*). We shall take over the store
and goods when Bombwe dies and not your children as you yourself
think, and I, being the only surviving brother, will take charge of them.
When Timoti, my other brother, died recently I took over his property
and the same will happen on Bombwe's death. So whatever you do
now, however hard you work, you are simply enriching me!' With
this NaBombwe exploded, saying, 'when my husband dies you will
not be able to treat me like you have Timoti's wife.[2] We shall keep
the wealth for I shall be caring for his children. And if you interfere
and try to cut me out then I shall burn down the store for I will not
suffer for nothing.'

Katwishi responded to this by replying that she dare not burn down
the store for she depended on it financially: 'Bombwe only married
you. You were poor. Bombwe has made you what you are. He has
given you good dresses to wear and provided you with money to buy
food to eat. But as yet Bombwe has not helped any of us; and this is
the reason why we shall hang on to the store. It is quite clear that
Bombwe now feels that he has wasted much on your family and now
wishes to give some to his own kin. We shall now tell him of your
intentions so that he can quickly divorce you. You will then look on
and see us enjoying his wealth. Bombwe, you see, is clever. He has sent
Pati to get to know his own kin and not yours, though according to

[1] *Cikanda* is an edible tuber grown on the dambo margins.
[2] Here she was probably referring to the way in which Katwishi, on hearing
of his brother's death, went immediately to Bancroft (Chililabombwe) and
removed from his house all the furniture and clothing; and how he later tried
to connive with Timoti's wife to get a large share of the compensation money
due to her on her husband's death.

Lala custom, Pati should have been taken to meet your people and not us. From all this, it is obvious that Bombwe wants his own kin to prosper from the store and not yours. Note too, that it is we who have the cattle, and not you or your kin.' Here NaBombwe interjected saying that her own brother had just returned from town and had purchased a grinding mill and would soon be making plenty of money. 'And when this is working we shall be much richer than your family.' Disregarding this point, Chiboli drove the wedge in further saying that since NaBombwe's kin at present had no cattle how could they have honoured Pati in the way in which the Lusefu people had done. Such words left NaBombwe very upset and she vowed that she would be leaving with Pati's mother in a few days when the lorry went to Kitwe.

Later that evening NaBombwe and Pati's mother discussed the day's events with my research assistant. Both expressed their disapproval of the way in which Pati had been received by the Lusefu family. They drew attention to the way in which Katwishi had been instrumental in persuading Pati to fetch more beer and criticized him also for being far too familiar with him. Katwishi was his 'father-in-law' and should therefore have been very much more reserved in his presence. He should not have eaten with him, nor have asked for money to improve his farm (as was alleged by the two women). He should certainly not have tried to extract gifts from him, in the form of beer or goods. (It was asserted that Katwishi had asked Pati to give him a suit or a jacket.) In short, he was far too friendly, behaving with Pati as if he were his 'brother-in-law' (*mulamu*). NaBombwe added that she could not understand why Katwishi had not learnt from her good example: 'I fear (*nkotina*) Pati. I do not talk with him like a friend. I do not eat with him like Katwishi does, nor do I enter his house.' Throughout the discussion Pati's mother corroborated what NaBombwe said and concluded that 'these people are country bumpkins (*kamushi*). What more can one expect?'

Day III

The next day was devoted almost entirely to beer drinking and many people from nearby settlements gathered at the store. The beer was sold as usual by Chiboli, but the proceeds went to NaBombwe. In the morning, however, Katwishi persuaded Pati to drive to the main road at Mulilima where they could buy bottled beer. In an unusually generous mood Katwishi bought Pati 12 pints of beer and Pati recipro-cated by buying two for him. They then returned with the beer and settled down in Pati's house to drink it. They were later joined by Lusefu.

During the course of their drinking several of Bombwe's kin arrived to offer gifts to Pati. Those who had not yet met Pati were introduced by Katwishi, the headman Lusefu assuming a completely passive role. The first person to arrive was Saulo's wife (II, D1). She brought a chicken and some millet flour and went straight into the house to make the presentation. NaBombwe had tried to get her to hand over the gift so that she might take it into Pati herself. However, Chiboli anticipated her move and insisted that Saulo's wife be allowed to enter the house and Katwishi supported her, arguing that she was Bombwe's 'sister' and must therefore meet Pati in person. NaBombwe stated that she accepted his point of view but asked 'who was to polish the floor of the house after people had trampled continually in and out of it? Eliza was fed up with sweeping the floor each time a village person (*kamushi*) entered the house. People who wear no shoes have dusty feet and leave large footprints behind.' Saulo's wife was obviously annoyed about it and made her stay as brief as possible. Outside she asked NaBombwe why it was that Pati and his wife were brought to live at the store at Kapepa school when they should have been taken to Lusefu Village where they could get to know Bombwe's matrikin individually and chat with them at their leisure. NaBombwe said that the village was dirty and unhygienic and that Eliza and Pati would get sick if they stayed there. Saulo's wife left in disgust.

The next person to arrive was Katwishi's second wife (II, D36) who brought *nshima* and chicken and gave it to Pati in the house. She wore shoes. Mwitwa (II, D40) followed her, also with *nshima* and chicken. Again he was allowed to enter the house without comment for he wore shoes. Later Mwitwa moved over to join one of the drinking groups outside and got talking to this group about 'townsmen' (*bena tauni*). He suggested that if one wished to bankrupt a townsman then one should give him many gifts when he arrived in the village so that on leaving he would feel obliged to give lots of gifts too. This would mean he would probably return to town with nothing but one shirt and a pair of trousers! He himself expected Pati to leave him a shirt or some money in return for his generosity.

Shortly after this Lameck (II, D37), Katwishi's classificatory brother, arrived in his motor-van. Lameck, the owner of a relatively prosperous peasant farm, lived about two miles away and did not normally use his vehicle when visiting the stores. He entered the house and was

N

formally introduced by Katwishi who said, 'Here is our elder brother Lameck, but from very distant ancestors. He does not belong to our kin group.' Lameck was extremely upset to be introduced thus and quickly left the house. Once outside, he complained to the rest of the Lusefu people, saying that Katwishi was trying to appear as the big man around the place so that Pati would give him many gifts. He also criticized him for being too familiar with his 'son-in-law', claiming that he should pay the customary gift of two or three shillings so that they might be permitted to talk freely together.[1] Lameck did not stay to drink beer with the others but returned home in his van.

Several other persons passing through or arriving for the beer drink called in briefly to greet Eliza and Pati. Among these was Zakeyo who went to inform Pati of the Jehovah's Witness Assembly to be held in a few days' time. Pati told Zakeyo he would probably go and would see him later to find out how to get there. His visit coincided with Pati's meal-time and so Zakeyo ate with him. Other visitors included Tomo, the local U.N.I.P. branch chairman, who only stayed for a few minutes and then joined one of the drinking groups outside; Saini, a peasant farmer, and Lacketi, who had recently returned from the Copperbelt. None of the other persons who came to the beer drink bothered to introduce themselves.

Outside several beer drinking groups had formed. For a time the conversation in each centred around Pati and his visit. Later I shall return to describe these conversations, but here I wish only to outline the composition of the various groups.

Group A consisted of the village headman, Sikelo, and two men from his village, Wilson, his sister's son, and Henry, a young man married into the village.

Group B was composed of the farmer, Saini, his friend Lacketi, and Bwalya, one of the teachers at Kapepa Primary School.

Group C consisted of Tomo, the U.N.I.P. chairman, and his friend and party colleague, Kunda, who was Bombwe's lorry driver. Both were young men in their twenties and had married into the same descent group. They later joined *Group A*.

Group D was similarly made up of two young men, Patrick, Chiboli's unmarried son, and Koda, Patrick's 'brother-in-law'.

At one stage in the drinking Sikelo and Henry attempted to join

[1] Here he inverted the normal custom of the son-in-law presenting a gift to the father-in-law (*kushikula shifyala*). Such a custom allows for a temporary relaxation of the expected norms of behaviour between in-laws.

Saini and Lacketi but were told to buy their own beer and not to beg it from others. After they had left Lacketi commented to Saini that it was no use drinking with villagers (*kamushi*) for they never paid their way properly, it was best to drink only with other *bena tauni*. That was why he, Lacketi, liked drinking with Saini.

Day IV

A beer drink was held at Lameck's farm on the fourth day, to which many of the Lusefu people went. Pati, his wife and the two mothers remained at the store throughout the day. They discussed the possibility of returning to Broken Hill (Kabwe) the next day. The composition of the beer drinking groups at Lameck's followed roughly the same pattern as at the store on the previous day. Saini and Lacketi were joined by three other peasant farmers and formed what they themselves called the 'gentlemen group'. Anyone who joined them had to be prepared to buy rounds of beer, for if they 'wanted to appear as "gentlemen" and "townsmen" then they must act like it'. The Lusefu people fell into two groups, one consisting of Katwishi and Lusefu, and the other made up of younger men who were married into the village. Sikelo, the other headman, drank with his wife and was later joined by others from his village and from other villages and individual settlements in the area. Katwishi and Lusefu discussed the problems concerning the store and the way in which NaBombwe had acted and it was decided that Lusefu should write a letter of complaint to Bombwe. This would be taken to him on the following day when the lorry left.

Day V

NaBombwe and Pati's mother returned to Kitwe with the lorry, but the former planned to travel back with another consignment of beer for sale. Lusefu came to the store to say goodbye to Pati's mother and presented her with four chickens, some Livingstone potatoes and some millet flour to take home to her husband. He gave Patrick the letter to hand to Bombwe. In it he criticized the way Pati had stayed at the store and not the village, the way in which he took over the best brick house, the way NaBombwe encouraged her daughter and husband to regard the village as a dirty place, the way in which people had been kept out of the house unless they wore shoes, and the general lack of respect shown to Bombwe's relatives.

During the night Bwalya had gone hunting with Patrick, using

Bombwe's gun that Pati had borrowed from Lusefu. Pati provided the ammunition and the arrangement was that Bwalya would give Pati the meat and in return would receive ammunition for his own use. One duiker was killed that night, which Pati's mother took to town with her. Pati planned to make this a permanent arrangement if he could get permission for Bwalya to use the gun. He would sell the meat on the Copperbelt. Later when Lusefu learnt that he was to receive no part of the killed duiker he was very disgruntled.

During the morning NaNason again visited Eliza, and when her husband beckoned her to return and cook for him, she refused. At this the husband came over to the store and dragged her away, threatening to beat her when he got her home. Eliza was enraged by his behaviour and told him he should not come near the house again for he 'was not yet awake (*taulashibuka*)'. He was 'still in the dark (*tabulaca*) and "primitive"'. During this fracas, Pati conveniently slipped away to clean his car.

While NaBombwe was away Lusefu managed to persuade the young couple to visit his village to meet his matrikin and see for themselves whether the village was dirty or not. That afternoon Pati and Eliza walked over to the village to see the place. While there they were offered various foods to eat but each time Eliza declined the hospitality and suggested that they give them some chickens and maize flour instead to take home with them, which they did. Later, back at the store, she was overheard telling her husband that her mother had been right: the village was dirty and she had no intention of visiting it again.

Day VI

Bwalya the teacher visited Pati to discuss the arrangement for hunting that evening. Pati had originally intended accompanying Bwalya but changed his mind because he said he had no old denims to wear.

Later in the day more gifts were brought by Bombwe's relatives. Malita (II, D9), his classificatory sister, arrived with a chicken and some millet flour. At the time of her arrival Eliza was busy in the kitchen and so she entered the house to present the gift to Pati himself. But after she had left Eliza ordered a young girl from the village to polish the floor and put the chairs outside so that if anyone else arrived they could sit outside. Kalikeka (II, C11) was the next to arrive. He brought a chicken; and Koda's wife, who was staying at the store with Chiboli, also presented a chicken. As NaBombwe was away, Chiboli wanted to cook a meal for Pati but Eliza refused to allow her, saying that she did not know enough domestic science to cook for Pati.

Day VII

Pati went to see Bwalya and drank some local beer privately with him. This was the first time he had tasted it. It was served hot and Pati likened it to hot tea. He told Bwalya that he had enjoyed it and would like to drink some more on another occasion.

In the afternoon Pati gave his wife a driving lesson around the school grounds watched by a number of local people. After this Lameck's wife arrived with some maize and beans for them. She walked straight into the house over the polished floor. This exasperated Eliza, who declared that she had finally given up trying to keep her house clean and would tell her father all about the way in which they had been treated since their arrival at Kapepa. Bombwe, she said, had tried to protect them from his dirty relatives by arranging for them to stay at the store, but their privacy had none the less been invaded.

NaBombwe's brother and her three sisters received quite a different reception when they arrived at the store, bringing gifts of maize flour and beans. They spent the afternoon in the house talking to Eliza and her husband, and later they were taken back along the road in the car to save them walking all the way home. On the drive back Eliza took the wheel and was stared at by various persons along the route who had probably never seen an African woman driving before.

In the late afternoon, Nason's wife popped in to have her hair styled once again by Eliza. Her husband was conveniently out of the way visiting friends.

Day VIII

In the morning Tomo, the U.N.I.P. branch chairman, arrived with his brother to ask Pati to drive them to Broken Hill (Kabwe) to attend their sister's funeral and offered to pay him £4 for the trip. Pati agreed and so they left immediately.

Just before dark the lorry from Kitwe returned bringing NaBombwe. She brought with her no beer as her husband had refused to let her bring another consignment, arguing that she had sold the first lot against his wishes and she might do the same again. When she learnt that Pati had gone to Broken Hill (Kabwe) she was furious and cursed the Lusefu family for allowing him to go. She said that they 'were stupid (*kutumpa*)' and that it would not have happened in the village where she came from. If anything happened to Pati on the road then they would be held responsible as they were supposed to be looking after him. This incident she said had finally made her decide to bring an end to the visit. They would be leaving as soon as Pati returned. When they got back to Kitwe she would report the difficulties they had experienced during their stay to Pati's father, telling him that the Lala were no good and that Bombwe's kin were totally irresponsible.

Day IX

Soon after Pati had arrived back in the early hours of the morning, NaBombwe ordered the driver to get packed up ready to leave at midday.

However before leaving Eliza and her husband visited a local herbalist to obtain medicines to make her pregnant as she felt she had waited too long for her second child. They left without saying goodbye to any of the people living at Lusefu Village and used the excuse that the local herbalist had advised them not to go near the village as there were malignant spirits (*ifibanda*) there that could nullify the medicines he had given her.

In return for the hospitality they had received at Kapepa they presented Chiboli and her lame sister, Changwe, with a dress each and gave Lusefu, the headman, a blanket. But Katwishi and others received nothing.

Analysis

I want firstly to analyse this case from the point of view of the interpersonal struggles that occurred and only later to discuss its wider ramifications. In order to do this, however, it is necessary to assess more fully the interests of the major participants and indicate briefly how each perceived this particular series of events.

Bombwe and his wife

I described earlier how the store was started and how Bombwe and his younger brother, Timoti, had both invested sums of money in it.[1] It had originally been managed by Katwishi but he left when the future of the store was in serious jeopardy. Bombwe's divorced sister, Chiboli, and her son, Patrick, replaced Katwishi and the business was put back on its feet. Bombwe and Timoti continued to contribute to the running of it and later purchased a

[1] See pp. 100–3.

motor-van and a lorry which they used to transport people and goods to and from town. It was generally recognized that Bombwe held the major share in the store and was therefore the senior partner and controller of the business. The store and the vehicles, for instance, were registered in his name, and when Timoti died there was no question of anybody else inheriting his share in the business.

Bombwe's daughter, Eliza, had married Pati in the early 1960's and since then Pati had assisted his father-in-law in meeting certain contingencies that arose in connection with the business. He had, for example, paid a £20 bill for vehicle repairs shortly before his visit to Kapepa and had regularly helped with the purchase of stock for the store. Pati had been a useful asset in other ways too. He had put Bombwe's eldest daughter, Ruth, through a domestic science college in Rhodesia, paying both her fees and her living expenses; and had looked after Ruth's two young children whilst she was away. He also provided school fees and living expenses for another of Bombwe's daughters who was attending a secondary school in Serenje; and had made numerous gifts to Bombwe in the form of clothing and household items. Thus when Bombwe first suggested that Pati should spend a few weeks at Kapepa it was seen by Pati as his father-in-law's way of rewarding him for what he had done for the family.

Bombwe intended more than this, however. The visit was part of a more general plan to persuade Pati to become a permanent business partner. By general standards, Pati was a wealthy and educated man whom Bombwe thought would make an ideal business partner. Pati himself was not hostile to the suggestion, though he said he would like to think over the proposition and weigh this against the alternative of his starting up independently. But he welcomed the opportunity to stay at Kapepa store for he could then, he claimed, make some assessment of the entrepreneurial possibilities in the parish.

At the time of the visit, which was less than a fortnight after Timoti's death, Bombwe was even more anxious to get Pati to come into the business. He was now alone and needed Pati's assistance to meet current running costs which were fairly high with two vehicles in use. But he had no way of pressuring Pati into partnership with him. Indeed as things worked out his wife and his own matrikin became major obstacles in his way, for by the end of the visit Pati had expressed a definite wish not to get involved in the politics of kinship surrounding Bombwe and the store.

Throughout the history of the store Bombwe had found it expedient to enlist the aid of various matrikin living in Kapepa. He needed someone to manage the store and someone to travel with the vehicle to collect fares. After Katwishi's unsuccessful management of the store, Chiboli and Patrick took on these jobs. Bombwe also relied on kin to look after his other assets. He had several head of cattle left in the care of Lusefu, his mother's brother, and four of these had been trained for ploughing by his younger brother, Katwishi, who used them at his farm. He also had a valuable rifle and a plough which were kept by Lusefu. It was tacitly agreed by Lusefu and the others that they would look after Bombwe's property until he returned from town, providing in the meantime they could put the items to their own use. Lusefu, the senior kinsman, acted as *inkoswe* or custodian of the property. The arrangement made with Chiboli and Patrick was that they would not be paid for their services but would be supplied regularly with foodstuffs and allowed from time to time to take certain household items from the store. The reason for the general vagueness about these arrangements was of course that they were never conceived of as being contractual in the strict sense. They simply arose as one aspect of Bombwe's relationships with them and were associated with sentiments of matrilineal kinship. Moreover the fact that Bombwe was utilizing these various links to safeguard his own interests and had invested considerable sums of money in Kapepa clearly showed that he intended some day to retire to his rural home and live off the fat of his years of urban employment.

Thus, although Bombwe himself did not appear on the scene during Pati's visit, it is clear from the details of the case that he aimed both at retaining the loyalty and support of certain strategic matrikin, whilst at the same time hoping to bring Pati, his son-in-law, into the business. In the original arrangements made for the visit Bombwe intended that this should also be an occasion for festivities among his kin. Several drums of *chibuku* beer and various food items had been promised for communal consumption and one of his beasts was to have been slaughtered and consumed by Pati and Bombwe's own kinsfolk. In point of fact, however, the

Lusefu group gained little from the visit as the plans were sabotaged by Bombwe's wife, who saw the visit as an opportunity to further her own private ends. Bombwe's chagrin for the way in which she operated was later made explicit by his refusing to allow her to transport a second consignment of beer.

Throughout her visit NaBombwe sought to assert control over the store and over the day-to-day organization of the visit. Immediately on arrival she criticized the Lusefu family for benefiting from her husband's wealth and ordered the selling of the beer he had sent. She then interfered with the serving of it, which she claimed was unhygienic, and later tried to enforce her right to sleep in the new store building. On both counts she was foiled by Chiboli, who regarded these incidents as a threat to her own position as store manager. In the morning NaBombwe took charge of the cooking and feeding arrangements and this time was able to exclude Chiboli from helping with these tasks by using her own cooking utensils and her own maize flour. She followed this by obtaining various other foodstuffs from the store, but was again challenged by Chiboli who also helped herself to store items. Then when the Lusefu people arrived to greet Pati formally NaBombwe intervened to stop them from entering Pati's house, arguing that they would dirty the floor with their bare feet; and she also prevented Pati and his wife from visiting the village which she claimed was 'full of disease'.

In all this NaBombwe was attempting to establish her right to have a major say in the affairs and property of her husband. This emerges most strikingly in the bitter disputes between her and Chiboli and Katwishi. During one of the vehement exchanges NaBombwe summed up her position, as she saw it, by stating that 'We shall share the wealth because I am caring for his children. . . . I cannot suffer for nothing.'

Yet her tactics throughout were to express her hostility towards Bombwe's matrikin by stressing the status differences which existed between her and the visitors, and the members of Bombwe's matrilineal kin group. She did this, it seems, so that she could win the support of Pati and his wife and the mother-in-law. In her estimation Bombwe's kin were nothing more than 'country bumpkins' (*kamushi*) who possessed none of the refinements of the townsman (*mwina tauni*). They were unhygienic when serving beer and when cooking food, were poorly dressed and totally unconcerned with the niceties of 'good living'. They would even enter a house without knocking. By framing her opposition in terms of the difference between the *kamushi*, whom she also regarded as essentially stupid and unenlightened, and the *mwina tauni* who possessed all the opposite qualities, she was strengthening her ties with Pati's mother and with her own daughter, Eliza, who were both townswomen born and bred, and who shared the same attitudes. By doing so she hoped indirectly to influence Pati in his decision to join forces with her husband. NaBombwe wanted to alienate Pati and Eliza from Bombwe's kin so that Pati would only decide to go into partnership with Bombwe providing the latter effectively curtailed the control that Chiboli, Lusefu and the others had over the store and the rest of his property. This she saw as in her own interests for she would then secure a tighter hold over Bombwe's property through the influence of her own daughter and son-in-law, and would be somewhat better placed to obtain a major share of the property when he died or at least to ensure that most of it went to her own children. Alternatively, if Pati chose to establish his own independent business then as his mother-in-law she might still be able to apply pressures upon him to obtain certain benefits. All in all, she had little to lose and much to gain by exacerbating the tensions between herself and her husband's matrikin, for she realized that her husband was unlikely to press for a divorce if the quarrels became serious, for to do so might mean that he would lose the support of Pati.

Although much of the antagonism between NaBombwe and her affines was framed in terms of status differences, NaBombwe was not beyond using other arguments when she considered them appropriate. For example, she tried to discredit Bombwe's kin by invoking certain customary norms. She reproved Katwishi for the way in which he was acting too familiarly with Pati, his 'son-in-law', and for the way in which he and others had shown disrespect towards Pati by begging from him when it was really their place to welcome him into the family by presenting him with gifts.

After the visit of Pati, Katwishi went to Kitwe to see Bombwe about the difficulties that had arisen, but returned to inform the Lusefu people that Bombwe wished now to repudiate his ties with them. Katwishi claimed that Bombwe had told him that as a result of the quarrels that had taken place he now considered their kin relationships broken. Following this, NaBombwe assumed more control over the store by travelling with the lorries to and from town. Yet throughout there was no suggestion that Bombwe really intended to sever his links with them. Indeed it would have been quite impractical for him to have cut off his links and it would have been most difficult for emotional reasons too. Bombwe had certain commitments towards his matrikin in Kapepa for the assistance he had received and felt closely attached to them because of bonds of matrilineal kinship. But he did attempt some appeasement of his wife by clearing away from the store the hangers-on (i.e. Koda and his wife and Chiboli's widowed sister) and by arranging for his wife to keep a closer watch over the affairs of the store.

Thus NaBombwe's strategy could only produce a partial solution to her problem, for her husband was already enmeshed in a complex set of ties which he simply could not repudiate. Bombwe was placed in an extremely ambivalent situation. On the one hand, he was bound to his kin, not because of matrilineal kinship *per se* but because of the way in which he had invested in these particular social relationships over the years; and on the other hand, he had his own nuclear family to consider. His ties with his own children were particularly important as they had all grown up away from either his or their mother's matrilineal kinsmen and in some cases they had contributed to the financing of the business. Thus Bombwe faced somewhat of a moral crisis which by its very nature could never be satisfactorily resolved. He was caught in mid-stream between two different currents of loyalty, each commending legitimate, though potentially conflicting, courses of action. Bombwe had somehow to balance the claims of different members of his nuclear and matrilineal-extended family for places in the business enterprise and also weigh the continued involvement of matrikin in the affairs of the store against the question of business efficiency.[1] Was he to continue to find places for various matrilineally related kinsmen in recognition of the past contribution they had made, or was he to bring Pati, his educated son-in-law who had additional capital resources at his disposal, into the business at the expense of his kinsmen? Bombwe had little option

[1] For treatment of a similar type of problem within a modern industrial setting, see Sofer, 1961; also Gluckman, 1965b, for a re-analysis of the case in Sofer's study.

but to do both; and it was this which gave rise to the bitter hostilities that occurred.

Bombwe's matrikin

I now examine the roles played by Bombwe's younger brother, Katwishi, his sister, Chiboli, and his mother's brother, Lusefu.

I have already described Katwishi's involvement with Bombwe as his first store manager and how he tried to wrest from Bombwe some of the profits accruing from the store. An important issue at the time was that Katwishi evidently saw his position as store manager not only in economic terms but also as a means of building up a following. His initial attempt took place in the context of the village, where he seems to have used his influence as store manager to try to win the support of a number of matrilineal kinsmen, though his plans were disrupted by the deaths of his mother and classificatory mother and by the accusations of sorcery which followed. He then re-built the store near Kapepa school and sought to gather round him a number of followers, this time largely on a non-kinship basis.

Shortly after moving near to the school he joined the local congregation of Jehovah's Witnesses and hobnobbed with several of the top men in the congregation. He was especially friendly with Zakeyo, the Assistant Overseer of the congregation, who assisted him with the building of the new Kimberley-brick store building and with the book-keeping. Later Katwishi made arrangements with Zakeyo to marry the latter's sister if he could obtain a divorce from his present wife, which he presumably saw as a way of cementing his relationship with him. But the marriage came to nothing, for Katwishi quarrelled with Zakeyo over the post of market supervisor to which the latter was appointed. Zakeyo was the owner of a grinding mill near Kapepa school, a leading member of the Kapepa School Committee and a man whom the District Commissioner respected both for his business efficiency and his honesty. Katwishi unsuccessfully contested Zakeyo's appointment, arguing that he was a more suitable candidate being the storekeeper at Kapepa. This led to bitter antagonism between Katwishi and Zakeyo and other Jehovah's Witnesses who, in the main, supported Zakeyo, an early pioneer of the movement in Chibale. Finally, Katwishi was expelled from the congregation on the grounds that he had taken to heavy beer drinking, and so his close bonds with Jehovah's Witnesses in the area came to an end. During these days he also tried to win the support of various peasant farmers in the parish by offering them free beer at his store, and developed useful links with the teachers at Kapepa and with the agricultural demonstrators in the area. But later he was removed from the store by Bombwe, who accused him of dissipating the profits by 'buying friends'.

He left the store in 1956 and established his own peasant farm. Earlier I discussed the ways in which he struggled to gain access to essential resources and argued that throughout the history of his farm Katwishi has constantly been beset by problems of insufficient capital and an unreliable labour supply. A few weeks before Pati's visit Katwishi had persuaded his younger brother, Timoti, to assist him financially and had received from him a 100-lb. bag of salt with which to take on hired farm hands. He also, it is said, got Timoti to agree to the financing of a new store which they intended to operate as a joint enterprise in competition with Bombwe. Timoti had been dissatisfied with his association with Bombwe for some time, as he argued that the latter kept most of the profits for himself, even to the extent of legalizing this by registering all the property in his name and not under some form of joint ownership. However, any plans that Katwishi and Timoti may have had were suddenly interrupted by the untimely death of Timoti.

Following this death, a series of disputes developed between various members of the Lusefu descent group over the inheritance of the deceased man's money and possessions and over the distribution of the compensation money awarded by the mining company. Katwishi's behaviour came under heavy criticism from many of his close matrikin. Bombwe, Lusefu and most of the women complained of the way he had removed furniture and clothing from Timoti's house before the others arrived for the funeral, and also of his attempts to try and inherit the widow. On one occasion Lusefu refused to have any part in the widow succession ceremony, for he believed that the fact that Timoti's wife was already living at Katwishi's farm indicated that the new union had been consummated without the proper ceremony. Similarly, Lusefu, Bombwe, Lameck and his wife, and Chiboli were annoyed about the distribution of Timoti's Provident Fund savings which was carried out at Serenje Boma. They asserted that Katwishi had manœuvred himself into a powerful position by undertaking to represent them before the District Officer and had falsified their genealogical relationships in order to get the lion's share for himself. Lusefu claimed that when Katwishi was in the District Officer's office he heard him give the sibling order as Katwishi, Chiboli, Chibuye, Changwe (II, D32), Ngosa (II, D31), Bombwe and Lusefu, and had denied that anyone of the deceased's parental generation survived. As a result, Katwishi received the sum of £35 and the rest only £10 each. Katwishi countered these charges by arguing that he had receive dmore money than the rest of his kinsmen because he was looking after the widow and children, and that his reason for claiming the major part of Timoti's property was because of the close bonds between them, the two of them having formed a 'company'.

Thus at the time of Pati's visit considerable tension existed between Katwishi and Lusefu and the rest of his kin at the village and store. Correspondence had gone back and forth between Lusefu and Bombwe and from this it appeared that Bombwe was supporting Lusefu and had threatened to return to Kapepa at his earliest convenience to put Katwishi in his place. By this time too Katwishi had lost favour with Timoti's wife, who had left his farm and was waiting at the store for transport to take her back to Kitwe.

The visit of Pati, however, brought about a temporary appeasement between Katwishi and certain of his kinsmen who presented a united front to NaBombwe when she commenced her attacks on Bombwe's kin. This emerged most clearly in the support that Katwishi gave Chiboli during her quarrels and in the discussions which took place between Katwishi and Lusefu. Katwishi was especially valuable to Lusefu for his willingness to engage in vitriolic exchanges with NaBombwe. Lusefu was happier playing a back-seat role as he wished to avoid antagonizing Bombwe himself. Thus the visit of Pati provided Katwishi with the opportunity to win the support of several of his close matrikin. Most of them, to a lesser or greater degree, had been incensed by the way Katwishi had operated over Timoti's inheritance, but when faced with a dragon like NaBombwe they willingly looked to him for support rather than to Lusefu, who seemed rather ineffectual in the situation. This was especially the case with Chiboli, who, like the others, had previously been highly critical of Katwishi's underhand methods during the Timoti affair. Chiboli had for some time been the main target for NaBombwe. She had more than once been accused of incompetent management of the store and had been branded a *kamushi*. As a result, Chiboli did not look forward to the arrival of NaBombwe and complained of these 'educated types' who must have everything spick and span. Hence, even before the arrival of Pati and the others, Chiboli knew that NaBombwe would again use the occasion to criticize her. Sure enough NaBombwe turned her fire on Chiboli almost immediately on arrival and continued to upbraid her during the days that followed. Throughout this Chiboli countered her attacks one by one and was ably supported by Katwishi, who lashed NaBombwe even more vehemently than the latter had done Chiboli. In a similar manner, Katwishi came to the assistance of Saulo's wife, his classificatory sister, when she was treated disrespectfully by NaBombwe.

Throughout the visit Katwishi spent a great deal of his time at the store trying to impress Pati and perhaps hoping that he might later put in a good word for him when he returned to Bombwe. Katwishi was there, dressed in his best suit, when the party arrived. He assumed the role of 'father-in-law' to Pati, stressing that it was he who deputized for Bombwe and it was he who was responsible for the day-to-day organization of the visit. Katwishi frequently moved between Lusefu Village and the store, arranging for the slaughtering of the beast, for the visits of kinsmen and for the *sundowni* (sundowner party) which was to be held as a climax to their stay. It was he too who persuaded Pati to drive to Broken Hill (Kabwe) to buy more *chibuku* beer and then to Mulilima, on the Great North Road, for bottled beer, though Pati complained later of the way in which Katwishi and Lusefu forced themselves on him and consumed most of it themselves. Katwishi also took it upon himself to introduce members of the Lusefu family as they arrived. This suggests that Katwishi wished to appear as the responsible and effective leader of the kin group, and as a sophisticated 'townsman' as well. He talked at length with Pati about his farming achievements, about the high standard of living he enjoyed at his farm, and about his urban experience.

It may have been that Katwishi saw this as a way of winning favour with Bombwe again. Yet whatever plans he had, these were spoilt by NaBombwe's interference and by her attacks on him and his kin. This had the effect of uniting Katwishi with his own close uterine kin against the hostilities shown them by NaBombwe, and of also alienating him more and more from Pati and his wife, Eliza.

Katwishi emerged as the most effective protagonist for the Lusefu group of kin. This led ultimately to a decrease in the control which Lusefu, their senior kinsman, could assert over them. Lusefu had shown himself to be a weak character in this situation and one who was probably too closely committed to Bombwe. Later when Katwishi returned from Kitwe, where he had seen Bombwe and discussed with him the difficulties which had developed over Pati's visit, Lusefu opened himself to sharp criticism from most of his matrilineal kinsmen. Katwishi reported that Bombwe had told him that their kin relationships were now broken and went on to argue that if this was the case then Lusefu should recognize it and divide up the property among the kin. Lusefu refused, saying that they should wait until Bombwe himself arrived to discuss matters. Katwishi called him Bombwe's slave and told him that he had lost his authority over his own female dependants, adding, 'Your days are numbered: we must brew beer to celebrate your death.' Following this incident, several of the remaining households made plans to leave the village and establish their own independent settlements. In conversation with them they said that they had been badly let down by Lusefu both in the dispute which occurred between them and Katwishi over Timoti's inheritance and during Pati's visit. By this time, Lusefu himself was a despondent old man who found it hard to face the prospect of living in a village of empty houses.

Thus, although Katwishi was really unable to make permanent allies of his matrilineal kinsmen (so much suspicion of him existed because of his past behaviour), he turned the Pati visit to his own advantage by undermining Lusefu's position in the kin group, and by restoring Chiboli's confidence in him. When I left the field in May 1964, Katwishi had high hopes that Lusefu would in fact be forced to divide up the property, and if so he would claim the oxen he had trained. He also was working hand-in-hand with Chiboli, advising her as to what she should do if Bombwe tried to remove her from the store, and making dresses for her to sell in the store. It appeared, then, that he was beginning to establish some basis of influence (if not authority) within the kin group, though a testing point would come in the next round with Bombwe and his wife.

In my discussion of the reasons for the fission of Lusefu Village I drew attention to the opposition which existed between Katwishi and his classificatory brother, Lameck, and classificatory sister's son, Kefas. The visit of Pati provides further illustration of the hostilities which existed between them. When Lameck visited the store to greet Pati, Katwishi antagonized him by refusing to acknowledge his membership of the same matrilineal descent group. He introduced him, saying, 'Here is our elder brother, Lameck, but from very distant ancestors. He does not belong to our kin group.' This was presumably calculated to upset Lameck to the extent of getting rid of him from the store; and in this he succeeded. Lameck was probably the greatest threat to Katwishi in that he was a wealthy peasant farmer whose style of life was closer to that of Pati and the visitors than anyone else's in the Lusefu family. He also had maintained a reasonably good relationship with Bombwe and had no desire to enter into the quarrels between NaBombwe and the Lusefu people. So far Bombwe had shown no wish to utilize links with his classificatory brother, Lameck, but it was at least a possibility that he might if matters continued to go badly with his own uterine kin. From Katwishi's point of view he wanted to keep Lameck out of the picture for he feared competition from him.

Kefas was less of a threat for he had nothing much to offer Bombwe and showed very little interest in the visit, and never even formally greeted Pati. Like many other classificatory matrikin, he kept clear of the quarrels at the store.

One interesting aspect of the way in which Lameck, Kefas and other classificatory kin operated in the situation is indicated by the pattern of gift giving. Apart from the gifts which Pati received from the teachers and agricultural demonstrator, most other gifts presented to him were from Bombwe's classificatory kin and not from uterine kinsmen. The exceptions to this were Katwishi, who sent his second wife with chicken and *nshima*, and Lusefu, who gave Pati's mother some chickens and flour to take back with her when she left. Only later when Pati and Eliza were persuaded to visit the village did they receive any gifts from the rest of Bombwe's close kin, and these appear to have been accepted somewhat

o

ungraciously as Eliza refused to eat the food she was offered and insisted on taking chickens and the like back with her instead.

From the few comments made by individuals who came to present gifts it appears that some of these classificatory kin were interested in short-term gains. Mwitwa, for example, said that he expected to receive either a shirt or some money from them before they returned to Kitwe; and Nason's wife hoped that Eliza would find her a handsome townsman whom she could marry. On the other hand, however, many of these classificatory kin saw this situation as an opportunity for furthering their own relationships with Bombwe in the hope that in future he might put more trust in them than in the Lusefu branch of the matrilineage. But more than this one cannot say.

Pati and his wife

So far I have said little about the part that Pati played. Because of the difficulties in the relationships between NaBombwe and Bombwe's matrikin Pati was placed in a delicate and rather vulnerable position. He could not interact too freely with any of Bombwe's kin, nor could he openly support NaBombwe for this would only exacerbate the hostilities further. He was forced then into withdrawing from the situation as far as possible. He spent much of his time either in the house or visiting a teacher at the school. On his arrival he had received several gifts from the teachers and this enabled him to strike up a friendly relationship with one of them, Bwalya, with whom he found he had much in common. Like Pati, Bwalya was a stranger to the chiefdom, being a Bisa from Mpika District. He was educated and enjoyed a standard of living which most closely approximated to Pati's own. Moreover, he was somewhat placid by disposition and well liked in the area and therefore had access to most of the gossip in the parish. His information on the Lusefu family was invaluable to Pati, who used him to work out how he should handle the situation. Bwalya was also a hunter of some renown in the parish, and Pati was quick to seize on the possible financial gain to be had from this. Before he left he made arrangements to supply Bwalya with ammunition, so that he could hunt and send the meat to Kitwe for sale. Bwalya did some hunting during Pati's stay in Kapepa, using Bombwe's rifle. This was the only point at which Pati was nearly drawn into the quarrels, for Lusefu had control over the rifle and expected to receive some share of the game killed by Bwalya. He was never in fact offered any and this annoyed him. But as far as Lusefu was concerned, the blame rested more with NaBombwe than with Pati and so he refrained from taking it up with him. Later when Pati sent ammunition to Bwalya via the store Katwishi intercepted it and claimed it for himself, stating that he had taken it in recompense for the service he gave to Pati during his visit.

Another opportunity for withdrawing from the store situation arose when Pati was asked to drive two local men to Broken Hill (Kabwe) to attend a funeral. At the time his mother and mother-in-law were in Kitwe and so he did not need to consult them. This incident, however, provided NaBombwe with more evidence for irresponsibility on the part of her husband's matrikin who, she argued, should have prevented him from going. This precipitated their leaving much earlier than they had intended.

A further factor to be considered when discussing Pati's behaviour is his religious affiliation. Like Bombwe, Pati and his wife were both ardent Jehovah's Witnesses, and this placed certain constraints on the kinds of behaviour they could legitimately adopt. Though strangers to the parish, Pati and Eliza were already known and quickly identified as members of this sect, the more especially as Zakeyo, the local congregation leader, regularly visited them on the pretext that he was arranging for them to attend a large Jehovah's Witness Assembly to be held in a few days' time.

The first way in which their religious commitment affected their pattern of behaviour arose over the question of participating in beer drinks. Although Jehovah's Witnesses generally disapprove of beer drinking, in Zambia this usually takes the form of refusing to drink in public. Hence if Witnesses drink at all they normally drink together in small groups in the home of a fellow churchman or friend, and most say there is nothing wrong in this providing it is done in moderation. This would partly explain why Pati and Eliza avoided drinking publicly with Bombwe's matrikin.

Secondly, being both townsmen and Jehovah's Witnesses Pati and Eliza exhibited a style of life which they considered appropriate to their social status. The ethic of Jehovah's Witnesses tends to place emphasis on attaining a *basambashi* way of life, which implies that one wears good-quality clothing, eats good foods, and acquires various consumer-durables, like furniture and household equipment. And one should also pay attention to both personal and household cleanliness. Thus Eliza's obsession for cleanliness, for eating the right kinds of foods and preparing them properly stemmed in part from the kind of status role she cast herself in. She regarded herself not only as a sophisticated townswoman and a nurse, but also as a Jehovah's Witness.

The idiom Eliza used when she upbraided Nason, the storekeeper, also contained certain Jehovah's Witness overtones. She accused him of 'not yet being awake', using the verb *kushibuka* which usually means 'to open the eyes', though here she was using it figuratively to mean 'not yet enlightened'. In Jehovah's Witness terminology, *kushibuka* is generally extended to mean 'to become enlightened concerning the Truth' and is the verb used for conversion. Nason himself had been a Jehovah's Witness for many years until his recent expulsion for deserting his first wife for a younger woman. The Nason case was common gossip throughout Eliza's visit and Eliza became very friendly with NaNason, the new wife, who came to her to have her hair styled, and who presumably told her all about the affair. Thus Eliza's comments to Nason probably expressed cryptically what most people felt, namely, that his faith had been of a very shallow kind indeed, otherwise he would never have behaved the way he did.

One of the most interesting aspects of the behaviour of Pati and Eliza was that they seemed consciously to avoid raising the question of their religious commitment. The main reason was that they wished to prevent this from also becoming an issue between them and Bombwe's matrikin, of whom only Patrick was a Jehovah's Witness. Throughout Zambia at this time rather tense relations existed between Witnesses and political party members. This arose primarily because Witnesses refused to buy party membership cards and to vote in local elections. To have introduced the religious question would have probably made for an extremely delicate situation, as several of Lusefu's people were staunch party men, and might have caused the hostilities to involve others outside the immediate kinship group. In view of this it is easy to understand why Pati avoided furthering his relations with Zakeyo and other Witnesses in the parish: not once did he attend the local Kingdom Hall, nor did he go to the assembly meeting.

On the other hand, Bombwe's own matrikin also refrained from mentioning their religious differences which they felt might antagonize Bombwe, who was himself an important Jehovah's Witness official in Kitwe. And, although NaBombwe was herself nominally a Jehovah's Witness on account of her husband's position, she too preferred to phrase the hostilities between herself and her husband's kin in terms of the differences which exist between townsmen and country folk, and not in terms of Witnesses and non-Witnesses. This enabled her to gain the support of Pati's mother, who was not a member of the sect.

General implications

The discussion so far has involved a detailed assessment of the parts played by the major participants, both from the point of view of how they behaved in this particular social situation and in terms of their more general interests. In order to deal adequately with this latter aspect it has been necessary to provide additional background material so as to make more explicit some of the critical factors in the situation. I want now to summarize the significance of the case for understanding the struggles for power occurring among a small group of kinsfolk.

In the first place it highlights the kinds of difficulties that now arise over inheritance and property holding. Under customary law only close matrilineal male descendants are eligible to inherit (i.e. uterine brothers or sisters' sons), though sons may receive a small bequest if the man leaves plenty of possessions. It is said, for example, that the father can bequeath a gun to his son if he has another gun to leave for his sister's son. Yet increasing involvement in a money economy, and the greater opportunities which it offers for capital accumulation, have produced a situation where the principles governing property inheritance are becoming more and more indeterminate. Many farmers and storekeepers now wish to leave their property to their own children rather than their sister's sons; but frequently they have maintained close contact with their own matrilineal kinsmen and have received considerable assistance from them in the establishment of their enterprises. This creates a potentially explosive situation which can erupt on the man's death, if not before. I suggested earlier that some farmers have tried to solve this difficulty through a form of anticipatory inheritance whereby they transfer during their lifetime some of their material assets to their sons so that the sons are already in possession of them at their father's death.

Many of the quarrels that developed between Bombwe, NaBombwe and the matrikin at Kapepa arose then out of the fundamental problem of who would inherit the store, and each of the parties concerned could invoke certain criteria by which to justify their claims. Bombwe himself, it seems, wished to play it both ways: he wanted to provide for his own children and at the same time satisfy his own matrilineal kin. Several of his matrikin already had strong claims to some share of his property, for they had worked for him at the store or had assisted in some other way. And yet he also wished to find a place for his own children and their spouses. In particular he wanted to get Pati into the business, which was as much for financial reasons as for any special attachment he had towards him and Eliza.

Despite the fact that strong values attach to membership of a uterine sibling group and to bonds of matrilineal kinship in general, in this case study uterine siblings and other categories of matrikin were ranged against one another in one situation but became allies in the next. This shows the constantly shifting pattern of alignments which often occur within such a group of close matrikin, and points to the importance of considering the various social and economic goals of the participants themselves. Moreover, from the details of the Bombwe case, it appears that nowadays competition between uterine brothers frequently arises for control over capital resources rather than simply for control of a group of female matrikin, though this does not exclude the possibility of marshalling support from these same kin if one sees this as a politically or economically expedient move.

Beer-drinking groups

I now consider the ways in which Pati's visit afforded an occasion for persons of different social standing in the community, who were not involved in the family quarrels which took place, to discuss their own views about social status, with particular reference to their evaluation of the townsman and villager.

On Day III of Pati's visit various individuals from nearby settlements came to the store to partake in a beer drink organized by NaBombwe and Chiboli. They formed themselves into several discrete drinking groups. *Group A* comprised a local headman, Sikelo, and two men from his village. This group was typically described as a *nshimishi* group, for each of the men was a villager by residence and a *citeme* cultivator who had little in the way of capital goods and who wore poor, denim clothing. Sikelo opened the discussion about Pati by complaining of the way Bombwe was lavishly honouring him and expressed disapproval of Pati's conduct. He interpreted Pati's withdrawal behaviour and his apparent unwillingness to reciprocate gifts as the kind of behaviour one might expect from a wealthy and educated person, implying that such individuals do not like to mix with ordinary people and jealously guard their riches. Sikelo's drinking companion, Wilson, agreed with him, saying that the trouble was that Pati wished to appear superior to others, and went on to remark that from the clothes that Pati's mother was wearing it was clear that Pati had no desire to help her but instead had showered gifts on his wife and mother-in-law. Wilson then reminisced about his own urban experience, recounting how he once tried to behave like a European when he worked as a bus driver but said that he had not wasted his money on his mother-in-law like Pati had. The third man, Henry, added that he did not really think that Pati even cared for his wife for she was expected to earn her own keep and buy her own clothes. None of these men went to Pati's house to greet him. To have done so would have been tantamount to approving of his behaviour and to recognizing his superior status.

During the days that followed other groups of people found occasion to discuss and evaluate the 'townsman', using Pati as their point of reference. Many of those who were *nshimishi* put forward similar points of view to Sikelo and his friends. They complained of the townsman's tendency to assume an air of superiority. One man, for example, said that the townsman often appears a somewhat brash and boastful individual who refuses to sit on the ground at beer drinks for fear of dirtying his clothes and who disrespectfully claims a chair when chairs are normally reserved for elders. Another made the point that when a townsman arrives at a beer drink he does not wish to drink with men 'who have patches on their trousers', even though he himself may only have one good pair of trousers to his name. 'He refuses to

mix with *cicommoni* (commoners).' Frequent reference was made
to the fact that one could easily distinguish the townsman from
the villager by the latter's concern for customary modes of be-
havious (*umulando wa mafunde*). The worst kind of townsman in
their view was the *lichona* (pl. *machona*), 'the lost one' who lives
for many years in town and neglects his kinsmen at home. He
becomes so thoroughly absorbed in town life that when he
returns he even rejects his mother because he finds she sleeps on a
reed mat (*mpasa*) on the floor.

Group B at NaBombwe's beer drink was composed of Saini,
a successful peasant farmer, and Lacketi, his friend who had
recently returned from Broken Hill (Kabwe). They were later
joined by Bwalya, one of the teachers at Kapepa school. Each of
them regarded themselves as townsmen (*bena tauni*) and were also
categorized as such by most persons in the parish. Though Saini
and Lacketi had both spent many years in Broken Hill (Kabwe)
where they had been regular drinking companions (*fibusa fya-
bwalwa*), Bwalya had only visited town to see his relatives. However all three enjoyed a standard of living which placed them in
the *basambashi* class, and it was by this criterion that they were
regarded as townsmen. During their drinking session at the store,
and again at Lameck's farm on the following day when they were
joined by three other farmers, Saini and Lacketi discussed the visit
of Pati and the requirements of being a proper townsman. Saini
argued that he was not jealous of any man however rich or educated he appeared to be, and that this was borne out by his
greeting Pati immediately on arriving at the store for the beer
drink. Moreover, he asserted that if one had spent as long in town
as Pati or Saini himself had, then one would become 'civilized' and
not 'half-civilized' like some people. The qualities of a civilized
man he suggested were that he would never quarrel with others
at beer drinks and would be equally at home with rich men, poor
men and educated persons, like the teachers. Lacketi concurred
with Saini and added that he thought Pati was basically a good
type of townsman, though he spent rather too much time shut
away inside his house and was said to drink only bottled beer. 'He
tried to be too much like a European, when in fact he continued
to eat *nshima* and not European foods.'

On the next day a similar discussion took place. On this occasion Saini and Lacketi made the link between being a townsman

and what they called the 'gentleman' or *muleme*. They insisted that one way in which one could demonstrate that one was a gentleman was by buying rounds of beer in the manner in which one does in the bars in town. On the previous day Sikelo and his associates were excluded from drinking with Saini and Lacketi on precisely these terms, and were called *kamushi* (country bumpkins).

These comments by Saini and Lacketi present a very different evaluation of the *mwina tauni* from that of Sikelo and his friends, and, like NaBombwe's tirades on her husband's matrikin, centre also on the opposite concept of *kamushi*, which is the term used towards a person who possesses none of the refinements of the townsman.

Hence, if one wishes to refer merely to the villager in a neutral, non-derogatory manner then one uses the term *nshimishi*, but if instead one wishes to discredit him, then *kamushi* is used. Typical comments about *kamushi* relate to his narrow field of interests, to his poverty and lack of cleanliness and to his low level of intelligence. *Bena tauni* frequently claim that they can recognize a *kamushi* by the way he speaks (he uses proper Lala and not town Bemba or *Cikoppabeliti*), by the way he dresses (he wears cheap clothing which often has patches on it and is dirty, and he does not know the techniques of dressing smartly, 'putting on'), and by the skills he practises (he knows how to cut *citeme* but that is all). Because of this, *kamushi* are dishonoured (*kusauka*).

The other two drinking groups at Bombwe store, *Groups C* and *D*, were composed of young men in their twenties. Tomo, the U.N.I.P. branch chairman, who lives at an individual settlement, was joined by Kunda, the driver for Bombwe's lorry, who is Tabwa by tribe and married into Chintomfwa Village. Both had spent their boyhood days on the Copperbelt and had worked for a while at one of the mines. Tomo had eight years' schooling and had worked for a short time as a clerk in the administration; Kunda's educational achievements were far less. Tomo and Kunda normally spent a fair amount of their spare time together as they had common political interests and were brothers-in-law married into the same family. Their discussion on Pati's visit was opened by Kunda, who commented on the reason why Pati preferred to segregate himself from the rest of the people. He suggested that Pati appeared very clean and decent (*bawoneka bwino*) as townsmen usually do, but feared to mix freely with people because of the possibility of becoming involved in quarrels, especially now that Bombwe's kin had started arguing among themselves. Tomo said, however, that he did not think that in terms of dress there was much difference these days between townsmen, whether living in town or living here in Chibale, and so-called villagers. Agricultural development and the work of the Party had changed all this. People like Pati should give up their urban employment and return to their home areas and lead a good life, having as many children as they liked and being able to feed them properly.

Group D consisted of Patrick, the son of Chiboli, the manager-ess, and his 'brother-in-law', Koda, who was married to a classificatory sister. Koda and Patrick had both had little formal schooling, though the latter had learnt to read and write through the local literacy class run by Jehovah's Witnesses; and neither of them had worked in town. Koda was still rather perturbed by the way in which Bombwe was honouring Pati. Koda was also a son-in-law to the Bombwe kin group and yet he had not been treated in this way. He could only conclude that it was because Pati was an educated townsman, and he was not. Patrick agreed with him that this was probably the reason why, but said that Koda was still a young man and could improve his own economic status either by going to work in town or by growing a successful crop of tobacco. In Patrick's estimation it was beyond dispute that townsmen always appeared 'heavy-heavy' (meaning by this very dignified) and full of riches (*wachumachuma*), and should therefore be accorded respect.

These comments by young men indicate that a favourable view of the *mwina tauni* may not be confined to members of an older, more prosperous or more urban-oriented stratum of the community. But, of the four young men, it is Patrick, who has had less urban experience and less formal education than the others, whose views are less ambivalent. Kunda recognizes the attributes of the townsman but is slightly ambiguous about evaluating him; Tomo believes that nowadays there are no striking differences in dress and style of life between townsmen and villagers; and Koda acknowledges the educated townsman's superior status position in the eyes of most people but implies that he finds it somewhat unwarranted. Only Patrick unequivocally regards the townsman of high status.

A possible factor influencing Patrick's attitude is his religious affiliation. He is a Jehovah's Witness, and of all status groups in the parish it is the members of this sect who present the most consistent ideology of status, stressing the importance of attaining a *basambashi* or a *mwina tauni* style of life. Similar views about the townsman were also expressed by Zakeyo when he visited Pati. On one occasion, having lunched with Pati, Zakeyo commented to his friends that he had enjoyed eating and talking with such a highly educated townsman because it made him too feel dignified (*kucindama*).

The last part of this chapter has been devoted to showing how the visit of Pati became an occasion for individuals and groups not directly involved in the quarrels over the store to express their own views on social status. The drinking groups at Na-Bombwe's beer drink were differentiated primarily in terms of socio-economic status and the views of each group differed both in their weighting of various prestige criteria and in the degree of conceptualization. Thus the *mwina tauni* and *nshimishi* groups presented coherent but opposing ideologies of status, whereas the groups of young men expressed a number of divergent, and sometimes ambivalent, views. This pointed, however, to the existence of definable groupings within the population which were composed of status equals and where the members evaluated their own group relative to other groups in terms of prestige, or, as Weber puts it, social honour.

CHAPTER VIII

RELIGION AND SOCIAL ACTION

At various points in the preceding chapters I have argued that as a group Jehovah's Witnesses differ significantly from the rest of the population in terms of a number of social characteristics. They tend to live outside the village in rather small settlements based on a nuclear or small extended family and many live at farms and stores. Proportionately more of them are utilizing the new economic opportunities brought by the introduction of new farming methods and cash-crop production, and more practise some additional non-farming skill from which they derive extra income. Also more of them are of high economic status.

Comparing Jehovah's Witness farmers with other farmers in the parish, we found that the Witnesses tend to be rather younger in age, to have spent less time in urban wage employment and to depend much less on non-contractual kin labour to solve problems of farm management. Instead they frequently utilize links with fellow churchmen to gain access to such resources as expertise, farming equipment and labour, though those who have sufficient capital will also take on hired hands to meet any additional requirements they may have.

In the chapters dealing with changing patterns of social status it was suggested that, although Witnesses operate within the same set of verbal categories when conceptualizing status differences, they place greater emphasis on the concept of *basambashi* which refers to style of life attributes rather than simply to such criteria as wealth and education. They tend also to interpret the various status distinctions that exist in the community in terms of a single major division between those of the New World (i.e. themselves) and those of the Old World, rather than in terms of a number of differentiating criteria or in terms of a town–country dichotomy. Thus, although a significant proportion of them would be categorized by non-Witnesses as *bena tauni* few of them would describe themselves as such and few in fact have spent lengthy periods of residence in the urban areas. They model themselves instead on their own conception of what they regard as a Christian way of life and set themselves somewhat apart from local systems of prestige, whether expounded by economic status equals or by other individuals or groups in the parish. Hence, they saw little value in answering a prestige rating questionnaire which required them to assess the relative respect accorded to various social positions in the local community.

All this, then, indicates that there is a close connection between being a Jehovah's Witness and engaging in certain forms of social and economic action.

The problem of the influence that certain religious ideologies can have on patterns of social and economic behaviour was first taken up by Max Weber in his study of *The Protestant Ethic and the Spirit of Capitalism*, where he argued that there was a close affinity between the ethic of ascetic Protestantism and 'the spirit of capitalism', in that certain types of Protestantism became the 'fountainhead of incentives that favoured the rational pursuit of economic gain' (Bendix, 1960, p. 57). Though much of his argument is devoted to a detailed exposition of the theological doctrines and pastoral writings of Puritans, the primary aim of his study was to investigate 'whether and at what points certain correlations between forms of religious belief and practical ethics can be worked out', and thus, indirectly, to show how religious ideas influence socio-economic behaviour (Weber, 1930, p. 91).[1]

It is the aim of this chapter to explore more fully, in relation to a specific empirical situation, the Weber thesis about the ways in which a religious ethic influences social behaviour.

Organizational aspects

Jehovah's Witnesses in Zambia form part of a wider international American-based organization which, in 1963, served 181 countries. The main headquarters of the movement is in Brooklyn, New York, where there is a printing press and a large administrative staff to maintain contact with branch offices throughout the world. The branch office for Zambia is in Kitwe, and it is here that the publications of the Watch Tower Bible and Tract

---

[1] Weber's thesis has of course been the subject of much controversy over the past 50 years and there still remain a number of difficulties over interpretation. See Bendix, 1960, for an excellent appraisal of Weber's contribution.

Society[1] are distributed throughout the country, that big assemblies are planned and records are kept concerning the overall running of the organization. In 1963 there were some 28,300 active Jehovah's Witnesses in Zambia, and the main publications were available in four languages, English, Bemba, Nyanja and Lozi (Jehovah's Witness *Year Book for 1964*).

Each church congregation is under local leadership, though attempts are made to prevent the local unit from becoming too autonomous. Firstly, there is a hierarchy of officials whose job it is to supervise the running of a number of local congregations and make reports to the branch office. Above the local congregation there are two main kinds of full-time workers: the Circuit Servant who has about 15 to 20 congregations in his charge and is generally a locally trained African speaking the vernacular of the region he is working in; and the District Servant who supervises the work of several Circuit Servants. In 1963–4 District Servants were mostly European missionaries. Each Circuit or District Servant regularly visits the congregations in his area to inspect the records and to discuss with local leaders any problems they may have, and after each visit he submits a report to the branch office in Kitwe.

Secondly, the branch office distributes booklets dealing with various organizational matters and requires congregation leaders to submit monthly reports on the progress of their congregations

[1] Three legal corporations act as co-ordinating bodies for the work of Jehovah's Witnesses, the Watch Tower Bible and Tract Society of Pennsylvania, the Watch Tower Bible and Tract Society of Brooklyn, and the International Bible Students Association whose headquarters is in London. Some confusion has resulted in central Africa from the use of 'Watch Tower' to cover both the African Watch Tower movement and Jehovah's Witnesses of the Watch Tower Bible and Tract Society. African Watch Tower groups, originally inspired by the doctrines of the Jehovah's Witnesses, have no official link with the Watch Tower Bible and Tract Society, though they do make use of the literature printed by the Society. They had a strong following in Northern and Southern Rhodesia, Nyasaland and the Congo before and during the Second World War, and small congregations of them still exist in some parts. On the other hand, Jehovah's Witnesses first established a permanent headquarters in Lusaka in the mid-1930's but their main phase of expansion came immediately following the last war. For further discussion of the distinction between the two movements see Shepperson, 1961; and Taylor & Lehmann, 1961, pp. 227–47. To my knowledge, there are no congregations of African Watch Tower in Serenje District at the present time.

and encourages them to write for advice when difficulties arise. The Society has its own printed forms for all reports and for the ordering of books and pamphlets, and a constant stream of literature goes out to all congregations.

The activities of each congregation centre around the main church building, called the 'Kingdom Hall', where the members meet regularly for worship. Each congregation is divided into sections and each section has a meeting place where Bible study periods are held. Kapepa Congregation, for example, has three sections (*ifitente*). At two of the sections there are pole-and-thatch shelters with blackboard and benches and the third section uses the Kingdom Hall itself. The Hall is a large, thatched, Kimberley-brick building with seats for about 100 persons. It is whitewashed inside, has a small room behind the platform, and a blackboard and notice board. The seats are in rows and are also made of brick, arranged with an aisle down the middle, and there is a raised portion from which the services are conducted. Close to the Hall is a settlement of about 20 pole-and-mud houses used to accommodate members at the weekends.

On Wednesday mornings each section meets for a study period, divided into two parts: a literacy class (called *shibukeni* from the Bemba verb *ukushibuka*, to awake) for those wishing to learn to read and write in the vernacular and for those needing some re-vision; and a Bible study period which is devoted to an exegesis of the book *From Paradise Lost to Paradise Regained*, the Society's main publication which outlines in an attractive manner their interpretation of the scriptures. Each section has a person held responsible for conducting these study sessions, called an Area Conductor. After the meeting people disperse for house-to-house preaching.

The important meeting of the week is held on Sunday morning at the Kingdom Hall. This generally consists of careful reading and discussion of the *Watchtower* magazine, but is opened and closed by hymns and prayers. The study of the magazine is led by a local official known as the Watchtower Study Servant, and the rest of the service by the Overseer of the congregation. Occasionally at Sunday meetings, or perhaps on Saturday, one of the more experienced members gives a public lecture relating to doctrine. The material used in such a lecture is taken from the Society's publications, though the speaker may develop his own line of argument. Frequently too, on Saturdays, classes are held to help members improve their house-to-house and public platform preaching. During these sessions various persons are invited to deliver short talks prepared beforehand and short plays are enacted to demonstrate how best to engage in house-to-house work. These classes are the responsibility of an official called the Theocratic Ministry School Servant. After these meetings members again go out to preach at nearby settlements.

Despite the fact that so much of the teaching is fairly strictly controlled by the use of publications, speakers often introduce local references. For example, at a meeting I attended, following the discovery that one of the congregation officials had taken another wife, the passage chosen for study was the story of Reuben in the Old Testament. Reuben was the firstborn of Jacob and should therefore have inherited his father's wealth and leadership of the people, but Reuben forfeited these because he knowingly committed adultery with his father's wife who was of slave descent. Nor did anyone in Reuben's family become a leader or prophet because of his sin (Genesis, chapter 49). The speaker went on to ask the congregation to compare this situation with the one they now saw before them. He argued that 'any leader who flouts the rules of the church will be treated like Reuben for he will become a "commoner" (*cicommoni*) and be deprived of all his authority'. This, he commented, would be a distressing experience. Again, when U.N.I.P. officials were criticizing Jehovah's Witnesses for not supporting the Party and for refusing to register as voters in local government elections, several of the public lectures at the Kingdom Hall used as their main text the passage from Matthew, chapter 24, where it says, 'Then shall they deliver you up to be afflicted, and shall kill you and ye shall be hated of all nations for My name's sake.'

All Jehovah's Witnesses must participate in house-to-house preaching and because of this are called *bakasabankanya* (publishers of the good news). A person is allowed to go out preaching after only a few months of joining the movement. He need not be baptized, though at first he will go with an experienced person. But each person who goes preaching must submit a weekly report of his preaching activities to one of the congregation officials, and is normally expected to complete a minimum of ten hours preaching per month and to have sold a number of books and

PLATE V

(a) *left:* a local storekeeper and his farmer friend. Both are Jehovah's Witnesses holding positions of responsibility in the local congregation

(b) *below:* inside the Kingdom Hall. The service is conducted by the Watch Tower Study Servant. Biblical references are written on the blackboard and a clock helps keep the Speaker to his schedule

PLATE VI

(a) *left:* woman Jehovah's Witness making notes before going out to preach from house-to-house

(b) *below:* a section of the congregation at the Kingdom Hall

pamphlets. His chances of promotion are increased if he does per-
sistently well in this work.

From among the *bakasabankanya* seven are appointed for special
duties: the Overseer or Congregation Servant who has overall
responsibility for the affairs of the congregation; his Assistant
whose main duty is the compilation of weekly reports for all
work done in the congregation and the keeping of detailed
records of attendances (he is a kind of secretary); the Servant of
Bible Studies who is responsible for all types of Bible study; the
Territorial Magazine Servant who orders and distributes maga-
zines, pamphlets and handbills, and is responsible for organizing
the preaching campaign (he is in effect the 'propaganda' expert);
the Servant of the Theocratic Ministry School who is in charge
of classes designed to improve teaching methods, and trains people
for public lectures; the 'Watchtower' Study Servant who teaches
the articles from this magazine; and lastly the Accounts Servant
or Treasurer who is in charge of the finances of the congregation.
All these officials have to make out reports concerning their duties.
In addition there are the Area Conductors, mentioned above,
though often they are also one of the seven. The seven officials
are referred to as the *Seven Committee* and together with the
Area Conductors are generally called *batumikishi* (ministers) or
babomfi (servants). An American District Servant told me that
three terms are commonly used of all Jehovah's Witnesses,
bakasabankanya, *batumikishi* and *bashimikila*, and that the terms are
roughly synonymous, meaning, those who publish, engage in
the ministry or preach. Yet in Kapepa Congregation I found that
batumikishi and *babomfi* were generally reserved for those holding
office.

The *Seven Committee* in Kapepa seldom met as a group but
there was a *Three Committee* consisting of the Overseer, his
Assistant and the Servant of Bible Studies which met fairly frequently to discuss matters affecting the congregation. Often their
meetings took place informally but when called in to settle a
dispute arising between members, they would hold a formal
session. Disputes involving only Jehovah's Witnesses did not
always find their way to the parish head or the chief's court.
As a general policy Jehovah's Witnesses preferred to handle
their own cases, especially matrimonial affairs, rather than take
them to the chief.

P

The Committee had two ways of dealing with misconduct. If the case was minor, a temporary lapse from the standards required, for example where a spouse had expressed remorse for having committed adultery, then the Committee could suspend the person from the church for a period of time. But if, say, a man became a polygynist and refused to get rid of his second wife, then the Committee could expel or 'disfellowship' him. Such a decision, however, would have to be ratified by the headquarters in Kitwe.

Local congregation officials are not elected by members of the congregation but are appointed by the Society. Should one of the seven appointments become vacant, then the other six officials can recommend to the District and Circuit Servants a suitably qualified *bakasabankanya*. He must be literate, he must have a good preaching record, he must be baptized and have been in the group for at least a year and be of good character. The District and Circuit Servants may endorse or reject the recommendation, but the formal letter of appointment must come from Kitwe. Nevertheless the members of the *Three Committee* appear to have a fair degree of influence over both the District and Circuit Servants and the headquarters staff concerning appointments, for the latter have to rely to a large extent on their knowledge of the people under their leadership.

From what I have said about the making of reports, the use of official literature and the appointment of leaders, it is clear that the local congregation is part of a highly bureaucratized religious organization. As Selznick writes, 'the most striking and obvious thing about an administrative organization is its formal system of rules and objectives. Here tasks, powers and procedures are set out according to some officially approved pattern. The pattern purports to say how the work of the organization is to be carried on, whether it be producing steel, winning votes, teaching children, or saving souls' (Selznick, 1957, p. 5). Jehovah's Witnesses constitute such an organization.

Although the organizational ideology of Jehovah's Witnesses emphasizes that all members of the congregation are of equal status and must engage in house-to-house preaching, there is nevertheless a hierarchical structure of offices with some posts carrying greater responsibility and accorded higher prestige than others. Thus the *batumikishi* are ranked above ordinary *bakasa-*

bankanya and the *Three Committee* constitutes the top status layer of *batumikishi*. Promotion comes only to those who have a good preaching record, judged by the number of hours put in and by the number of converts made, and who are well versed in Watch Tower publications and doctrine. Thus within the bureaucracy, emphasis is placed on individual achievement and self-discipline as prerequisites for advancement within the church hierarchy. 'The apostle Paul says, at I Timothy 3:1 (N.W.): "If any man is reaching out for an office of overseer [Congregation Servant], he is desirous of a right kind of work." Every one of God's servants should train himself and cultivate his talents and abilities and the fruitage of the spirit so that he will be able to be used, if necessary, by God's organization, for it is a very honourable work' (*Watch Tower Bible and Tract Society*, 1955, p. 230).

Doctrine and ethic

The doctrines of Jehovah's Witnesses centre on the belief that we are now living in the 'time of the End' after which God will inaugurate a new heaven and a new earth. The end is imminent but no one knows how soon it will happen. This last phase before God's New Kingdom is characterized by a mounting lawlessness on earth which will culminate in the battle of Armageddon, the final struggle that will take place between the Powers of Evil and the Powers of Good. Satan and his protagonists will be crushed and God will emerge as victor. Only those who have been faithful to Jehovah God will survive the onslaught and inherit the new paradise on earth. Christ will remain in heaven along with 144,000 specially chosen companions but will rule earth from heaven. Theocratic government will replace all forms of secular government and God will appoint 'princes' to be Christ's agents on earth from among the survivors of Armageddon. According to Jehovah's Witnesses, Bible chronology indicates that Christ's rule started to become effective on earth from 1914, when He was enthroned in heaven, but it cannot be totally effective until after the battle of Armageddon when the faithful will, with God's help, re-build the earth.

Everyone who lives through Armageddon will have a part in this good work. Paradise will be earth wide. Every person will be making something good and useful. No-one will be working for another man.

Each man will enjoy the results of his own labour and the work of his own hands. Isaiah 65 : 21–22 gives a picture of what it will be like: 'they shall build houses and inhabit them; and they shall plant vineyards, and eat the fruit of them. They shall not build and another inhabit; they shall not plant and another eat; for as the days of the tree are long and fruitful shall be the days of my people, and my chosen ones shall enjoy the work of their hands. . . .' The cleansed earth, ruled by Christ under the direction of the Great Gardener, Jehovah God, will be a place of even greater plenty than that ancient promised land was (*Watch Tower Bible and Tract Society*, 1958, p. 221).

There will be no death, no sickness and no hunger. 'Nation shall not lift up sword against nation, neither shall they learn war any more' (Micah, chapter 4, verse 3).

Jehovah's Witnesses see themselves as 'the chosen people', who have been set the task of warning others about the coming destruction. They describe themselves as God's theocratic organization on earth, 'the New World Society', and believe that salvation can come only to those who accept the faith. All other Christian bodies are Satan-influenced and their adherents will not enter the New Kingdom. Baptism is a milestone on the way to salvation but salvation itself can only be attained through continued good works. All Jehovah's Witnesses should therefore go out preaching, study the Bible thoroughly and be attentive to the needs of their families. And this leads to an examination of the religious ethic as expressed by Witnesses in Kapepa Parish.

Before a person can be baptized he has to undergo a period of biblical instruction, but baptism is by no means the end of Bible education. Official publications all lay stress on the fact that being a Jehovah's Witness is a *process* and not a *state*. One must progress spiritually. One must become mature in the knowledge of the Bible and must acquire the ability to teach others, and of course to do this one must be able to read the scriptures, hence the importance of holding literacy classes in African rural areas. Moreover, spiritual advancement means also that each individual must pay attention to his own personal organization: 'He must have organization about everything he does including his personal appearance, his living quarters and all his actions, in order that the high standard of God's Ministry may not be found fault with (II Corinthians 6 : 3)' (*Watch Tower Bible and Tract Society*, 1955,

p. 261). A Witness should therefore keep a record of his preaching activities and devise a schedule for such work and for his own Bible study. Also, as one man explained:

A disciple of Christ should appear clean and decent because then he will preach a clean gospel and his message will be received well by all. He will appear dignified (*bawoneka bucindami*). In Old Testament days people did not shave because they had no razor blades, but in these days we do have such things and should make use of them, for dirtiness is associated with evil and cleanliness with God.

In a discussion with another Witness about the well-groomed appearance of many members he said, 'We are looked upon as *basambashi*.' As I described earlier, the word *basambashi* is used to refer to someone who has a reasonably high standard of living, who dresses well, eats well and possesses plenty of furniture and other property items. The importance that Jehovah's Witnesses as a group attach to this concept is illustrated in the following texts.

When talking of acquiring skills one Witness emphasized that,

Everyone should make use of the opportunities available for obtaining skills, like those given by the Government training centres. There are various reasons why particular individuals attend courses but my reason was that I thought that I should train for something that would give me a good living for I did not complete my education properly. The Bible teaches, even from the very early history, that each individual should have his own special work. The prophets had work for the body and work for God. Jesus and his disciples had their own special skills as well as work for God. Today every Christian must have a job so as to help himself. Everyone must have work for himself in order to reach the level of *basambashi* and follow the ways of God. If a person attains this balanced life then he will have a life of abundance in the New World. A person who neglects the teachings of the Bible and who makes no effort to advance will have nothing in the New World.

On another occasion it was argued before the congregation that it had been God's original intention to make men eternal *basambashi* but that Adam chose to reject God's laws:

Thus it was our disobedience that brought death and suffering, they were not part of God's design. It is now up to us to achieve the level of *basambashi* in this world, for being Jehovah's Witnesses we are already part of the New World Society. At the end of the world we shall be rewarded even more. God has planned for his people just as the Mine Management or Government plans for their people. A person who works for the mine for 20 or 30 years need not ask for a pension, because the arrangement is that he will receive one. So also with the Kingdom of God. God will give pensions too, yet no one will ask for one, for only God will decide who deserves one.

As Isaiah taught that the world would be re-built by God's chosen people, so the Witnesses of Kapepa Parish believe that by acquiring such skills as bricklaying, carpentry, tailoring; by using improved methods of cultivation and by raising their own standards of living, both materially and spiritually, they are preparing themselves for the new life and the tasks ahead. One zealous Witness went so far as to declare that, 'Those among us who now practise as carpenters and bricklayers will continue to do so in the New Kingdom, whilst those who are unskilled will remain as labourers.'

Wealth in itself is not considered evil, but a man should not try to hide his wealth from God or from other men, for Jehovah knows all. One man explained that if having wealth made one desirous of more wealth and of having riches for their own sake, then it would be better to be poor for one would lose faith in God. Money alone would not get one into the New World, but money together with the knowledge of God can help one to provide for one's family properly and in the New Kingdom one will inherit wealth in abundance. Wise investment is encouraged: 'Do not squander your money away on beer and cigarettes.' 'Keep your family well clothed and well fed.' By 'family' Jehovah's Witnesses generally mean nuclear family and some say that the traditional Lala matrilineal system of descent and inheritance is not God-ordained for the Bible makes no mention of it. One Witness farmer explained that he had decided to leave his property to his eldest son and not to his sister's son as custom required, because 'my son is of my blood (*umulopa wanji*) and not my nephew'. Also husband, wife and children should eat together and not separately as is customary among non-Christians and they should sit together as a family when attending religious meetings.

Jehovah's Witnesses regularly organize large District Assemblies, which last for about four days and which are attended by people from many congregations in the area. Such assemblies generally attract about 2,000 or more people, and are occasions when the baptisms take place. In addition a National Assembly is arranged every four years or so. The last one was held in May 1963 at Kitwe and was attended by about 24,000 people who came from all over Zambia and from some of the neighbouring territories. Assemblies are designed to instruct members in basic doctrine, preaching methods and how to conduct themselves in daily life. A regular feature of them is the performance of short plays used to illustrate various themes. A study of these plays provides a useful way of collecting data on the social ethic preached by Jehovah's Witnesses, and material gathered from both District and National Assemblies indicates that there is an ethic which is general for Witnesses throughout Zambia, though here I am concerned with the ethic as expounded by Kapepa Witnesses.[1]

In May 1964, I attended a District Assembly held in Chibale Chiefdom, which was organized by the two Circuit Servants responsible for congregations in the area. At this assembly several plays were staged to characterize conversion and to exemplify other aspects of 'ministerial' work. The following extracts taken from these plays serve to highlight some of the points made earlier and isolate other features of the local ethic.

Play I
The first play focused on the need for cleanliness and for appearing smartly dressed when out preaching, and emphasized the marked contrast that should exist between Jehovah's Witnesses and the unconverted with respect to these matters.

Scene One portrayed a Jehovah's Witness preaching to a 'typical' non-Christian. The Witness was wearing a black suit, clean white shirt and tie and highly polished black shoes; the non-Witness no jacket, dirty denim trousers, a tattered and grubby white shirt and no shoes. The Witness instructs the man on how a Christian should dress smartly and be clean if his gospel is to be accepted. He argues that just as the Word of God is pure and clean so must the preacher be clean in heart and appearance. He tells him of the work of Jehovah's Witnesses,

---

[1] For an account of a play performed at the 1963 National Assembly, see my paper on Jehovah's Witnesses, 1968.

quoting the passage in Matthew, chapter 28, where Christ commissions his disciples to go out and preach among the nations of the earth about the coming Kingdom of God, and emphasizes that Jehovah's Witnesses are now completing this task. He concludes by saying that Witnesses are so enthusiastic in their work that they sometimes continue to preach and teach by candle-light; yet even at night they still pay attention to their personal appearance.

In Scene Two the Jehovah's Witness pays a return visit to the man. He is pleasantly surprised to find that the man has learnt something from their first encounter. His house is clean and he has washed his shirt and ironed his trousers, though he is still without shoes. The Witness advises him to work harder on his gardens and take better care of his domestic livestock so that he has some surplus of produce for sale with which to buy a pair of shoes. In support of this he argues that the devil is always depicted in the Bible as clad in rags, with nothing on his feet. This, he says, symbolizes that God has condemned him to a life of sinfulness.

A commentary on this play was then provided by one of the Circuit Servants, who said that if you ask anyone how a man looks when he wears dirty clothing and has unkempt hair with bits of grass in it, the answer will be that he looks a slovenly fellow (*musali*).

The first thing to remember when you go out preaching is that householders prefer a clean man to enter their houses rather than a dirty man. If a dirty man enters a house he will make the furniture in the house dirty. Secondly, if you yourself appear clean and smart, wearing a jacket and tie and polished shoes, then what you preach will be acceptable to the people you meet. Also remember that the words you speak come from your mouth, and that your teeth show when you pronounce your words. If you do not clean your teeth householders will chase you from their homes for you will be dirty and unwholesome (*kununke fibi*). If a rotting carcass of an animal is nearby do you like it?

He then quoted the text from Deuteronomy, chapter 7, verse 6, where it stresses that 'yours is a people set apart for its own God', and asked them to ensure that they lived up to the standards required of God's chosen people.

Play II

A fuller account of the process of conversion was given in the second play. Here changes in style of life, in attitudes towards gaining literacy and in preferences towards certain kinds of occupation were well illustrated and some attempt was also made to show how pressures operate to turn one away from the faith.

The first scene showed how a female Witness received training from the Theocratic Ministry School Servant before going out to preach. When the woman goes out she preaches to a woman householder, and after preaching she instructs the woman to tell her husband about the good message she has brought.

After revising the texts for her preaching the Witness calls once more on the household and makes an arrangement with the woman to visit her again with the School Servant so that they can meet the husband and discuss matters further.

The next scene showed the female householder bringing food to her husband, who had just returned from cutting *citeme*. The husband wanders in from the gardens, carrying an axe over one shoulder and dressed in dirty clothing, and sits down at the table to eat his *nshima*. His wife tells him about the visits made by the Jehovah's Witness.

Meanwhile the two Witnesses prepare their preaching schedule and dress to go out. When they arrive they find that the wife has cleaned up the house, put flowers on the table and brought out a clock which she has placed in the middle of the table. She has also dressed in her best clothes ready for their visit. The Witnesses immediately remark on the decent clothes she is wearing, on the tidy house and on the handsome looking clock. During their preaching they find that it is the wife who shows greatest interest in the lesson. This, they deduce later, is because the woman is literate and her husband not. But after they have left the husband asks his wife to teach him to read and write. He has been very impressed by the fact that the woman Witness can read fluently from Watch Tower publications and feels he himself should learn to do this.

The following scene showed how the woman was visited by a friend who is an ardent U.N.I.P. member. The U.N.I.P. woman tries to persuade her to go off and drink beer with her at a nearby settlement, but she refuses, saying that the Witnesses have told her to read the Bible for a whole week and not to go out beer drinking. The U.N.I.P. woman asks her whether she realizes that being a Jehovah's Witness involves a lot more than just this. For example, she will have to abstain from eating meat that has not been properly bled, and this means refusing to eat meat of any animal found dead in a trap or any animal that has not had its throat slit to allow proper bleeding after being killed.[1] From this she argues that as the woman's husband is a hunter using traps she will have to go hungry when he returns home with a kill. The other woman takes her point and states that in this case she will probably have to violate church rules. The U.N.I.P. woman then makes her second point: she suggests that because Jehovah's Witnesses refuse to vote in government elections they will not achieve high positions in government service. They will probably have to take work as domestic servants.

The next scene showed the husband exposed to outside influences. He is visited by a friend who asks him to go fishing, but he refuses, saying that he is studying the Bible for a week and learning to read and write. His visitor tells him that this is not the way to get rich, he cannot do this by reading books. He can become rich by selling fish. Moreover he cannot feed his children by reading the Bible.

The final scene portrayed the two Jehovah's Witnesses making a return visit to the household. They find that during the week the husband and wife have been subjected to so many external pressures from kin and friends that they have now set their minds against the faith. However, through skilful argument, backed by numerous Biblical references, they are able to convince them that they should once again return to the path of righteousness. They suggest that the husband should give up his interest in hunting and fishing and should instead aim at becoming a storekeeper or cash-crop farmer. Being a store-keeper they argue is probably the best kind of occupation to have, because it enables one to be always clean and well dressed and there are plenty of opportunities for preaching. As for the wife, they assure her that by being a good house-proud wife she is living in accordance with Christian principles, though she must also devote some time to reading the Bible and teaching her husband to read and write. Lastly they commend them on the way in which they have cleaned up the house and donned smart clothing. Jesus, they argue, always dressed in white clothes to symbolize the purity of the gospel he preached. By

[1] Jehovah's Witnesses quote a number of Old Testament texts to support their views on this (e.g. Genesis 9 : 3–4; Leviathan 3 : 17; Samuel 14 : 32–33). See *Watch Tower Bible and Tract Society* pamphlet on 'Blood, Medicine and the Law of God'. They also refuse blood transfusions.

the time the Witnesses leave it emerges that the householders have given their sincere assurance that they now wish to become part of this New World Society.

After the play was finished the Circuit Servant summarized the main aspects of it and described how the family had eventually expressed a desire to become mature in the faith. This, he said, was evidenced by their wish to improve their own standard of living and by their interest in the Bible. He suggested that they would later attend the Kingdom Hall meetings and learn more about the part to be played by Jehovah's Witnesses in this world of sin. He stressed that they would also invest in better household furniture and clothing, and learn to care for their children in the proper Jehovah's Witness fashion.

Main features of the religious ethic

From the comments elicited from Kapepa Witnesses and from the content of the ethic preached at their assemblies, it appears that Jehovah's Witnesses commend a certain style of life. A Witness should be well dressed (which for men means wearing a jacket and tie, especially when out preaching or attending religious meetings) and clean in his habits. He should be attentive to the needs of his family, both spiritually and materially. He should aim at acquiring various household equipment and at gaining some special skills so that he has the means of purchasing these things. In short, he should struggle to attain the level of *basambashi*. Importance is also attached to becoming literate, for only by being literate can one satisfactorily perform one's religious roles. Jehovah's Witnesses do not see their secular style of life as separate from their religious ways. To them it is rather an extension of their religious approach: to be a member of the New World Society means spiritual advancement and promise of a new life, but this also implies a certain practical orientation towards life in this world.

As part of this New World Society, Witnesses contrast themselves with those of the Old World who have failed to respond to the message of the New Kingdom. They see themselves apart from the old way of things, and preach a form of millenarianism. Yet at the same time they hold a this-worldly oriented ethic which focuses on individual achievement and self-discipline, the rationale for this being that they are preparing themselves for the great day when Jehovah's Kingdom is established on earth.

An individual is held responsible for all his actions and the rules and objectives set out in the various publications of the Watch Tower Bible and Tract Society serve to guide him. The ethic itself also has ascetic elements. There is a strong ban on polygyny, and smoking, drinking, and too much dancing are disapproved of. Time and money are valued and should not be wasted; they should be spent improving oneself spiritually, socially and economically. Throughout there is an emphasis on individualism and industriousness, and church organization and discipline work to uphold the values of the group.

A close correspondence exists between certain aspects of the religious ethic as expounded by Jehovah's Witnesses in Kapepa and the actual characteristics of the members of the congregation as outlined earlier. Witnesses tend to live in small independent settlements based on a nuclear or small extended family and depend to a lesser extent on kin labour at their farms; and congruent with this is the importance that the ethic places on the nuclear family as a fundamental Christian grouping. Proportionately more of them follow occupations from which they derive some cash income, more are skilled and of higher economic status; and the ideological counterpart of this is the value that is attached to capital investment, to the acquisition of skills, to the attainment of a *basambashi* standard of living, and to the need to prepare oneself for the new life ahead by utilizing the new opportunities now available in the changing economy.

In addition, Witnesses may be distinguished from the rest of the population by their smart dress. Most of the men wear jackets and ties and carry briefcases when attending religious meetings or when out preaching and this reflects the style of life they have adopted. Here too, they receive backing from the ethic which states that one must pay attention to one's personal appearance when propagating the 'good news'. Similarly, if we compare Witnesses with non-Witnesses in the parish in terms of literacy and level of education, we find that 87·2 per cent of male Witnesses and 31·9 per cent of female Witnesses are literate as against 51 per cent male and 11·7 per cent female non-Witnesses. Also proportionately more have completed three or more years of formal schooling (See Table VII, Appendix). And this ties in with the ideological stress placed on becoming literate in the vernacular and on gaining first-hand knowledge of the scriptures and the publications of the Society.

The close affinity, then, between the religious value-orientation and the social characteristics of the members of the congregation suggests that the ethic serves to legitimize and to provide religious sanctions for the mode of life, achievements and status aspirations of Jehovah's Witnesses in Kapepa. Hence those individuals who have responded, or who wish to respond, to the changing social situation by taking on new socio-economic roles, perhaps at the expense of certain customary modes of behaviour, and who are Jehovah's Witnesses, find that their religious commitment offers them some moral justification for their actions which, because it is set within the bounds of a specific doctrinal and institutional framework, forms a coherent ideology for action.

Earlier I indicated in my analysis of particular social situations how individual Witnesses used their religious affiliation as a way of justifying certain actions, for example, moving out of a village to establish an independent settlement, or refusing to allow matrikin to live at their farms or to work for them except on a strictly contractual basis. Yet even if a person seldom verbalizes this aspect of the ethic it nevertheless remains a basis for influencing and legitimizing particular courses of action and can always be employed situationally to justify certain modes of behaviour or certain attitudes. Hence Jehovah's Witnesses will sometimes give their religious affiliation as a reason for investing in particular social relationships at the expense of others, whilst in other situations they may cast their arguments solely in terms of the rights and obligations customarily associated with particular categories of kinsfolk. This allows them to manipulate a wide range of social ties based on a number of different criteria, such as kinship, friendship, and membership of a common religious congregation; and in part explains why it is that several Jehovah's Witnesses with relatively little in the way of capital resources have become successful farmers or businessmen.

So far I have discussed the relationship between religion and social action from a general standpoint, showing how the religious ethic of Jehovah's Witnesses serves as an ideology for changing patterns of social and economic action. I now turn to examine the process of religious conversion and discuss the

factors which seem to predispose an individual towards becoming a Jehovah's Witness.

The conversion process

Religious conversion is not only a response to a person's religio-
psychological needs but relates also to the total social milieu
within which the individual has grown up and now lives. Hence
it is essential to examine the process of conversion within the context of the life history of the individual so that the main sociological background factors affecting his decision to become a Jehovah's
Witness may be isolated.

I propose therefore to present in detail the life histories of two
converts and on the basis of these to construct a paradigm representing the crucial variables involved. The paradigm will then be
tested out over a wider body of data to determine the extent of its
generality. The examples chosen and the material used in the
analysis which follows relate only to males under 40 years of age
at the time of my enquiries and to those Witnesses converted
during the 1950–63 period. I have found it necessary to limit my
discussion in this way in order that as many variables as possible
relating to social change could be held constant. I shall later briefly
describe the characteristics of those Jehovah's Witnesses who fall
into the older age category or who were converted prior to 1950,
before the introduction of the various agricultural and other
changes described in earlier chapters.

In the two examples which follow I describe where and with
whom the individual grew up, giving prominence to those
persons whom the informant considered important to him
during various periods of his life (childhood, first town experience, marriage, etc.), and where possible I document the specific
content of these relationships, and outline his present-day network
of kin and friends.

CONVERSION HISTORY I

Daiman (II, D16) was born in 1929 and converted to the faith in 1951,
during a short period of residence in the parish in between spells of
urban employment. He was converted by Zakeyo, his mother's sister's
husband, who was an early pioneer of the movement in Chibale
Chiefdom and at the time an official of Kapepa Congregation.

Daiman's early years were spent in Kasuko Village with his mother and her matrikin, the father having divorced her and moved to Shaibela Chiefdom in Mkushi District. Although Daiman later went with his mother to a nearby village, most of the friends and kin he has since kept contact with had originally lived in Kasuko at the time when he was there and several of them had been early Jehovah's Witness converts. Zakeyo had lived there during his early years of marriage and so had Kaisa, another mother's sister's husband, whom Daiman later stayed with during a period of employment in Luanshya. Zakeyo and Kaisa and their wives became Witnesses in the late 1930's and have remained in the movement since. Both hold positions of leadership within the congregations they now attend and are reasonably prosperous men, Zakeyo owning a grinding mill and growing tobacco as a cash crop, and Kaisa owning a lorry which he uses to transport goods and people between Luanshya, where he works as a Boss boy at the mine, and Chibale, where his son runs a peasant farm. Another man, Sabuni, who is a distant patrilateral relative, had also lived in Kasuko Village for a while and was friendly with Daiman's elder brother Godfrey, his contemporary. Later, when Daiman stayed in Luanshya he also developed a close friendship with Sabuni, who was already a convert to the faith. In 1963-4 Sabuni held the post of Assistant Congregation Servant in another congregation in Chibale Chiefdom.

After completing approximately three to four years schooling in Chibale, Daiman left to join his elder brother, Godfrey, who was working in Broken Hill (Kabwe), and within a month or so obtained employment at the mine as a labourer. This was in 1949. But he worked there for only a year, returning to Kapepa to assist his classificatory mother's brother, Mukwenda, who had recently become a farmer at the farming block. Although Daiman had not seen a great deal of Mukwenda during his days at Kasuko Village as Mukwenda was working on the Copperbelt, Daiman found him to be a senior matrilineal kinsman to whom he could turn in times of difficulty, for example, when he needed money for school fees. Moreover, Daiman's mother had no male uterine siblings and Mukwenda himself no female siblings and so both Mukwenda and Daiman readily accepted their roles as uncle and nephew. On the invitation of his uncle, Daiman returned to Kapepa to work with him at the farm. Daiman saw this primarily as an opportunity to learn the techniques of plough cultivation. Unlike the others mentioned above, Mukwenda had never been a Jehovah's

Witness, either in town or in Chibale, but he was a man well known for his town ways and respected for his success at farming.

Daiman worked for him for about two years, helping with all kinds of farm work. On an adjacent farming plot at the block farms lived another classificatory mother's brother, Amos, who was later joined by Godfrey when the latter returned from town in 1950. Amos had given up headmanship of a village to become a peasant farmer and had been converted a Jehovah's Witness in the late 1940's though he never took a very active part in the affairs of the local congregation. Occasionally Daiman would be asked to assist with farming tasks and was often at the farm when Zakeyo visited to conduct Bible study periods in Amos' house.

During this period of Daiman's life, he commenced negotiations with Lusefu (II, C6) the headman, for marriage with one of his daughters Enala (II, D15). Zakeyo acted as Daiman's go-between as he was very friendly with Lusefu and lived in a nearby village. In this way Daiman renewed his earlier acquaintance with Zakeyo, and from time to time did carpentry jobs for him. Daiman had learnt the basic skills from Mukwenda, who had worked as a carpenter in town.

Then, in 1952, Daiman applied for admission to the Development Area Training Centre at Serenje to train for six months as a bricklayer, but was turned down, he claims, because of his low educational qualifications. So instead he obtained employment at the Centre as a labourer assisting in the training scheme and through this gained the necessary know-how to practise the trade himself. Thus, in the latter half of 1952, he left Serenje for Luanshya to stay with Kaisa who held a good post at the mine and who offered accommodation to Daiman for as long as he might need it. Kaisa, it will be recalled, was another zealous Witness and a congregation official.

For a while Daiman tried to find employment as a bricklayer, but finally had to content himself with a labouring job with one of the building contractors in Luanshya. However, finding the prospects rather poor, he resigned after only a few months and used Kaisa's contacts at the mine to secure an unskilled, underground job. As the job carried with it housing and other benefits, Daiman sent for Enala and arranged to marry her in Luanshya. They were married in December 1952.

During his stay at Mukwenda farm Daiman, it seems, first became interested in becoming a Jehovah's Witness, though he had of course been in close contact with several prominent Jehovah's Witnesses during his early years at Kasuko Village. On his arrival in Luanshya and

PLATE VII
(a) *above:* temporary grass encampment to accommodate Witnesses during a
District Assembly. The large building on the right is the cookhouse
(b) *below:* the gathering at a District Assembly. The stage and pavilion were
specially constructed for the Assembly, which lasted for four days

PLATE VIII
(a) *above:* new converts being led off for baptism at a District Assembly
(b) *below:* baptism by total immersion at a District Assembly

throughout the months he spent living in Kaisa's household he became more and more encapsulated within a Jehovah's Witness network of kin and friends. Kaisa and his son Steven, Sabuni, Daiman's patrilateral 'brother', and many of Daiman's work mates were Jehovah's Witnesses. When discussing the friends he made in Luanshya Daiman gives greatest emphasis to the friendship he developed with a Lala from Muchinda Chiefdom who worked underground with him and who now has a farm on the Muchinda–Chibale boundary. Daiman still keeps contact with him and they frequently visit each other and exchange gifts. Daiman's Muchinda friend was an ardent Witness in Luanshya and remains so to this day.

Daiman's involvement in a Jehovah's Witness network in Luanshya finally resulted in his joining the church and participating in house-to-house preaching. He was baptized in Luanshya in 1954. His wife was not converted until much later. Some of her patrilateral kinsmen (e.g. Bombwe (II, D25) and Timoti (II, D34)) and her elder brother had been members of the church for a number of years, but the rest of the Lusefu residents were non-Christian. As she had had no schooling and was illiterate, Enala was unable to participate fully in the activities of the church, and so Daiman himself undertook to teach her to read and write. By 1958 she had begun to show some interest in the meetings at the Kingdom Hall, but it was not until 1960 that she was baptized.

Daiman worked at the mine until May 1955 when he left to settle in Lusefu Village so that he might give service to his in-laws. During his stay there he converted three members of the village, Kabichi (II, D18), and the headman's son (II, D21), and his wife (II, E14). One of his converts commented later that his attention was drawn to the 'truth' by witnessing the care which Daiman always took over his personal appearance, by his industriousness as a bricklayer, and by the way he conserved his money, even to the extent of refusing to buy beer or join in beer drinks. This man was of Standard VI education and had worked as a tailor in Broken Hill (Kabwe). Within six years of baptism he had achieved a prominent position in Kapepa congregation as Watchtower Study Servant.

In 1959 Mukwenda died and Daiman inherited from him various farm equipment and oxen. This enabled Daiman to move out of the village and start his own farm.

In Chapter III, I described how he established his farm, assisted by his brother Godfrey, and how later the two of them financed

Q

the opening of a store. I also drew attention to the fact that the close bonds of co-operation that existed between Godfrey and Daiman and their nuclear families were strengthened also by their common religious outlook. Like Daiman, Godfrey had become a Jehovah's Witness on returning from urban employment, and so too had the younger brother, Boniface, who was placed in charge of the store.

My analysis of the pattern of farm organization at the farms of Daiman and Godfrey stressed the extent to which the brothers relied on each other's assistance in most agricultural tasks and on hired labour to meet peak requirements. Neither of them made any determined effort to recruit other permanently resident kinsmen-workers, either matrilineal or patrilateral kin. Moreover when they did utilize certain kinship or affinal ties to acquire extra hands during the harvesting and weeding times, or for picking and stringing of tobacco, they tried to avoid the build-up of a series of potentially burdensome reciprocal obligations by treating them as ties of a strictly contractual nature. That they were able to do this was facilitated by a number of factors; they had sufficient capital resources available to engage hired hands when they needed them and their farms were located at some distance from many of the matrilineal kinsmen, and those who did live close were either well set up as farmers themselves or had married into families with wealth of their own. A factor of significance was their common religious commitment which served to legitimize their repudiation of close bonds with certain of their kinsfolk, whilst at the same time strengthening their ties with others who were of similar religious affiliation. Daiman's involvement in the activities of the local congregation of Jehovah's Witnesses has led to his developing a number of close friendships with other unrelated persons with whom he interacts beyond the reach of church activities. He has also, through his interest in commercial farming, become friendly with certain non-Jehovah's Witness farmers in the vicinity and regularly visits them to talk over various farming matters; but he has only minimal contact with non-Christians of lower economic status except for his affines at Lusefu Village, whom he designates as 'greeting friends'. We can conclude from this that a high proportion of the kin and friends with whom Daiman regularly interacts on a basis of reciprocal gift-giving and mutual assistance of various kinds are Jehovah's Witnesses or persons of roughly similar economic status.

CONVERSION HISTORY II

Frank was born in 1926 in Chilembalemba Village in Chibale Chiefdom. His mother died during his childhood and so he was sent to live with Kalale, an elder brother who was working as a lorry driver in Kitwe. He lived with Kalale for many years and completed five years of formal schooling. He then returned to Chibale to live with other matrikin; first, with his mother's sister Manyala, who resided in Chilembalemba Village, and then with his elder brother, Zakeyo, in Kasuko Village.

During his stay with Zakeyo, Frank came under the influence of Jehovah's Witnesses, though he was not converted till some years later. As I mentioned earlier, Zakeyo was an important official in the local congregation and there were several other Witnesses living at Kasuko. One of these was Musukwa, who later provided accommodation for Frank when he went to Broken Hill (Kabwe) and was instrumental in finding him a job. While living with Zakeyo, Frank learnt the rudiments of tailoring, as the former owned a sewing machine and had himself worked for a number of years as a tailor in Luanshya and other Copperbelt towns.

In 1946, Frank left Kasuko for work in Broken Hill (Kabwe). Through Musukwa he found a job as a tailor in an Indian store. Musukwa had built up a considerable number of contacts with local businessmen, partly through his occupational position as a shop assistant at one of the Indian stores, and partly through his Jehovah's Witness network.

Whilst in Broken Hill (Kabwe) Frank made friends with many Jehovah's Witnesses and began to attend some of their meetings. According to Frank his best friend was Laketi, a Witness and a Lenje by tribe. Frank claims to have first met him when Laketi was touring stores in Broken Hill (Kabwe) looking for work. They became friendly, and Frank later taught him tailoring and eventually got him a job as a tailor in the same store as himself.

In 1949, Frank returned to Chibale Chiefdom to marry Alice Musonda, a daughter of Misheck Kasubika, the village headman. Alice had recently become a Jehovah's Witness, though she was not yet baptized. The Misheck family was well known to Zakeyo, as the latter had worked in town with Misheck and his brother Edward, and had converted Edward to the faith. He was now hoping to convert the rest of the group. In view of this Frank asked Zakeyo to make the arrangements for his marriage and returned to Chibale when everything was fixed up. He made no marriage payments as the girl was his patrilateral cross-cousin.

After the marriage Frank returned with his wife to Broken Hill (Kabwe), where they spent another two years. In 1951, they came back to Kapepa Parish to live at the wife's village so that Frank might do service for his in-laws, and in the same year the couple were baptized at a District Assembly.

In the following year Frank and his wife went to Pemba in the Southern Province in response to a letter from an old school friend. After several weeks there he found work in a local store as a tailor and stayed there for two years. During this period Frank's interest in the movement and his preaching activities fell away as there was no local congregation of Jehovah's Witnesses.

In 1954 they again spent a short time in the wife's village. Here he began attending religious meetings again and developed close links with other congregation members. Later, through one of them he found a job as tailor at one of the stores at Serenje Boma, where he worked for several months. During these months at Serenje he became well integrated into the local Jehovah's Witness congregation and made a lasting friend of the Overseer, who operated a licensed hawker's business. Since this time Frank has lived in Kapepa Parish, first with his in-laws completing his service to them, and later at his own farm which he established in 1958.

During the mid-1950's the Development Area Training Centre at Serenje carried out extension work in the parish and Frank took this opportunity to learn bricklaying. He then built several brick houses for his in-laws, and also earned cash building for local farmers, and working as a bricklayer on the local school buildings.

By 1958 Frank had sufficient capital to buy two oxen and one plough, and with these he moved out of the village to establish his own farm. Although during the first year he relied to some extent on money given him by his two older brothers, Zakeyo and Matson, to hire a local farmer to help with the ploughing and clearing of his land, later he acquired the necessary expertise himself and received assistance from various Jehovah's Witness friends.

The first site Frank chose for his farm was a bad one as the soils were poor, and so he later re-sited his farm in close proximity to three farms owned by Jehovah's Witnesses from the same congregation. At the new site Frank was able to get the assistance of these farmers and their families and, in return, has helped them to build brick houses and barns, and has assisted with the training of oxen. In 1963, the main team for ploughing, weeding, sowing and harvesting, consisted of Frank and his wife and a daughter, but he received additional help from these neighbouring farmers and their families, and from several of his own and his wife's matrikin. As his sales of maize and other food crops are not yet very substantial, he does not have sufficient capital to take on hired hands, but hopes that his tobacco crop (which he was growing for the first time in 1964) would enable him to do so.

Though Frank continues to have regular contact with several of his matrikin living in Sikelo Village and occasionally ploughs for them, he also has, as he puts it, 'many friends through the Society', as an analysis of his present network of kin and friends would clearly show. In 1963-4, Frank was one of the most active proselytizers of the congregation and had high hopes of becoming one of the *Seven Committee*.

Paradigm of main factors which predispose an individual towards becoming a Jehovah's Witness

We are now in a position to isolate the main sociological factors which incline an individual towards the church.

In the first place, the individual should normally have had close contact with a number of Jehovah's Witnesses during his childhood or early adulthood. He has frequently grown up in a village where there was a small but active group of Witnesses, and where some of these were his senior kinsmen or affines (i.e. of the adjacent ascending generation to the individual in question). Often, as was the case with Daiman and Frank, he has also lived for some years as a member of a household run by a Jehovah's Witness and/or has received the assistance of some Jehovah's Witness kinsman, affine or friend in finding urban employment, in marriage arrangements or in some other important way. Through these experiences the individual not only acquires an early knowledge of the content of beliefs and the religious ethic of Jehovah's Witnesses, and comes to appreciate the nature of the bonds uniting members of the sect, but also develops close ties and obligations to some of these Witnesses which may later be activated by either party on some future occasion. The likelihood of the person developing close links with kin or friends who are Jehovah's Witnesses is of course increased where the latter are of reasonably high economic status with extra-local connections which may prove useful, and where there are relatively fewer non-Jehovah's Witnesses of comparable standing. This was clearly so with Daiman and Frank, and has also been found to be the case with many other converts.

A second predisposing factor is that the individual should normally have had a minimum of three years' schooling and is therefore already literate in the vernacular. Being literate means that the teachings are easily accessible to him, for he can study the Bemba literature put out by the Society with a minimum of instruction from practising Witnesses. Moreover, if he joins with some degree of formal education and is presumably already acquainted to some extent with bureaucratic procedures, then, providing he engages energetically in proselytizing and lives up to the moral standards required of him, he can generally expect a quicker rise to some position of responsibility within the local congregation. Daiman and Frank had both received some formal education and in 1963–4 were favourites for posts in the congregation as soon as they fell vacant.

A third factor to consider is the individual's status position in his matrilineal descent group. Here the tendency appears to be for younger male siblings to become Jehovah's Witnesses during their youth and for older siblings, if they join at all, to be converted at a later phase in their life histories. This is exemplified in the first conversion history and is also characteristic of other cases. The reason for this, I suggest, is related to the individual's expectations for leadership within his group of uterine siblings and their descendants. It can generally be expected that the eldest male sibling will become *inkoswe* or warden of the group, which apart from any customary rights and duties that may attach to such a position, will now often carry with it the role of banker. Because of his senior age and greater experience in kinship affairs, an elder brother is frequently more strategically placed for winning the support of his siblings, and may also be better placed for succeeding to the position of an important mother's brother who may be a man of considerable influence in the community. Though being a Jehovah's Witness would not preclude a man from taking on certain of these responsibilities, he may find that religious commitment interferes with some of his duties (e.g. participating in divination procedures, offering advice on cases involving sorcery accusations or widow inheritance, none of which would be approved of by the church). Thus those individuals who have greater expectations of succeeding to some position of authority within the kin group will be less likely to be attracted to the church, and in the main, these persons are older rather than younger brothers. Conversely, younger brothers who are less well placed for winning the support of their uterine siblings seem more inclined to become Jehovah's Witnesses. It may be that a younger brother will initially see the church as an alternative way of gaining power and status, though religious proselytization may result in the conversion of his own uterine siblings, which he can then turn to political advantage. Nevertheless, it appears that younger brothers are more prone to become Jehovah's Witnesses than older brothers, who, if they do join the church, tend to be converted later in life, following the conversion of one or more of their junior siblings.

A fourth factor of significance, and one which is really a complex of interrelated factors, is the nature of the individual's urban experience. Earlier I suggested that individuals who have close contact with Jehovah's Witnesses during their youth often utilize these same links when they go to town to seek employment, even though they themselves may not yet be Witnesses. One reason for this is that many Witnesses maintain widespread extra-local connections which are regularly renewed when they attend the District and National Assemblies or when they visit town. As a result of his using such links in town, the individual often becomes involved in a fairly close-knit network of Jehovah's Witness ties (at least during the early months of urban residence) which tends to seal him off from other urban influences. Frequently the individual finds it somewhat difficult to move outside this circle as he quickly develops a whole number of obligations to Witness friends for assisting him with accommodation, and for finding him a job. Thus in many cases there is a striking network continuity between country and town for persons of this background.

Like most young labour migrants the individual generally experiences a fair degree of occupational mobility during his first years of urban experience as he tries to secure a job to his liking. But persons who later become Jehovah's Witnesses differ somewhat from others of comparable age and town experience in that there is often a marked discrepancy between their job expectations and the type of employment they eventually find. Many of them have already acquired some trade before going to town, as was the case with Daiman and Frank. This they do either by learning the trade from some kinsman or friend in Chibale or through attending the Development Area Training School at Serenje. Having been trained as bricklayers, carpenters or tailors they are then motivated to seek work in town in these trades. Yet when they arrive they mostly find that there is fierce competition for skilled jobs of this kind and they do not have the necessary financial resources or contacts to set themselves up as self-employed tradesmen. Hence they finally have to resign themselves to taking poorly paid, un-skilled employment, very often as domestic servants or gardeners. Only a minority get employment at the mines as these better-paid jobs are also somewhat difficult to obtain. The small number who do eventually obtain work in their trades (like Frank) often do so through exploiting their various Jehovah's Witness con-tacts even when they themselves are still not practising church members. But the vast majority never reach this stage and after a couple of spells in urban employment return to Kapepa Parish, where they can use their skills to better advantage now that there is more cash circulating in the local economy.

The pattern that emerges is that those individuals who already have a trade and who are anxious to obtain skilled employment in town possibly experience a greater degree of disaffection with their unskilled occupational status and thus are more likely to return earlier to Kapepa, where the opportunities for practising their trades are better, and where they can move into cash-crop farming if they can raise the initial capital. These men often be-come Jehovah's Witnesses.[1]

Their educational background may also contribute to increase

[1] Although more detailed research is needed on the social characteristics of Jehovah's Witnesses in town, it emerges from the survey of the 'line-of-rail' population undertaken by Mitchell in 1951–4 that a high proportion of Witnesses fall into the domestic servant, gardener and petty trading occupa-tions. Only a small minority find employment in clerical or skilled occupations. From labour histories collected in Kapepa, I would suggest that it is generally those Witnesses who stay on in town for an extended period who gravitate towards petty trading and not those who are in their early years of urban employment.

their expectations of town life. It was found, for example, in the prestige rating study that school children of Standard V level tended to accord greater prestige to persons of higher educational standing, like the teacher and agricultural demonstrator, and their comments indicated that, in their view, a characteristic of persons of this status was that they displayed a typically *basambashi* style of life. It may be, therefore, that a person with a number of years formal schooling goes to town expecting that he can quickly obtain some semi-clerical or skilled job which will enable him to achieve a *basambashi* style of life. But when he arrives there he finds that competition for such posts is keen and his educational quali-fications are poor when compared with others.

If more published data were available on the urban *milieux* and on the attitudes to urbanization expressed by Witnesses whilst in town, one might be able to extend the argument further by discussing the apparent discrepancy which exists between expec-tations and achievements in terms of a theory of 'relative depriv-ation'. On this basis one would aim to show that certain indivi-duals experience a greater relative deprivation in terms of their economic and social status when in town than do others of similar age and urban experience, and that a substantial proportion of them in fact become Jehovah's Witnesses or join other sectarian movements. Membership of these sects offers them some compen-sation for the low occupational status they occupy in the urban mass, a highly articulate ideology of social status which matches their own style of life aspirations, and the promise of a better life in the New Kingdom to come.

However, leaving aside the complex problem of exactly how this type of individual responds to the urban scene and the question of the utility of such theories of relative deprivation as advanced by certain sociologists of religion,[1] it seems beyond dispute that those individuals who are predisposed to becoming Jehovah's Witnesses will normally have about two spells of urban wage employment, frequently in some unskilled occupation, and will have spent something like a third or less of their working life in town.

[1] A recent discussion on relative deprivation theory as applied to religious commitment is found in Glock & Stark, 1965, Chapter 13, where the authors argue that it is important to distinguish analytically between several different kinds of deprivation: economic, social, physical, ethical and psychic.

Table XVII: Association of predisposing factors for married men under 40 years of age for Jehovah's Witnesses and non-Witnesses

Patterns of association	Close contact with Jehovah's Witnesses	3 or more years' schooling	Urban employment in unskilled occupation	Possessed skill prior to going to town	Jehovah's Witnesses	Non-Witnesses	Totals
4 factors	+	+	+	+	16	1	17
3 factors	+	+	+	−	4	3	7
	+	+	−	+	2	4	6
	+	−	+	+	0	1	1
	−	+	+	+	0	1	1
2 factors	+	+	−	−	1	0	1
	−	−	+	+	0	1	1
	+	−	+	−	1	1	2
	−	+	−	+	0	5	5
	−	+	+	−	0	15	15
	+	−	−	+	0	1	1
1 factor	−	+	−	−	0	1	1
	−	−	+	−	*3	21	24
	−	−	−	+	0	6	6
No factors	−	−	−	−	0	16	16
TOTALS					27	77	104

+ Means factor present   − Means factor absent

* These are the only Jehovah's Witnesses who did not have contact with Witnesses during their childhood and early adulthood. The reason for this was that they married into the parish from areas where there were no congregations of Jehovah's Witnesses.

These are the factors which seem important for predisposing an individual to becoming a Jehovah's Witness. Stated in the form of a hypothesis, we can say that if all these major factors (early and continuing contact with a number of active Jehovah's Witnesses, three or more years of formal schooling, low expectations for leadership of a kin group, urban experience in some unskilled occupation but possessing some trade) are present in the individual's life history then the likelihood is that he will be converted. But before testing this hypothesis I wish to emphasize that the paradigm tells us nothing about where a man will be converted for this in itself does not appear to be a critical factor. Of those men under the age of 40 and converted during the 1950–63 period, most claim to have been converted in the rural area, though for many the crucial period came whilst in town. Jehovah's Witnesses tend to think of conversion in terms of when they first commenced house-to-house preaching, and for most men this work was begun after returning to Kapepa Parish. However, the period of initial instruction and preparation for this work frequently occurs whilst in town and must be seen as a response to an urban as well as a rural environment. Similarly the baptisms generally take place in the rural areas, but often shortly after returning from urban employment or during a spell of leave.

I shall now examine the general validity of the hypothesis formulated above. In order to do this I have compared all men under the age of 40 in terms of their contact with Jehovah's Witnesses during their childhood and early adulthood, their education, their urban employment and their skills before conversion. I have excluded from the analysis the question of expectations for leadership in a kin group, as this raises a number of difficult analytical points concerning the availability and social ambitions of siblings and of senior matrilineal kinsmen, but I shall return to this later.

Using a simplified factorial analysis one can show the association of these factors one with another for each of the individuals in the sample. Table XVII shows the results. From this it emerges that those persons who later became Jehovah's Witnesses differed markedly from the rest of the population, as the table on p. 232 demonstrates most clearly. This shows that the hypothesis has a high predictive value and suggests that the paradigm is substantially accurate in its formulation.

	Totals	No. of Witnesses	% of Witnesses
All factors present	17	16	94
3 factors present	15	6	40
2 factors present	25	2	8
1 factor present	31	3	10
No factors	16	0	0

The question of the individual's expectations for leadership of a kin group is rather more difficult to test adequately, for it depends on a number of additional factors: the number of male and female siblings available, their relative ages, the individual's goal-orientation, values and abilities against those of his siblings, etc. It is not easy therefore to devise a control group with which to compare Jehovah's Witnesses. However, the suggestion that younger male siblings are more prone to become Witnesses can partly be validated by the fact that of the 27 Witnesses some 14 are younger male siblings. In nine cases out of the 14, an elder brother has been converted subsequent to his younger brother, and in the remaining five he has not yet joined the church.

Up to now the discussion has concentrated on the pre-conversion period and has examined the sociological background to becoming a Jehovah's Witness. From this it has emerged (for the younger category of convert anyway) that a certain type of individual is attracted to the church who in some respects already possesses some of the attributes of the typical Jehovah's Witness as characterized in their ethic, though he has not yet achieved high economic status. He is literate, skilled, and has some knowledge of the wider, more urbanized sector of society, and probably aspires to achieve status outside the bounds of the 'traditional' prestige system. He has also, through his early dependence on Jehovah's Witnesses of a senior generation for assistance of various kinds, begun to develop a network of relationships with a number of Witnesses, and already has some acquaintance with their doctrines.

His joining the church takes the form of a gradual process of induction into the movement, and probably offers him some compensation for the relatively low position he occupies in the urban system of social prestige, and a way of putting to good use his literacy and associated skills. Moreover, becoming a Jehovah's Witness adds a new dimension to the relationships he has developed with members of the sect, and enables him to extend his range of contacts when he returns to Kapepa. As I showed in the chapter on farm management, several of these contacts may later be of use to him if he moves into commercial farming or store-keeping.

The fact that a high proportion of converts have had continuous contact with Jehovah's Witnesses over a number of years (even if they themselves were not brought up in a Witness household) suggests that many of them have probably already internalized some aspects of the ethic before they actually commit themselves to the faith. Thus the particular form the ethic takes in Kapepa is both a rationalization of certain aspects of religious dogma developed by individuals placed in similar empirical situations and experiencing similar life histories, and also an independent factor operating through and influencing the life histories of these same persons.

The post-conversion period

The most typical pattern of conversion for Witnesses who fall into the younger age range is that they take their steps towards becoming a church member towards the end of their second or third spell of urban employment, as exemplified in the two life histories described above. Their conversion frequently occurs shortly before their marriage to a local girl and several of them find their wives through house-to-house preaching.[1] Later the husband and wife are often baptized at the same District Assembly; and any delay on the wife's part can usually be attributed to the fact that she has not fulfilled the literacy requirement and not because she is uninterested.

I cannot here discuss in detail the reasons why certain women become Jehovah's Witnesses, but it is clear that if a woman has some degree of education and some experience of living in town the likelihood is that she will be attracted to the church if other

---

[1] Although Jehovah's Witnesses emphasize the importance of finding a wife from within the church, most in fact marry outside. Thus proselytization provides a means by which one can meet and court one's future wife. The same point has emerged from a recent study of marriage patterns in Broken Hill (Kabwe) made by Bruce Kapferer.

aspects of the situation are conducive to her joining. The vast majority, however, do not have this kind of background and simply join at the behest and influence of their husbands, though the prospect of becoming literate through the literacy classes organized by the Society, or the promise of fecundity in the New Kingdom, for women who are barren, are added incentives for some women.

On returning to Kapepa the man normally lives for some years in his wife's village or settlement, where he does service for his in-laws. During this time he re-establishes his links with various kin and friends and extends his network to include many Jehovah's Witness associates. Also, if he has a trade or sufficient resources to operate a licensed hawker's business, he will devote much of his spare time to developing a regular clientele. Many of his customers will be fellow churchmen.

Later, when he has completed several years' service for his in-laws, he will move out of their settlement and either take his wife to live with his own matrikin, or establish his own individual settlement or peasant farm. In a previous chapter I argued that more Jehovah's Witnesses move out of their villages to establish independent settlements and that most of these settlements become peasant farms or stores. I want now to develop this argument further to show that Jehovah's Witnesses are more likely in fact to hive off earlier from their wife's place of residence than non-Witnesses of comparable age.

Table XVIII relates type of residence to the number of children in the family for married males under the age of 40, and separates out the Witnesses from the non-Witnesses. Though the figures are small for the Witnesses, the pattern that emerges is that proportionately more non-Witnesses continue to reside uxorilocally after the birth of their third child than do Witnesses; or conversely, that Witnesses tend to spend less time in uxorilocal residence than do non-Witnesses. Of the 17 Witnesses who have left their wives' settlements, two have gone to join their own matrikin and two to their fathers' farms; the rest have established their own independent settlements away from both matrilineal and patrilateral kin. In contrast, of the 15 non-Witnesses living virilocally, 13 are resident at a village or settlement where they have a body of matrikin, and eight out of 11 have set up their own settlements and have since been joined by various matrilineal kinsmen.

Table XVIII: *Type of residence against number of children for married men under 40 years of age for Jehovah's Witnesses and non-Witnesses*

No. of children in family	Type of residence for Witnesses					Type of residence for non-Witnesses					TOTALS
	Uxori-local	Viri-local	Intra-village	Own settlement	Sub-totals	Uxori-local	Viri-local	Intra-village	Own settlement	Sub-totals	
0–1	4	2	2	3	11	23	2	4	2	31	42
2	4	1	—	2	7	9	6	—	2	17	24
3+	2	1	—	6	9	15	7	—	7	29	38
TOTALS	10	4	2	11	27	47	15	4	11	77	104

Index of Representation relating membership of Jehovah's Witnesses and place of residence:

Uxorilocal 67
Virilocal 81
Intra-village 128
Own settlement 192

Index of Representation relating membership of Jehovah's Witnesses and number of children in family:

0–1 Child 101
2 Children 112
3+ Children 91

The Index of Representation is 100 when the observed frequency exactly equals expected frequency.

Thus, although many Witnesses who hive off from their wives' settlements are men who practise some trade and might be motivated to leave the settlement to gain greater economic independence from affines, a significant factor appears to be their religious affiliation. The indices of representation relating membership of Jehovah's Witnesses to place of residence, and to the number of children in the family shown in Table XVIII substantially confirm this interpretation.

Another point to note is that several of these Jehovah's Witnesses have since achieved high economic status. Eight out of the 11 men in Table XVIII are now commercial farmers or storekeepers, as against only four out of 11 non-Witnesses. From this one can infer that their religious conversion has been an important factor contributing to their economic success. The two conversion histories illustrate how two of these farmers were able to exploit their links with both kinsmen and fellow churchmen to obtain certain resources, and also suggest that their religious ethic prompted them to organize their farms with a minimum of assistance from matrilineal kinsmen.

Before concluding this chapter, it remains to summarize very briefly the characteristics of those male Witnesses not included in the sample, but I cannot here discuss the reasons for their joining as this would take us outside the scope of the chapter. There are ten Witnesses who were converted prior to 1950 and these constitute the early pioneers of the movement in Kapepa Parish. Eight of them are cash-crop farmers or storekeepers. A further ten Witnesses, over the age of 40, were converted during the 1950–63 period. Of these, three came from outside the parish to establish peasant farms and have since joined the church. Another is married into a village where he practises as a part-time bricklayer, and another is a tailor for one of the Jehovah's Witness storekeepers. The remaining five are all old men and take little part in the work of the congregation.

CHAPTER IX

CONCLUSION

The argument

This study combines a socio-historical account of the major processes of economic and social change in Kapepa Parish with a type of situational analysis which explores the dynamics of change in different fields of social action. A central theme throughout has been the question of the sociological concomitants of agriculture development. It was argued that the technological changeover from axe to plough, together with the development of commercial production, have brought about certain innovations in the organization of agricultural labour, have affected attitudes towards land holding, and have led to an expansion of the local economy. Case studies on the strategies of commercial farm management showed how particular farmers gained access to essential resources and utilized them in the development of their farms. Differences in farm organization were related to differences in the levels of resources available and to differences in the farming objectives and the social characteristics of the farmers themselves. It was found for instance that there were essentially two different categories of farmers: those who had recently returned from town, having spent a considerable period in wage employment and who had sufficient capital to set up as peasant farmers; and those who were younger, with less urban experience, less capital and who had gradually moved into cash-crop farming after several years in some part-time trade such as bricklaying, carpentry or tailoring. While the former relied heavily on resident kinsmen for labour and expertise, especially during the early years of establishing a farm, the latter category (who were predominantly Jehovah's Witnesses) tended to rely more on help from neighbouring farmers and on contract labour.

The rapid fragmentation of the village into smaller residential units was also shown to be partly a response to changing economic and ecological circumstances. An analysis of the precipitating causes of secession in the recent history of two villages illustrated the interplay of various social and economic factors and showed how new types of socio-economic inducements were operating to persuade people to leave their villages and set up independent settlements. Some account was also given of the new types of residential grouping in the parish and of the social characteristics of their founders. Here it was argued that farms and stores differ significantly from individual settlements in terms of their composition and patterns of growth. Whereas individual settlements resemble villages during their early developmental phase and tend to increase in size with the incorporation of additional kinsmen, farms and stores are typically smaller (often consisting of a single nuclear or small extended family) and shed some of their dependants as they become more established. One of the reasons for this is that many commercial farmers and storekeepers attempt to limit the number of resident dependants so that they might conserve their resources, though this does not prevent them from soliciting short-term assistance from various nonresident kinsmen and affines when necessary. Many of these farmers and storekeepers were practising Jehovah's Witnesses.

The analysis of settlement growth and fission introduced another set of components which, though closely connected with the various economic changes taking place, provided an added dimension to the situation. These components were primarily related to the question of changing patterns of status evaluation.

My discussion of social status opened with an account of the declining position of the village headman which was attributed to a number of interrelated factors: the breakdown of the village and the proliferation of smaller settlements without recognized headmen, the circumscription of the headman's administrative responsibilities with the creation of the parish system of local government, the falling away of the headman's politico-ritual functions, and the emergence of new criteria of prestige and of new forms of leadership within the community. This led to a fuller examination of the kinds of criteria used to assess social status and to a brief discussion of the ways in which persons of different socio-economic standing in the community evaluated various prestige criteria. I then explored, through the analysis of a specific social situation, the struggles taking place within the context of a small group of kinsmen and affines and showed how competition for control over certain capital resources was expressed through the idiom of status differences. This dispute ramified into the wider community and became an occasion for different status groups to formulate their own views on social status with particular reference to the concepts of the 'townsman' and the 'villager'. Here I demonstrated the existence of new forms of social coalition which cut across existing descent groups and described the new types of status ideology.

The final part of the study focused on a problem which was germane to both economic development and social status. This concerned the differential social responses to economic change shown by Jehovah's Witnesses as compared with the rest of the population. At various points in the preceding analysis it was established that Witnesses occupied a prominent position in the changing social and economic organization of the community, and the last chapter attempted to explain this. In it, I firstly concluded that, like the correlation that Weber suggested between the Protestant ethic and 'the spirit of capitalism', there existed in Kapepa a close correspondence between the religious ethic of Jehovah's Witnesses and their social and economic behaviour. Hence the ethic legitimized and provided religious sanctions for the mode of life, achievements and socio-economic aspirations of members of the sect, and was used situationally to justify the repudiation of certain social relationships (often of a so-called 'customary' nature) and to sanction the utilization of ties of a different kind.

An examination of the main sociological factors underlying the process of religious conversion revealed that persons who later joined the sect already possessed some of the characteristics of the Jehovah's Witness as typified by their ethic. Their joining did not take the form of a sudden conversion but was a gradual awakening to the faith, and a way of cementing a network of relationships which they had built up with Jehovah's Witness friends and kinsmen. This emphasized the intricate interplay of ethic and action and stressed the need to examine both sides of the causal chain.

Conversion was also in part a response to the urban situation. Many of those who became Jehovah's Witnesses underwent the critical period of induction during a spell of urban employment. Here I postulated that becoming a Witness served in some way as compensation for their low occupational status whilst in town and might be explained in terms of some theory of relative deprivation.

Their conversion and subsequent return to Kapepa, however, provided the opportunity by which they could rise in socio-economic status, for sect membership afforded them the chance to mobilize assistance and to develop a clientele outside the network of relationships they had with kinsmen and affines. Thus being a Jehovah's Witness made for greater upward economic mobility. This was substantiated through an analysis of the post-conversion period where it was shown that Witnesses were more likely to hive off from their wives' settlements at an earlier date than others, and more likely to set up peasant farms and stores.

Wider implications of the study

It has not been within the scope of the present study to relate these findings to a wider body of theory on the sociology of religion, nor to discuss their relevance for studies of economic development in developing countries. However, before concluding, it is important to indicate briefly some of the broader issues raised by the study.

In the foregoing analysis of Jehovah's Witness ideology and action I showed the usefulness of the Weberian thesis concerning the ways in which a religious ideology can influence social and economic behaviour, but in order to clarify the argument further it is necessary to discuss the relationship of religious ethic to dogma.

During the account I isolated only those aspects of doctrine which seemed to me to be important for understanding the ethic. My main interest was the believers' orientation towards the practical affairs of everyday living, and this is what I meant by 'religious ethic'. Obviously, however, the link between doctrine and ethic is an intimate one in that what Weber calls the 'annunciation and promise' of a religion and its evaluation of the life-situation very largely determine the kind of ethic that can evolve. Hence Weber argued that the Protestant ethic was associated with various Puritan sects and not with Catholicism or with Hinduism (Gerth & Mills, 1948, pp. 267–362).

But social, economic and cultural factors also play their part. Thus the ethic of a particular religion or denomination may vary somewhat according to the social and economic circumstances of the believers when the doctrine remains essentially the same. This, I think, would clearly emerge from a comparative study of

Jehovah's Witnesses found in different areas of Zambia. For example, in the economically less developed parts of Serenje District one finds in their ethic a greater emphasis placed on the imminence of the millennium and on the rewards that the faithful will receive in the New Kingdom, rather than on the need to prepare oneself for the new life by engaging in certain new forms of socio-economic action as described for Kapepa Parish. Similarly, in fishing areas (e.g. on the Bangweulu swamp fringes or in the Luapula region) where the population is concentrated in large villages along the river banks, one would expect to find a slightly different religious ethic with perhaps less emphasis on the nuclear family, though Witnesses may still, as Cunnison observes, be 'associated with the more prosperous class of commoners . . . and have an entrepreneurial attitude to industriousness and diligence in their domestic tasks' (Cunnison, 1958, p. 13; see also Cunnison, 1951, p. 160). And one would expect the situation to be even more varied in the urban areas.

This points to the inherent flexibility of a religious ethic and suggests that within the same doctrinal framework different groups of adherents may select out for elaboration different aspects of dogma (and even stress different aspects of the ethical theories developed by their church leaders) and thereby present rather different religious ethics.[1] Yet each form the ethic takes will bear some relation to the felt needs (spiritual, social, economic, etc.) of the particular group of believers who operate within a specific socio-cultural setting. It requires further comparative and historical research on the ethic and social composition of Jehovah's Witnesses in Zambia and elsewhere to establish how far it is meaningful to speak of a general ethic and to examine the relation of this to various local versions.

An interesting parallel to the situation described here is found in Gluckman's contribution to the Tonga report (Allan, Gluckman, Peters & Trapnell, 1948). Gluckman records a 'perfect correlation' between membership of the commercial farmer category and membership of the Seventh-day Adventist Church among the Plateau Tonga of Zambia;[2] and several reasons are put

[1] This is an extension of the point made by Weber in his essay on the Protestant ethic (Weber, 1930, footnote 12, p. 197, and footnote 42, p. 267).
[2] Two passages in Colson's studies on the Plateau Tonga support Gluckman's findings. In the preface to *Marriage and the Family* (1958, pp. xii–xiii) she states

forward to explain this. One is that 'while the able and educated men of other denominations usually find remunerative employment, Seventh-day Adventists of the same calibre tend to work for themselves and, in Mazabuka, to take up farming as the most remunerative occupation available' (Allan, *et al.*, p. 179). He also quotes one Seventh-day Adventist pastor who argued that 'there were two reasons why Seventh-day Adventist people have become big growers. We don't drink beer and we are taught to work for ourselves and not to rely on others or on employment which might involve breaking the Sabbath.' Moreover, the Seventh-day Adventist mission sets high value on individualism, business efficiency and the Christian family as the basis of the State, and adherents tend to set up their own settlements outside their areas of origin. The mission provides instruction in carpentry, building and digging of wells and latrines, and dismisses employees for adultery, divorce and polygyny and has a ban on beer drinking.

Thus a close similarity exists between the content of the Seventh-day Adventist ethic among the Tonga in the late 1940's and the ethic of Jehovah's Witnesses in Kapepa Parish in 1963–4. It is possible therefore that the type of explanation offered here might also have been applicable to the Tonga situation of a decade or two ago, though with the general expansion of commercial agriculture in Tongaland it seems unlikely that the correlation of religious affiliation with economic success would appear so evident nowadays. Further investigations might show that initially the Seventh-day Adventist ethic was an important factor making for the acceptability of new farming techniques and of commercial agriculture, as was the case in Kapepa Parish, where many of the first persons to register as peasant farmers, to grow Turkish tobacco and to open stores in the area were Jehovah's Witnesses.

Another example of the influence that a type of ascetic Protestantism has had on the responses to economic change in Africa is among the pastoral Ankole of Uganda, where Anglican Revivalists (*Balokoli*) have become more oriented to the cash

---

that in Mujika neighbourhood, Mwansa Chieftaincy, 'considered by the Tonga as progressive, as a place where people are trying to live like Europeans . . . many of the people are adherents of the Seventh-day Adventist Mission'; and she makes a similar point in her essay on 'Ancestral Spirits and Social Structure' (Colson, 1962).

economy and express different attitudes towards pastoralism than do their fellow tribesmen. Their patterns of consumption and their attitudes towards hygiene are also noticeably different (Stenning, 1965).

From this emerges the wider problem of how far certain religious ideologies have facilitated the processes of social and economic development in Africa as has been reported for parts of south-east Asia and the Americas (see, for example, Geertz, 1963; Hagen, 1962; and Willems, 1964). Although much more detailed research is needed, it is my view that we are unlikely to advance beyond the general Weberian argument unless we examine the patterns of religious recruitment, enquire into conversion histories to assess the underlying sociological reasons for joining, and look closely at the question of the economic mobility of members during both the pre- and post-conversion periods. We may also have to develop ways of measuring the levels of religious commitment. But we should be cautious about inferring from a particular study that the ethic and social composition of one congregation will necessarily be the same for other congregations in the same religious organization.

The present study stresses that religious values are used situationally. Although Jehovah's Witnesses in Kapepa accept the general standards of behaviour approved by their church and express an antipathy towards certain customary modes of behaviour, they do not thereby reject all forms of 'traditional' relationships and values. In certain situations they utilize these just as do others in the community. For example, although Jehovah's Witness farmers cannot increase the labour input at their farms by taking a second wife—this would conflict with a major point of doctrine—they can, and do, recruit temporary workers from among their kin and affines. This may be on a contractual or non-contractual basis and may be rationalized in terms of some appropriate kinship norm. Hence their religious commitment does not exclude the possibility of selectively exploiting a wide range of relationships and values, providing these can be shown to be consistent with their basic doctrinal position. This emphasizes the importance of examining the relationship of ideology to action from a situational viewpoint and not merely in terms of a set of abstract ideas which are supposed to entail certain types of behaviour.

Certain religious ideologies may indeed provide ready-made ideologies for social and economic change, but we should be sceptical of formulations which posit a simple one-to-one relationship between religious affiliation and economic success. This point is well illustrated in Geertz's study (1963) of the differential responses to economic growth in two Indonesian towns. Geertz shows how, in one town, the entrepreneurs arose out of the ranks of a small group of petty shopkeepers who belonged to a Moslem reformist sect, whilst in the other they came predominantly from a class of Hinduized noblemen. Both types of entrepreneur successfully mobilize the necessary resources for economic modernization by capitalizing on certain existing relationships and values and by legitimizing their actions through an appeal to different, but equally compelling, norms, values and beliefs. Geertz's explanation rests on a detailed analysis of the various social and cultural transformations taking place in the two towns during their pre-take off periods.

The present study follows this lead and has discussed the interplay of economic, social and cultural factors in the life of a small rural community in Zambia. Although in the latter part of my analysis I have concentrated on Jehovah's Witnesses as an important group of socio-economic innovators, I have also tried to set this within the context of the broader social and economic changes taking place, and have described the responses shown by other social categories and groups within the population. This has enabled me to explore the implications of various types of social change for persons occupying different positions within the community. Later it will be necessary to re-examine some of the sociological problems raised in a wider, more comparative perspective.

A COMPARISON OF THE SOCIAL CHARACTERISTICS OF JEHOVAH'S WITNESSES AS AGAINST THE REST OF THE POPULATION

In order to avoid any possible sampling difficulties that might have arisen when comparing Witnesses with the rest of the population, it was decided to limit the unit for analysis to the area within which recruitment to this particular religious congregation took place, and to collect survey data on all persons resident within it, rather than to work simply in terms of the administrative Parish of Kapepa. The universe for the following numerical data (as also for all other quantitative information presented in the main text of the study) relates strictly to the 'congregation area' and *not* to Kapepa Parish, though the two were closely coincident.

Table I: Residence patterns for adult Witnesses and adult non-Witnesses

Type of settlement	Witnesses	Non-Witnesses	Totals
Village	23 (25·3)	243 (59·9)	266 (53·6)
Individual settlement	24 (26·4)	82 (20·2)	106 (21·3)
Peasant farm	35 (38·5)	74 (18·2)	109 (21·9)
Store	9 (9·8)	7 (1·7)	16 (3·2)
TOTALS	91 (100·0)	406 (100·0)	497 (100·0)

Percentages in brackets

Combining all non-village dwellers (i.e. persons residing at individual settlements, peasant farms and stores):

$$n = 1 \quad x^2 = 34\cdot35 \quad p < 0\cdot001$$

Tables V and VI compare male Witnesses and male Non-Witnesses with respect to economic status and are based on the analysis of ownership of major property items. To place individuals into three economic status categories, I have used a form of Guttman scale analysis (see

Table II: *Primary occupations of male Witnesses and male non-Witnesses*

Occupation	Witnesses		Non-Witnesses		Totals	
Subsistence cultivator	23	(48·9)	135	(80·8)	158	(73·8)
Subsistence cultivator growing tobacco	8	(17·0)	13	(7·8)	21	(9·8)
Peasant farmer	3	(6·4)	2	(1·2)	5	(2·4)
Peasant farmer growing tobacco	9	(19·2)	11	(6·6)	20	(9·3)
Storekeeper	3	(6·4)	2	(1·2)	5	(2·4)
Storekeeper growing tobacco	1	(2·1)	2	(1·2)	3	(1·4)
Government employee	—	—	*2	(1·2)	2	(0·9)
TOTALS	47	(100·0)	167	(100·0)	214	(100·0)

Percentages in brackets. *Both are chief's messengers.
Combining all those deriving some cash income (i.e. all but 'subsistence cultivators' category):

$$n = 1 \quad x^2 = 17·7 \quad p < 0·001$$

Table III. *Proportion of male Witnesses and male non-Witnesses skilled*

Whether skilled or not	Witnesses		Non-Witnesses		Totals	
Non-skilled	20	(42·5)	131	(78·4)	151	(70·6)
Skilled	27	(57·5)	36	(21·6)	63	(29·4)
TOTALS	47	(100·0)	167	(100·0)	214	(100·0)

Percentages in brackets

$$n = 1 \quad x^2 = 21·05 \quad p < 0·001$$

below). The data have been processed under two separate clusters of five property items each. Table V gives the results for the first cluster made up of (1) hand grinding machine, (2) farm implements other than plough, (3) four or more cattle, (4) plough, and (5) bicycle. Table VI gives the results for the second cluster of property items comprising (1) motor vehicle, (2) radio, (3) Western-type furniture, (4) sewing machine, and (5) brick house.

In processing the data the assumption made (following Guttman) was that the five selected attributes (or in this case property items)

Table IV: *Type of agriculture practised by male Witnesses and male non-Witnesses*

Type of agriculture	Witnesses	Non-Witnesses	Totals
Citeme only	15 (31·9)	121 (72·5)	136 (63·6)
Plough only	22 (46·8)	30 (17·8)	52 (24·3)
Plough and *citeme*	10 (21·3)	16 (9·7)	26 (12·1)
TOTALS	47 (100·0)	167 (100·0)	214 (100·0)

Percentages in brackets

$n = 2$ $x^2 = 23·07$ $p < 0·001$

Table V: *Economic status of male Witnesses and male non-Witnesses: first cluster of property items*

Economic categories	Witnesses	Non-Witnesses	Totals
I (High)	10 (21·3)	12 (7·2)	22 (10·3)
II (Medium)	22 (46·8)	64 (38·3)	86 (40·2)
III (Low)	15 (31·9)	91 (54·5)	106 (49·5)
TOTALS	47 (100·0)	167 (100·0)	214 (100·0)

Percentages in brackets

Category I (High)	(1) Those possessing all five items.
	(2) Those possessing all but grinding machine.
	(3) Those possessing cattle, plough, and bike only.
Category II (Medium)	(1) Those possessing plough and bike only.
	(2) Those possessing bike only.
Category III (Low)	Those possessing none of the five items.

$n = 2$ $x^2 = 9·24$ $0·01 > p > 0·001$

could be ranked so that if a man possesses the first attribute of the series then it is likely that he will possess the rest. If he possesses the second and not the first, then it is still consistent with the ranking that he possesses the third, fourth and fifth. Theoretically there will be 32 possible combinations of the five items. Six of these will be 'perfect-scale types' representing patterns of attributes consistent with the

Table VI: Economic status of male Witnesses and male non-Witnesses: second cluster of property items

Economic categories	Witnesses		Non-Witnesses		Totals	
I (High)	10	(21·3)	6	(3·6)	16	(7·5)
II (Medium)	18	(38·3)	71	(42·5)	89	(41·6)
III (Low)	19	(40·4)	90	(53·9)	109	(50·9)
TOTALS	47	(100·0)	167	(100·0)	214	(100·0)

Percentages in brackets

$$n = 2 \quad x^2 = 13·08 \quad 0·01 > p > 0·001$$

Category I (1) Those possessing all five items.
(High) (2) Those possessing all but motor vehicle.
  (3) Those possessing furniture, sewing machine and brick house only.

Category II (1) Those possessing sewing machine and brick house only.
(Medium) (2) Those possessing brick house only.

Category III Those possessing none of the five items.
(Low)

assumed ranking. If the symbols '+' and '−' are substituted for 'possessing' and 'not possessing' the attribute, then the six perfect-scale types can be represented thus:

$$+++++$$
$$-++++$$
$$--+++$$
$$---++$$
$$----+$$
$$-----$$

where $+++++$ means that the person has all five and $-----$ means that he has none of the five attributes. The ranking of the items arrived at by this method reflects the significance of those items in discriminating amongst those possessing and those not possessing them.

The final ranking of the items for the two clusters is given above. The distribution of the 214 males over the 32 possible combinations enabled me to group them into three arbitrary economic status categories. But in order to do this I had to allocate those inconsistent patterns to scale types on the basis of image analysis. For more details on scale analysis and for application of this technique to a specific anthropological problem, see Garbett, 1961.

Table VII: Literacy and level of education of adult Witnesses and adult non-Witnesses

Education/ literacy	Males		Females		Totals
	Witnesses	Non- Witnesses	Witnesses	Non- Witnesses	
Illiterate	6 (12·8)	82 (49·0)	30 (68·1) 211 (88·3)		329 (66·2)
Literate no formal education	10 (21·2)	14 (8·1)	9 (20·5)	4 (1·7)	37 (7·4)
1–4 years schooling	17 (36·2)	40 (24·5)	3 (6·8)	16 (6·7)	76 (15·3)
5–8 years schooling	14 (29·8)	31 (18·4)	2 (4·6)	8 (3·3)	55 (11·1)
TOTALS	47 (100·0)	167 (100·0)	44 (100·0) 239 (100·0)		497 (100·0)

Percentages in brackets

Combining all literate groups:

$$\text{Males:} \quad n = 1 \quad x^2 = 18·53 \quad p < 0·001$$
$$\text{Females:} \quad n = 1 \quad x^2 = 10·34 \quad 0·01 > p > 0·01$$

BIBLIOGRAPHY OF WORKS CITED

Census of Northern Rhodesia (1963).
Chitambo Mission Records, National Library, Edinburgh, Scotland.
Native Authority Rules and Orders (1947), Serenje District.
Report on Native Affairs for quarter ending 30 June 1904, B.S.A. Company.
Serenje District Notebook, National Archives, Lusaka, Zambia.

ALLAN, W. (1965) *The African Husbandman*. Oliver and Boyd.
ALLAN, W., GLUCKMAN, M., PETERS, D. U., AND TRAPNELL, C. G. (1948)
   *Land Holding and Land-Usage among the Plateau Tonga of Mazabuka
   District*. Rhodes-Livingstone Paper No. 14.
BAILEY, F. (1960) *Tribe, Caste and Nation*. Manchester University Press.
BARNES, J. A. (1954) *Politics in a Changing Society: A Political History of the
   Fort Jameson Ngoni*. Oxford University Press; 2nd edition, 1967,
   Manchester University Press.
BARTH, F. (1963) *The Role of the Entrepreneur in Social Change in Northern
   Norway*. Bergen: Norwegian Universities Press.
BENDIX, R. (1960) *Max Weber: An Intellectual Portrait*. New York: Doubleday.
CLAYTON, E. (1964) *Agrarian Development in Peasant Economies*. Pergamon
   Press.
COLSON, E. (1958) *Marriage and the Family among the Plateau Tonga of Northern
   Rhodesia*. Manchester University Press.
— (1962) *The Plateau Tonga of Northern Rhodesia: Social and Religious Studies*.
   Manchester University Press.
COSTER, R. N. (1958) *Peasant Farming in the Petauke and Katete areas of the
   Eastern Province of Northern Rhodesia*, Dept. of Agriculture Bulletin
   No. 15. Government Printer, Lusaka.
CUNNISON, I. G. (1951) 'A Watch Tower Assembly in Central Africa. *Inter-
   national Review of Missions*, xl, 160.
— (1956) 'Perpetual Kinship: A Political Institution of the Luapula Peoples'.
   Rhodes-Livingstone Journal, xx.
— (1958) 'Jehovah's Witnesses at Work'. *The British Colonies Review*, 1st
   quarter, 29.
— (1959) *The Luapula Peoples of Northern Rhodesia*. Manchester University
   Press.
EPSTEIN, A. L. (1958) *Politics in an Urban African Community*. Manchester
   University Press.
FALLERS, L. A. (c. 1956) *Bantu Bureaucracy: A Study of Integration and Conflict
   in the Political Institutions of an East African People*. Heffer.
FIRTH, R. (1964) *Essays on Social Organization and Values*. The Athlone Press.
FORTES, M. (1953) 'The Structure of Unilineal Descent Groups'. *American
   Anthropologist*, 55.
GARBETT, K. (1961) *Growth and Change in a Shona Ward*. Occasional Paper,
   University College, Salisbury, Rhodesia.
GEERTZ, C. (1963) *Peddlers and Princes*. University of Chicago Press.

GERTH, H. H., AND WRIGHT MILLS, C. (1948) *From Max Weber*. Routledge & Kegan Paul.

GLOCK, C. Y. AND STARK, R. (1965) *Religion and Society in Tension*. Chicago: Rand McNally & Company.

GLUCKMAN, M., MITCHELL, J. C., AND BARNES, J. A. (1949) 'The Village Headman in British Central Africa'. *Africa*, xix, 2.

GLUCKMAN, M. (1950) 'Introduction', *The Lamba Village: Report of a Social Survey*. Cape Town: Communications from the School of African Studies, 24.

— (1958) *Analysis of a Social Situation in Modern Zululand*. Rhodes-Livingstone Paper No. 28.

— (1965a) *Politics, Law and Ritual in Tribal Society*. Basil Blackwell.

— (1965b) 'Moral Crisis and Secular Solution'. Unpublished Marett Lecture.

HAGEN, E. E. (1962) *On the Theory of Social Change*. Homewood, Ill.: Dorsey.

KAY, G. (1964) 'Aspects of Ushi Settlement History: Fort Rosebery District of Northern Rhodesia', in STEEL, R. W., AND PROTHERO, R. M. (eds.), *Geographers and the Tropics: Liverpool Essays*. Longmans.

LAMBO, L. (1948) 'Etudes sur Les Balala'. *Bulletin des Juridictions Indigènes du Droit Coutumier Congolais*, 8.

LONG, N. (1968) 'Religion and Socio-economic Action among the Serenje Lala of Zambia', in *Christianity in Tropical Africa*, BAËTA, C. G. (ed.), Oxford University Press.

MACLEAN, H. A. M. (1962) *An Economic Appraisal of African Grown Turkish Tobacco in Northern Rhodesia*. Lusaka: Ministry of Agriculture.

MARWICK, M. (1965) *Sorcery in its Social Setting: A Study of the Northern Rhodesian Cewa*. Manchester University Press.

MIDDLETON, J. (1960) *Lugbara Religion: Ritual and Authority among an East African People*. Oxford University Press.

MIDDLETON, J., AND WINTER, E. H. (eds.) (1963) *Witchcraft and Sorcery in East Africa*. Routledge & Kegan Paul.

MITCHELL, J. C. (1956) *The Yao Village*. Manchester University Press.

MITCHELL, J. C., AND EPSTEIN, A. L. (1959) 'Occupational Prestige and Social Status among Urban Africans in Northern Rhodesia'. *Africa*, xxix.

MITCHELL, J. C. (1960) *Tribalism and the Plural Society*. Oxford University Press.

— (1966) 'Theoretical Orientations in African Urban Studies', in *The Social Anthropology of Complex Societies*, BANTON, M. (ed.) London: Tavistock Publications.

MOORE, W. E. (1963) *Social Change*. New Jersey: Prentice-Hall, Inc.

MUNDAY, J. T. (1939) 'Some Traditions of the Nyendwa Clan of Northern Rhodesia'. *Bantu Studies*, xiv, 1.

— (1948) 'Spirit Names among the Central Bantu'. *African Studies*, vii, 1.

— (1961) *Kankomba*. Rhodes-Livingstone Communication No. 22, Lusaka: Rhodes-Livingstone Institute.

PETERS, D. U. (1950) *Land Usage in Serenje District*. Rhodes-Livingstone Paper No. 19.

RICHARDS, A. I. (1939) *Land, Labour and Diet in Northern Rhodesia*. Oxford University Press.

RICHARDS, A. I. (1950) 'Variations in Family Structure among the Central Bantu', in *African Systems of Kinship and Marriage*, RADCLIFFE-BROWN, A. R., AND FORDE, C. D. (eds.), Oxford University Press.

SELZNICK, P. (1957) *Leadership in Administration: A Sociological Interpretation.* Evanston, Ill.: Row, Peterson & Company.

SHEPPERSON, G. (1961) 'The Comparative Study of Millenarian Movements', in *Millennial Dreams in Action*, THRUPP, S. L. (ed.), Comparative Studies in Society and History, Supplement 11, The Hague: Mouton & Co.

SMYTH, N. W. (1958) *Unpublished Report on Agriculture in Serenje District.* Lusaka: Ministry of Agriculture.

SOFER, C. (1961) *The Organization From Within.* London: Tavistock Publications.

STEFANISZYN, B. (1954) 'African Reincarnation Re-examined'. *African Studies*, xiii, 3-4.

— (1964) *Social and Ritual Life of the Ambo of Northern Rhodesia.* Oxford University Press.

STENNING, D. (1965) 'Salvation in Ankole', in *African Systems of Thought*, FORTES, M., AND DIETERLEN, G. (eds.), Oxford University Press.

TAYLOR, J. V., AND LEHMANN, D. (1961) *Christians of the Copperbelt.* S.C.M. Press.

TRAPNELL, C. G. (1943) *The Soils, Vegetation and Agriculture of North Eastern Rhodesia.* Lusaka: Government Printer.

TURNER, V. W. (1957) *Schism and Continuity in an African Society.* Manchester University Press.

VAN VELSEN, J. (1964) *The Politics of Kinship.* Manchester University Press.

— (1967) 'Situational Analysis and the Extended-Case Method', in *The Craft of Anthropology*, EPSTEIN, A. L. (ed.), London: Tavistock Publications Ltd.

Watch Tower Bible and Tract Society (1955) 'Qualified to be Ministers'.

— (1958) 'From Paradise Lost to Paradise Regained'.

— 'Blood, Medicine and the Law of God'.

— (1964) *Yearbook of Jehovah's Witnesses.*

WEBER, M. (1930) *The Protestant Ethic and the Spirit of Capitalism.* George Allen & Unwin.

— (1947) *The Theory of Social and Economic Organization.* Glencoe Ill.: The Free Press of Glencoe, Paperback Edition, 1964.

WILLEMS, E. (1964) 'Protestantism and Culture Change in Brazil and Chile', in *Religion, Revolution and Reform*, D'ANTONIO, W., AND PIKE, F. B. (eds.), New York: Praeger.

INDEX

agricultural demonstrator, duties of, 17, 18, 19; prestige evaluation, 158

agriculture, patterns of, 3, 12–20, 237; *citeme*, 3, 12, 25–6; hoe, 13; plough, 18, 20; Turkish tobacco, 3, 19, 20, 34n.1; introduction of cassava, 16; and diversification of local economy, 33–4; *see also* labour, land holding, peasant farming scheme

Allan, W., 16n.1, 241, 242

Ambo, 138

Ankole, 242–3

'anticipatory' inheritance, 122–3, 194

Bailey, F., 9n.1

Barnes, J. A., 6, 9n.2, 132

Barth, F., 5n.1

Bemba, 2, 12, 15, 80, 138

Bendix, R., 201, 201n.1

Bisa, 2

Bombwe, and the store, 100–3, 178–84; economic ties with Timoti, 166, 178–9; reasons for wanting Pati in business, 179; types of assistance from matrikin, 180; conflicting claims of matrikin and nuclear family, 183–4

British administration, the beginnings of, 81–3; and the village headman, 139–40

British South Africa Company, 81–3

Broken Hill (Kabwe), and Copperbelt towns, economic links with, 3, 15, 18, 32

bureaucratic administration, 143

Cewa, 124

Chibale Chiefdom, location of, 1–2; ecology of, 2–3; population, 2–3, 81–2, 83; population density, 14; ratio of *citeme* to hoed gardens, 15

Chief, judicial and administrative powers, 137–9; as 'owner' of the land (*mwine mpanga*), 27, 138; prestige evaluation, 152

Chintomfwa Village, 106–19; establishment of, 106–7; fission of, 107–110; causes of fission, 110–19;

internal conflicts generated by succession to headmanship, 112–118; on brink of disintegration, 120

citeme, see agriculture

Clayton, E., 39n.1

Colonial Office rule, establishment of, 83

Colson, E., 123n.1, 241–2n.2

Coster, R. N., 16

court clerk, duties of, 153; prestige evaluation, 154

critical population density, under *citeme*, 14

Cunnison, I. G., 80n.1, 110, 111, 241

Daiman, inherits farm property from mother's brother, 68; co-operates with brother Godfrey to establish farm, 68–9; opens store with Godfrey, 69; income and expenditure of, 70; factors facilitating independence from kin, 71–2, 222; life history and religious conversion, 218–23

— Farm, 67–72; few restrictions on development of, 71; and store, 70

Department of Agriculture, 15; and peasant farming scheme, 16–18; labour input study for Turkish tobacco, 25; block land administered by, 28; loans for peasant farmers, 17, 52

District Commissioner, 139–40

district messenger, 161

division of labour between sexes, under *citeme*, 21; under hoe, 21–2; under plough, 22; at peasant farms, 73–4

ecological change, 14–15, 26; and village fission, 96, 124

economic differentiation, 33–8

Epstein, A. L., 9n.2, 145

extended-case method, 8–10

Fallers, L. A., 6, 143

Firth, R., 9

Fortes, M., 8

253

Frank, life history and religious conversion, 223–5

Garbett, K., 249
Geertz, C., 243, 244
Gerth, H. H., 240
Glock, C. Y., 229n.1
Gluckman, M., 1, 6, 90, 91n.1, 132, 142, 152, 183n.1, 241
grinding mills, 33
Guttman scale analysis, 35–7, 245–9

Hagen, E. E., 243

individual settlements, defined, 87; size of, 89–90; social composition of, 94–6; growth pattern of, 121; social characteristics of founders of, 126–7
inheritance of property, 30; difficulties over, 193–4; *see also* 'anticipatory' inheritance
inkoswe, see village headman
in-laws, labour service to, 20–1, 116, 234; son-in-law/father-in-law relationship, 116

Jehovah's Witnesses, church organization, 155, 201–7; doctrine, 207–8; history, 155, 202n.1; religious ethic, 78, 191–2, 208–17, 240–1; social characteristics of, 6, 37–8, 200–1, 245–9; residence patterns of, 37, 126–9, 234–5, 245; type of agriculture practised by, 38, 247; economic status of, 6, 38, 127–9, 247–8; socio-economic mobility of, 234–6, 240; occupations of, 37–8, 246; education of, 216, 226, 249; kinship status of, 226–7, 232; urban experience of, 127–9, 227–9; interpersonal networks of, 225–6, 230–1, 233; status attitudes of, 161–162, 191–2, 199, 200–1, 209–210; sociological background factors to conversion, 225–33, 239–240; conversion histories, 218–25; post-conversion period, 233–6; National Assembly of, 211; District Assembly of, 211–15; and labour recruitment, 76–8, 122; women converts, 233–4; and United National Independence Party, 156,

192, 204, 214; *see also* Watch Tower Bible and Tract Society

Kabwe, *see* Broken Hill
Kapepa Parish, location of, 1–2; population of, 2; estimated population density, 26; and 'congregation area', 245
Kapferer, B., 233n.1
Katwishi, as store manager for Bombwe, 62, 100–2, 184; friendship with Zakeyo, 65, 184; quarrels with matrikin over store, 101–2, 105–6, over Timoti's inheritance, 185–6; quarrel with NaBombwe, 171–2; attempts to enlist aid of Timoti, 185; temporary alliance with matrikin, 186–8; tactics during Pati's visit, 186–9; undermines Lusefu's position 188–9
— Farm, 61–7; establishment of, 62–3, 65–6; attempts to expand, 64, 66; social constraints affecting development of, 67
Kay, G., 96

labour, organization of, 20–7; under *citeme*, 21–2; under plough, 22; hired labour, 22–4; *citeme* labour input, 24; plough labour input, 25; Turkish tobacco labour input, 23; composition of labour force at peasant farms, 72–9
labour migration, rate of, 31–2; effect on composition of villages, 93; capital investment by labour migrants, 3, 34; farms established by recently returned labour migrants, 17, 58, 74–5
Lala, history and location of, 2; migration of, 2, 16n.1; raided by Yeke, Ngoni and Bemba, 80
Lambo, L., 2
land holding, system of, 27–31, 51; under *citeme*, 27–8; under plough, 28; prior rights to land, 27–8; disputes over land, 28–30; land as an economic asset, 30; land transactions, 30; Peters' land usage survey, 13–15
Lehmann, D., 202n.1
Long, N., 211n.1